Why Study Baptists?

A Festschrift to Bill J. Leonard

The James N. Griffith Series in Baptist Studies

This series on Baptist life and thought explores and investigates Baptist history, offers analyses of Baptist theologies, provides studies in hymnody, and examines the role of Baptists in societies and cultures around the world. The series also includes classics of Baptist literature, letters, diaries, and other writings. For a complete list of titles in the series, visit www.mupress.org and visit the series page.

—C. Douglas Weaver, Series Editor

Why Study Baptists?

A Festschrift to Bill J. Leonard

Coedited by

Keith Harper and C. Douglas Weaver

MERCER UNIVERSITY PRESS
Macon, Georgia

Dedicated to students of the

Baptist Way(s)

Acknowledgments

It is always a joy to work with Mercer University Press and this project was especially gratifying. Marc Jolley, Marsha Luttrell, and Jenny Toole are top-notch professionals who go above and beyond the call of duty in their given tasks. Moreover, they make the publication process a lot of fun. Also, we would like to thank Faith Steele for her editorial assistance in this project's earliest stages. We want to express our heartiest appreciation to you all.

Keith Harper
Doug Weaver

MERCER UNIVERSITY PRESS

Endowed by

Tom Watson Brown
and
The Watson-Brown Foundation, Inc.

Contents

Contributors | viii

Introduction | 1

A Reckoning on Ninth Avenue: Southern Baptists, Race, and the
  Becoming Episode," Keith Harper | 5

The Shantung Revival: Baptists, Pentecostals, and Spirit-Led
  Experience, C. Douglas Weaver | 30

A Baptist on Capitol Hill: The Progressive Evangelicalism of Mark O.
  Hatfield, Randall Balmer | 67

Evangelical Faith, Politics, and Race in Black and White, 1945–2020,
  Edward R. Crowther | 85

"The True Ekklesia and the Hope of the World": Martin Luther King
  Jr. and the Theo-Politics of Black Baptist Ecclesiology, Corey D. B.
  Walker | 105

"Bold Mission Thrust" and White Baptists in the South: Beyond the
  Offense of Objectification toward a Theology of Mutual Regard,
  Robert N. Nash Jr. | 128

"There Is No Area of Religious Privilege Fenced Off for the Exclusive
  Use of Men": Baptist Preaching Women, 1630–2000, Pamela R.
  Durso | 147

"Do You See Her?" A Sermon on Luke 7:36–50,
  Meredith Stone | 183

The Mountain behind the Mountain: The Spirituality of Appalachian
  Mountain Religion Seen from the Life of an Appalachian
  Mountain Preacher, Linda McKinnish Bridges | 190

Studying with *Doktor Bruder*: On Being Bill Leonard's First Graduate
  Student and Living to Tell about It, Andrew Manis | 220

Wrapping the Gospel in Humor and Fidelity: A Tribute to Bill J.
  Leonard, Molly T. Marshall | 239

Contributors

RANDALL BALMER, the John Phillips Chair in Religion, Dartmouth College

LINDA MCKINNISH BRIDGES, Founding Faculty Member and Final President of Baptist Theological Seminary at Richmond, Virginia

EDWARD R. CROWTHER, Emeritus Professor of History, Adams State University

PAMELA R. DURSO, President, Central Baptist Theological Seminary

KEITH HARPER, Senior Professor of Baptist Studies, Southeastern Baptist Theological Seminary

ANDREW MANIS, Professor of History (retired), Middle Georgia State University

MOLLY T. MARSHALL, President, United Theological Seminary of the Twin Cities

ROBERT N. NASH Jr., Professor of World Christianity, McAfee School of Theology, Mercer University

MEREDITH STONE, Executive Director, Baptist Women in Ministry

COREY D. B. WALKER, Dean of the Wake Forest University School of Divinity, Wake Forest Professor of the Humanities

C. DOUGLAS WEAVER, Barbara Jo Beard Driskell Professor of Historical Studies and Department Chair, Department of Religion, Baylor University

Introduction

Why on earth would anyone want to study Baptists? Ask anyone and they will tell you: Baptists do not agree on anything. Baptist theology, or theologies, are all over the place. Baptists bicker like spoiled children. There is no fortune to be made in studying Baptists—any fame that comes with such inquiry is another story altogether. Still, those same people will likely tell you that there is something endlessly fascinating about the Baptist story that compels a telling, or in many cases, a retelling. Bill J. Leonard is one of those who tells the Baptist story, and he is a master of the craft.

Those familiar with Bill's career know that he has written extensively on topics ranging from Appalachian Christianity and personal spirituality to religious freedom and denominational politics. In fact, it would take a separate, rather extensive volume to comment on all of his writings. But Bill is more than a chronicler of the Baptist experience because there is more to it than telling a story. There is an interpretive element to the Baptist experience and a corresponding element that seeks both to explain what it means to be a Baptist and why it is important. To this end, three of Bill's works are especially influential and instructive.

First, consider *Baptist Ways: A History*. Writing partisan history is a serious temptation for anyone writing about denominational life. That is, it is tempting to write as an "insider" for other insiders. By the same token, denominational historians are frequently tasked with training others to live and work in a specific denominational context, hence they tend to write along carefully proscribed, almost scripted lines. According to *The Handbook of American Denominations*, there are more than sixty different Baptist groups in the United States, and that does not count other groups worldwide. In *Baptist Ways*, however, Bill reminds readers that there is more than one way to be a Baptist, notwithstanding our peculiarities and proclivities. The book's title is simple, suggestive, and brilliant. Point taken!

Beyond mapping and detailing the nuances of Baptist faith and practice, one might ask, What about application? How have Baptists applied their theology? These are great questions. Take conversion, for example. Whereas some Baptists decry infant baptism, Bill has angered more than a few parents by questioning a practice he calls "toddler baptism," or baptism for those barely able to walk a church aisle by themselves. Churches or associations do not keep a tally of those requesting a "second" baptism after having been baptized at an early age because they decided later that they had not really been converted. Doubtless, that would be an embarrassing statistic! But toddler baptism is not the only point where Baptists would do well to reflect on what they preach and how they conduct themselves. Bill's *The Challenge of Being Baptist: Owning a Scandalous Past and an Uncertain Future* is a sobering work, especially chapter 5, "Once Saved, Almost Saved." Again, the title is on point: it *is* challenging to be a Baptist.

It may go without saying, but calling one's fellow laborers to reconsider what they believe to be absolute truth requires both courage and integrity. Few know that better than Bill Leonard, and *God's Last and Only Hope: The Fragmentation of the SBC* is arguably his most remarkable work. Written in the heat of the most recent Southern Baptist controversy, Bill focuses on the creation and erosion of what he describes as "the Grand Compromise" in *God's Last and Only Hope*. Moreover, Bill describes the protracted battle that engulfed the denomination toward the end of the twentieth century in clear, balanced prose, and in doing so, he captures an understated irony. Southern Baptists have always styled themselves as a missionary people, but those who attacked the Grand Compromise's missionary consensus were seemingly oblivious to the fact that once the consensus was undermined, they could never return to it—at least, not the way it was—and post-controversy events have demonstrated this to be true.

So, why on Earth *would* anyone want to study Baptists? Maybe they know someone who challenged them to think differently. Maybe they read something about Baptists they found instructive. Maybe they respect someone with the courage to say what they believe needs to be said—or maybe they are familiar with the life and ministry of Bill J. Leonard. We have found Bill to be all these things: courageous, instructive, challenging, *funny*, and, above all, kind. Quite a skill set for a Baptist historian!

Contributors to this Festschrift have a variety of special connections to Bill Leonard. Three (Andy Manis, Rob Nash, and Doug Weaver) wrote their PhD dissertations under his guidance. All three call him mentor and friend and joined him in the ranks of studying the history of Baptists, American

Introduction

religion, and the world throughout their careers. Manis's chapter is a personal reflection; Nash's chapter reflects his longtime study of Baptist missiology (burdened in racism), a study that began in his dissertation; and Weaver's chapter speaks to the interaction between Baptists and Pentecostals, his interest in the topic no doubt tied to his dissertation on divine healer William Marion Branham, a Baptist who ministered in the Pentecostal subculture.

Molly Marshall and Corey Walker were academic colleagues of Bill's—Marshall at Southern Seminary and Walker at Wake Forest. Marshall offers a personal tribute and speaks to how she and Bill worked alongside one another. Walker's chapter notes Leonard's interest in the importance of the black Baptist church tradition in the Baptist story. Linda Bridges, another academic colleague, offers a chapter on Appalachian religious experience. Those who know Leonard remember how he took classes to the Appalachian Mountains and revealed a deep commitment to understanding those believers (including snake-handling religion) not always understood. Bill Leonard has long been an advocate for women in ministry, seen not only in Molly Marshall's tribute, but also in the chapter by Pamela Durso and the sermon from Meredith Stone. The inclusion of the insightful material on women and preaching is an important reminder that Professor Leonard is not simply known as an academic but as a popular, powerful preacher in Baptist circles. Randall Balmer, well-known historian of American Evangelicalism, has been a special friend to Bill as both have traveled the journey of noted historian of American religion in academia, and both are popular commentators about religion in the public square and on social media.

Ed Crowther knows Bill as a scholar, academic fellow traveler, and dialogue partner (often on emails from Keith Harper...and Doug Weaver) about religion and politics. Crowther's article reminds us of Professor Leonard's interest in how religion and politics intersect in Southern Baptist life. Keith Harper is, like Leonard, a historian of Baptists with a keen interest in Southern Baptists and culture, a topic he and Bill have talked about many times. His work on a preparatory event before the Southern Baptist conflict of the late twentieth century reminds us that Bill Leonard (and Harper) have been noted interpreters of recent Baptist events.

WHY STUDY BAPTISTS?

Harper and Weaver collaborated on this volume—both with deep appreciation for Dr. Bill J. Leonard's influence on their work and their lives. The coeditors give thanks to all of the contributors for their important work. We offer these essays with our profound gratitude and believe they are a worthy tribute to our friend, professor, mentor. And last, but certainly not least, we offer a shout-out of love to Bill and his spouse, Candyce, and their special daughter, Stephanie, whose birthday is the same day of the year as Doug Weaver's—a bit of trivia celebrated by both. Festschrifts are, in their own way, an academic birthday present of scholarly work that seeks to be top tier in quality but deep in grace-filled friendship.

Keith Harper
Doug Weaver

A Reckoning on Ninth Avenue:
Southern Baptists, Race, and the *"Becoming* Episode"

Keith Harper

In the fall of 1971, the dust appeared to be settling somewhat from the social upheaval of the 1960s. But before the nation could catch its collective breath, a controversy erupted within the Southern Baptist Convention (SBC) that caused great embarrassment for the nation's largest non-Catholic denomination. The issue involved the apparent censoring of educational material, and what might otherwise have been an in-house editorial matter quickly drew attention from local, state, and national media.

The controversy centered on the Southern Baptist Sunday School Board (SSB), the denomination's publication agency, and material prepared for Training Union, essentially a Sunday evening version of Sunday school. Titled simply *Becoming*, the literature in question had been written for fourteen-to-fifteen-year-olds on the theme of race relations. After the material had been printed, the editorial staff suddenly decided to pull it and edit one lesson and rewrite another just prior to distribution. The editors considered a picture of an African American male talking to two white females, in one lesson, especially vexing. As a result, some 140,000 booklets along with 18,000 booklets for teachers were scrapped at an estimated cost of $8,000.[1] News of the material's destruction leaked to the media, and what came to be known as the *"Becoming* episode" generated a firestorm of criticism that ranged from charges of racism and censorship to the Board's apparent failure to lead well in crisis. By the time the controversy subsided, an editor had resigned and the SSB's executive

---

[1] James L. Sullivan, "Sullivan Directs Revision of Quarterly After Printing," Baptist Press, October 28, 1971, Sunday School Board. Executive Office Records. James Lenox Sullivan Papers, Southern Baptist Historical Library and Archives, Nashville, Tennessee. Correspondence File, AR 795-345, Box 19, Folder 18. All letters cited are from the Sullivan Papers unless otherwise noted and will follow an abbreviated format for box and folder numbers, noted in parentheses.

secretary-treasurer, James Lenox Sullivan, found himself scrambling to regain trust among Southern Baptists.

The Sunday School Board had been a regular feature of Southern Baptist life since its beginning in 1891. Located at 127 Ninth Avenue North, in downtown Nashville, Tennessee, the SSB produced educational material for Southern Baptists. While churches were not obligated to purchase educational material from Nashville, the SSB soon gained a strong following, largely because it supported the discipleship efforts of local churches and promoted the denomination's broader mission interests. Historian Bill J. Leonard argues that prior to 1990, Southern Baptists operated according to the "Grand Compromise," whereby theology and theological disputes were subordinated to missionary enterprises. That is, cooperating Southern Baptists could "agree to disagree" on any number of specific theological tenets while maintaining fraternal relations for the sake of missionary ventures.[2] Over time, the SSB began generating an impressive publication list ranging from Sunday school literature to Bible commentaries. By the early 1970s, the SSB had grown into a multi-million-dollar corporation and served as the parent company of both Broadman Press and Convention Press.[3]

The SSB had faced controversies before, but none quite like the *Becoming* episode. Within a month of the story breaking, the Board received 391 letters, with the negative responses outpacing the positive responses more than four to one.[4] Beyond the letters, SSB staff counted twenty-two

---

[2] Bill J. Leonard, *God's Last and Only Hope: The Fragmentation of the Southern Baptist Convention* (Grand Rapids, MI: Erdmans Publishing Company, 1990) 31–54.

[3] For overviews of the Southern Baptist Sunday School Board, see Robert A. Baker, *The Story of the Sunday School Board* (Nashville, TN: Convention Press, 1966) and James T. Draper Jr., *Lifeway Legacy: A Personal History of Lifeway Christian Resources and the Sunday School Board of the Southern Baptist Convention* (Nashville, TN: B & H Publishing, 2006). It is important to note that the SSB's origins are tied closely to race at the turn of the century. See Keith Harper, "The Fortress Monroe Conference and the Shaping of Baptist Life in America at the Turn of the Century," in *Mirrors and Microscopes: Historical Perceptions of Baptists*, ed. C. Douglas Weaver (London: Paternoster, 2015) 110–28.

[4] In-house tabulation, November 23, 1971 (19–18). The recorded numbers were 314 unfavorable, 77 favorable, for a total of 391.

editorials or columns in eighteen different Baptist state papers, with Tennessee, Missouri, Mississippi, and South Carolina supportive, and Maryland, Indiana, North Carolina, Texas, California, Illinois, Kentucky, Georgia, and DC critical.[5] Further, seven states and numerous churches, associations, and student organizations drafted resolutions opposing the action, but support for and opposition to the Board's decision was more complex than a simple yea or nay. In North Carolina, the Department of Interracial Ministries surveyed messengers to the state's annual meeting and reported 72 percent either agreed or strongly agreed that the SSB was "correct in withdrawing the picture," and 74 percent either agreed or strongly agreed that "withdrawing the picture probably did more harm than good."[6]

What made *Becoming* such an explosive issue? Assuming that the North Carolina survey was not flawed, how does one explain a large majority who both approved of withdrawing the literature while maintaining that the action caused more harm than good? While the *Becoming* episode is specific to Southern Baptists, it sits within a much larger context. The American South was experiencing large-scale cultural and economic transformation thanks to the New Deal and war industries.[7] Many Southerners received the government's bounty with thanksgiving, except when it came

---

[5] Ibid. Assuming the tabulation is accurate, four papers were neutral. Of course, this tabulation came at an early point in the controversy, and the other four papers might have become more vocal over time.

[6] Results of a survey conducted by NC Department of Interracial Ministries, November 23, 1971, Sullivan Papers (19-17). The survey had space for respondents to indicate whether they lived in Western North Carolina, the Piedmont, or Eastern North Carolina. These numbers are not recorded in the materials submitted to the SSB.

[7] The literature on the postwar South is extensive, but two examples may suffice. See Numan Bartley, *The New South, 1945–1980* (Baton Rouge: Louisiana State University Press, 1995) and Charles P. Rowland, *The Improbable Era: The South Since World War II* (Lexington: University Press of Kentucky, 1975). The literature on the civil rights movement is also extensive. For a general survey, Harvard Sitkoff's *The Struggle for Black Equality* (New York: Hill and Wang, 2008) is helpful. For a nuanced exploration of the intricacies of the civil rights movement, see Jacquelyn Dowd Hall, "The Long Civil Rights Movement and the Political Uses of the Past," *Journal of American History* 91/4 (March 2005): 1233–63.

to programs aimed at equality for African Americans. It is impossible to know the number of Southern Baptists who supported the so-called Dixiecrats. It is safe to assume that many did, however, and in 1954, the *Brown v. Board of Education* decision only stiffened their resolve to keep the region segregated. On the other hand, many Southern Christians fought for equality and desegregation. In Mississippi, Southern churchgoers were so preoccupied with civil rights that historian Carolyn Renee Dupont claims, "No other issue so occupied the religious attention of white Mississippians nor worried church leaders, and nothing elicited greater religious energy or creativity."[8]

When it comes to Southern Baptists, Dupont's assessment of Mississippi is applicable to the SBC. As the nation struggled, so, too, did Southern Baptists, and as subsequent events unfolded, at least three things became clear. First, the *Becoming* episode tapped a simmering unrest among Southern Baptists over social and cultural issues. Vietnam, feminism, and an expanding welfare state all contributed to what historian Allan Matusow described as the "unraveling of America."[9] Southern Baptists felt the nation's multiple stresses, but they were especially sensitive to any issues stemming from the civil rights movement. Beyond highlighting persistent racism among some Southern Baptists who feared that the SSB was endorsing racial mixing and even interracial marriage, the *Becoming* episode demonstrated the frustration among those who were actively seeking to improve race relations. These Southern Baptists felt a deep sense of betrayal in what they saw as the Board's cowardice, and they were not shy in expressing themselves.

Second, by the 1970s, a distrust of denominational leadership permeated SBC life beginning at the church level and extending into leadership structures themselves. Southern Baptist leaders such as agency heads had always counted on good will and interagency cooperation from high-profile pastors, editors of state papers, and denominational workers at the state

---

[8] Carolyn Renee Dupont, *Mississippi Praying: Southern White Evangelicals and the Civil Rights Movement, 1945–1975* (New York and London: New York University Press, 2013) 2.

[9] Allan Matusow, *The Unraveling of America: A History of Liberalism in the 1960s* (New York: Harper & Row, 1984).

level. But the *Becoming* episode revealed internal stresses that made it increasingly difficult for denominational leaders to sustain a workable mission-oriented consensus. Thus, institutional inter-cooperation and interdependency, staple themes in SBC life, became increasingly tenuous.

Finally, the *Becoming* episode demonstrated that SSB leaders were committed to what they saw as a centrist, denominationally focused approach to publishing. But the soft center was at odds with competing forces that pitted those who sought improved race relations against those who sought to preserve segregation. Historian Mark Newman argues that after 1963, Southern Baptist "progressives" began calling for integration. "Clearly, at every turn, progressives followed behind secular developments inaugurated by the civil rights movement and the federal government, but, nevertheless, they played a vital role in helping Southern Baptists to adjust to and accept the demise of legal segregation."[10] The SSB served a broad, diverse community, and it was simply impossible to please everyone. Yet no one on Ninth Avenue could afford to be bullied into favoring an extreme position, regardless of the issue. Newman's assessment is correct, but it was a hard-fought battle. Unrest, failure to maintain a workable consensus, and a commitment to denominational centrism all represented serious problems in SBC structures, and these fault lines, which figured prominently in another controversy, alternately known as the "Conservative Resurgence" or the "Fundamentalist Takeover" of the SBC, were clearly evident nearly a decade earlier during the *Becoming* episode.[11]

Chronology of Events and Reaction

Allen Comish became director of Church Services and Materials Division at the SSB in March 1971. Georgia's state Baptist paper, *The Christian*

---

[10] Mark Newman, *Getting Right with God: Southern Baptists and Desegregation, 1945–1995* (Tuscaloosa and London: University of Alabama Press, 2001) 206.

[11] For "The Controversy," see David Morgan, *The New Crusades, the New Holy Land: Conflict in the Southern Baptist Convention, 1969–1991* (Tuscaloosa: University of Alabama Press, 1996) and Jerry Sutton, *The Baptist Reformation: The Conservative Resurgence in the Southern Baptist Convention* (Nashville, TN: B & H Publishing, 2000).

Index, described Comish as a "mighty big ex-Georgian" who was making important changes in Nashville. Prior to coming to the SSB, Comish served Waldrop Memorial Baptist Church in Columbus, Georgia, and claimed he brought a pastor's perspective to his new role. It was Comish who first spied problems with the *Becoming* quarterlies. He believed the picture of the African American male and the two white females was grainy, but he also believed the lessons were potentially inflammatory.[12] Sullivan agreed, and the material was revised.

Twyla Wright wrote the two lessons that came under editorial scrutiny. A Phoenix resident, Wright's first lesson focused on God's image in humanity. In comparing her original lesson with the edited version, one finds no changes in the two texts. Ironically, the second lesson, titled "When Brothers Dwell Together in Unity," caught Comish's eye. In it, Wright began by recounting in positive terms a story about an African American who joined a white church. She ended her lesson by asking, "Have you ever visited a black church? a Spanish church? a Cuban church? an Oriental church? How would you react to a person of another race asking for membership in your church? Why?" Anne Craig of Nashville supplied the "revised" version of Lesson Two, which emphasized freedom and evangelism. She muted any mention of race by asking readers if they were willing to accept others based on individual worth. As for the photographs, the original lessons featured two interracial photographs, one for each lesson. The edited material likewise featured a picture for each lesson, neither of which included an African American.[13] It was an internal, editorial decision the Board made on Friday, October 22, 1971.

Word of the SSB's action somehow leaked to the Religious News Service (RNS), which ran the story on Wednesday, October 27. The next day, Sullivan responded by issuing an extended statement through Baptist Press (BP). Sullivan claimed responsibility for failing to distribute the Training Union quarterlies and corresponding teacher's material for fourteen-to-fifteen-year-old youths. The press release quoted Comish as

---

[12] Jack U. Harwell, "Big Georgian Making Big Changes in Nashville," *The Christian Index* (December 2, 1971): 12.

[13] The original lessons and the revised lessons are available in the Southern Baptist Historical Library and Archives, Nashville, TN.

saying, "A review of the materials in the publishing process dealing with sensitive issues led us to observe that misunderstandings could result from release of this issue in its original form." He further claimed, "One of the photographs which depicted a black boy and two white girls in conversation was subject to misrepresentation, as was some of the textual material.... It could have been construed as improper promotion on the part of the Sunday School Board of integration in the churches, which is an individual church matter under Baptist polity." The BP article noted that the SSB followed regular editorial procedures but decided at the last minute that the material might be too sensitive for some localities. In the end, the Board reprinted the materials and noted that this was not the first time that items had been revised prior to distribution.[14]

If Sullivan thought his statement would solve potential misunderstandings among Southern Baptists, he was wrong. Media outlets pounced and the frenzy was on. Even before *Newsweek* ran its story on November 15, the SSB was inundated with letters from irate Southern Baptist church members, ministers, local associations, and state conventions. The writers were either unaware of the BP statement or they simply ignored everything Sullivan had said.

Fielding complaints about training material was nothing new for the SSB. Sullivan had experienced something similar in 1963 when Anderine Farmer wrote a piece titled "Red and Yellow, Black and White" for *The Baptist Training Union Magazine*. Farmer served as the Baptist Student Union (BSU) director at the University of Kansas, and the title reflects a line from the children's song "Jesus Loves the Little Children." Farmer used the line to describe a recent worship service in her church where she noticed that the morning's soloist was Chinese. On that day, the church baptized a Native American girl, and Farmer noticed two African Americans, one of whom had visited before and returned because the church was friendly. "Perhaps this is what 'love' and 'precious' mean in that song," she

---

[14] Sullivan, "Sullivan Directs Revision of Quarterlies After Printing," BP, 10-28-1971.

WHY STUDY BAPTISTS?

mused, "that red and yellow, black and white can worship together as children of God, bound by a common salvation."[15]

The reaction to Farmer's article was mixed. A few hailed it as a positive step forward in SBC race relations, but most reactions were negative. The prevailing sentiments were probably best expressed by Harper L. Tillman, who labored under the impression "that our denomination was staying clear and clean of the political, racist, and communist instigated race question." In his view, integration served no one's best interest. Besides, Baptists had experienced remarkable growth "without at this time taking sides with the World Council of Churches and the Catholic Church." He even implied that Farmer had fabricated the story because "there were too many coincidences to have been absolute facts."[16]

As the *Becoming* episode gathered steam, Sullivan felt confident that the leak came from someone on the inside who aimed at radicalizing the SSB. He feared that "some group may be planning labor agitation—negro employment.... Extremists who can't find a point of penetration may use violence." As a result, he called upon his staff to "rewrite procedures to safeguard us from material being fed in." He also noted, "Somebody is maneuvering at crucial points. We had a Malaysian artist, Missouri editor, Arizona writer, and Kentucky supervisor. Nobody to look at it from the *deep south*." Even worse, the number of complaints from denominational leadership indicated even bigger problems. The notes for this staff meeting conclude with "we have *internal problems and interagency relationships*."[17]

While there was no handbook that specified the parameters for interagency relations, there were assumed relationships that agency leaders counted on for the SBC to run smoothly. Southern Baptists organize themselves denominationally around state conventions, each with an executive to direct Southern Baptist doings within the state. Traditionally, SBC agencies counted on mutual support and solidarity from leaders in

---

[15] Anderine Farmer, "Red and Yellow, Black and White," *Baptist Training Union Magazine* (September 1963): 8–9.

[16] Tillman to Harris, 9-6-63; Correspondence File, "Segregation," SBHLA, Sullivan Papers, AR 795-354 (35-33).

[17] Minutes of SSB staff meeting, November 1, 1971 (19-18). The notes do not specify who recorded them or list all participants. Emphasis mine, both instances.

the states. Sullivan could continue to steer "middle course" if he received support from other denominational agency leaders as he dealt with complaints from Southern Baptist laity and ministers. Unfortunately, he faced criticism from those whom he counted on most. The majority of state executives were disappointed in the decision and the uproar it caused. They noted they had cultivated relationships with African Americans who no longer trusted the SSB, and they did not blame them. They, too, felt mounting pressure from the *Becoming* episode, and Sullivan soon discovered that many of the SBC's faithful were not going to toe a strict party line if it smacked of racism.

As Sullivan assessed the situation, letters flooded the SSB offices on Ninth Avenue, some from as far away as England and Israel. The letters may be coded into three broad groups. One group supported Sullivan. They agreed with the decision to pull the literature, and they minced no words in registering their contempt for integration or for assigning blame. For instance, Mr. J. B. Hillman of Beaumont, Texas, thought Sullivan "did right" in not publishing the material. "All this integration popy cot [sic]," he said, "is ruining our Baptist Churches, we ought to go on like we have for 100 years, teachers and preachers should not even mention the word integration or Racial."[18] According to E. C. Hand of Andalusia, Alabama, "Until the Communists came along and stirred up all this stink, we were making reasonable progress in race relations in this country but they have set it back many years."[19] Manning Kirby of Nashville did not blame Communists for civil unrest. Rather, he blamed Nashville's local newspaper, *The Tennessean*, saying, "A certain newspaper has had much to say about what happened. I believe this paper would sell the United States to Russia for $100,000.00 if they could do so and not have to pay income tax on the deal."[20]

Some of Sullivan's supporters offered their own personal reflections on the situation. Too many people had confused "the Great Society with the Kingdom of God," mused Robert S. Magee from Ruston, Louisiana. Proper preaching would correct that. In fact, proper preaching would set

---

[18] Hillman to Sullivan, November 29, 1971 (19-17).

[19] Hand to Sullivan, December 3, 1971 (19-17).

[20] Kirby to Sullivan, November 6, 1971 (19-14).

many things straight, but when it came to the real issue bedeviling most Southern segregationists, no one spoke more pointedly than Edna Evans from Kress, Texas: "If you emphasize black and white togetherness too much in Sunday School literature," she intoned, "then pretty soon the young people will begin to think it is alright and will start dating one another." From there, Evans claimed that intermarriage would produce children that would not be accepted by either whites or blacks.[21] Perhaps Sullivan's most hateful letter came from E. S. "Doc" Boggs, who denounced interracial worship in no uncertain terms. "Frankly," he declared, "I don't like to mix with a bunch of smelly bastards. I am a Christian. I am ordained. I worship with whites—you tell me I am wrong."[22]

A second group of letters offered measured support for Sullivan and the SSB. That is, they regretted the incident happened, but, overall, they trusted Sullivan's leadership. James E. Humphries of Forest Hill, Tennessee, and Ronald R. Owens of Elkin, North Carolina, assured Sullivan that any complaints leveled against the SSB did not represent rank-and-file Southern Baptists.[23] Paige Patterson, pastor of First Baptist Church, Fayetteville, Arkansas, and future president of the Southern Baptist Convention, offered Sullivan words of encouragement. Patterson claimed that he served an integrated church and boasted, "We have no racial problems—thank the Lord!" He concluded by wishing Sullivan well.[24] Even W. A. Criswell, pastor of First Baptist Church, Dallas, arguably the most high-profile individual in the SBC and previously on record as a segregationist, admonished Sullivan to "stay down the middle of the Bible—neither right nor left—just with this Lad—just as you are, and this will give us every continuing victory."[25]

---

[21] Evans to Sullivan, February 29, 1972 (19-21).

[22] Boggs to Sullivan, January 2, 1971, Sullivan Correspondence, "Race" AR 795-354.

[23] Humphries to Sullivan, November 23, 1971 (19-15); Owens to Sullivan, November 17, 1971 (19-15).

[24] Patterson to Sullivan, December 1, 1971 (19-17).

[25] Criswell to Sullivan, November 26, 1971 (19-17). See also Curtis Freeman, "Never Had I Been So Blind: W. A. Criswell's 'Change' on Racial Segregation," *The Journal of Southern Religion* 10 (2007). http://jsr.fsu.edu/Volume10/Freeman.pdf.

By far, the majority of the letters came from a third group of people who were angered by the SSB's action. Even when writers tried to appreciate Sullivan's position, they could not believe that integration was such a divisive issue. Julius H. Avery of Jacksonville, Florida, queried, "Will the day ever come when the Sunday School Board will not have to gear its publishing work to the lowest common denominator in the denomination? Why do the reddest red-necks on race issues and the least educated among our preachers have to determine the course of our Sunday School Board?"[26] Many like Dan Hagan announced they were leaving the SBC altogether, stating, "I am now looking for a new denomination that presents the Gospel and does not worry which parts are 'inflammatory' because God's truths are often uncomfortable for us—Ain't they?"[27]

Other letters raised questions bearing on missionary work. If social mixing caused such consternation and outrage, should Southern Baptists even conduct international mission work? How were pastors to explain the SSB's action to African American members of mixed congregations? For that matter, how were they to explain the SSB's action to African American preachers in their community? Georgia governor and future president of the United States Jimmy Carter said, "Your recent action in expunging a photograph from our Sunday School literature of black and white children standing five feet apart was embarrassing to me as a Christian and has seriously damaged Southern Baptists' ministry. Do the two of you really feel that the autonomy of Baptist churches depends on bigotry and censorship?"[28] James C. Comer, special assistant to Indiana senator Vance Hartke, queried, "For God's sake, when is the Board going to take a stand on something? For Comish to state publicly that it is 'improper promotion' for the Board to try to influence their constituency to take Jesus seriously is more than I can take." Comer then encouraged Sullivan to make a motion at the next SBC meeting that churches no longer observe Race Relations Sunday. That way, the denomination could at least be consistent. "In

---

[26] Avery to Sullivan, November 19, 1971 (19-15).

[27] Hagen to Sullivan, November 11, 1971 (received) (19-14).

[28] Carter to Allan Comish, answered by Sullivan, November 14, 1971; November 24, 1971 (19-14). Emphasis Carter.

the meantime," Comer said, "I will try to keep secret here in Washington the fact that I am a Southern Baptist."[29]

Miss Pat Strother of Louisville, Kentucky, had raised similar questions and received a speedy response. In a follow-up letter, she noted, "This is to acknowledge receipt of and to express my appreciation for your prompt reply to my letter of 11/3/71. It is good to know that you have received so many letters of this nature that it became necessary to compose a form letter with which to reply."[30] Strother had no way of knowing it, but Jimmy Carter and James C. Comer had received form letters, too.[31]

Those who were angered by the SSB's action were divided in assessing the fallout. Some believed the SSB either supported segregation or pandered to segregationists because of economic advantage. But then, Sullivan and the Board would not understand such things because they were out of touch with Southern reality. At least, that is what William C. Haskell from Louisville believed. "You see, Dr. Sullivan," he claimed, "it's like this: You are comfortably situated in your offices in the Sunday School Building, carefully shielded from irate parishioners and deacons—not to mention the 'forgotten people of the land'—which is really a tragic situation."[32] Shielded from irate deacons and parishioners, perhaps, but James Sullivan was not shielded from irate Southern Baptists who seemed oblivious to the fact that the material was intended for Training Union, not Sunday school.

Amidst the controversy, Sullivan received a letter from Twyla Wright, the author whose material had been withheld from publication. She was sorry for the fuss the incident caused. She, too, had been bombarded by media questions, and she had answered them to the best of her convictions and ability. She appreciated her relations with the SSB and concluded by saying, "Forgive me if any of my printed statements have

---

[29] Comer to Sullivan, November 12, 1971 (19-14). Race Relations Sunday appeared on the SBC calendar as early as February 14, 1963. See SBC Annual, 1963, 80.

[30] Strother to Sullivan, November 12, 1971 (19-14).

[31] Comer responded to Sullivan tersely, "I would have preferred it if you had simply ignored my previous letter to you than to insult my intelligence by your inane response." See Comer to Sullivan, November 30, 1971 (19-16).

[32] Haskell to Sullivan, December 10, 1971 (19-17).

caused you trouble."[33] Sullivan thanked her for her gracious letter and her integrity in handling her interviews. He assured her that what she had written was not the problem. He hoped they could talk someday, and he encouraged her to continue writing.[34]

Under Siege

As an entity of the Southern Baptist Convention, the Sunday School Board was accountable to a sizable constituency, a significant number of whom were disappointed, angry, or both. Before Sullivan could deal effectively with the SBC at large, however, he faced more pressing issues on Ninth Avenue. Some of the letters had raised good questions. How had the redesign of Training Union literature generated such controversy? Who was responsible for leaking the news? How should he address the crisis? He claimed the "truth" would ultimately come out, but that was not likely, seeing that Sullivan refused requests for the unedited versions of *Becoming*.

Before Sullivan could fully assess his predicament, Frank Grayum, the editor directly responsible for the *Becoming* literature, resigned. In a prepared statement, he said, "I believe that in order to fulfill the objectives of my personal ministry as I see it, I need to seek another opportunity and avenue of service." He added, "I look forward to an opportunity to serve in some situation where I can reconcile my personal philosophy, theology, and objectives with those of any institution or group of which I may become a part."[35] Grayum did not say that he had been forced to resign; perhaps James Sullivan did that for him. "When we become a part of an agency like the Sunday School Board," Sullivan intoned, "we either adopt the philosophies and objectives of the agency, changing our own views to bring them into alignment; or we seek through appropriate channels to influence the agency's positions. Those who are not able to reconcile their

---

[33] Wright to Sullivan, November 3, 1971 (19-19).

[34] Sullivan to Wright, November 9, 1971 (19-20).

[35] Frank Grayum, "Becoming Editor Resigns," Baptist Press, Press Release, November 13, 1971.

views with those of their employer may understandably desire to seek other avenues of fulfillment."[36]

Reaction to Grayum's resignation mirrored the rest of the *Becoming* correspondence that flooded Sullivan's office. Some applauded the editor for his courage and offered encouragement. Others were less than charitable. Harry Williams congratulated Grayum for resigning and said, "I think that Southern Baptists would be better off if hundreds more with your views would resign and use their own funds and time to expound their ideas."[37]

Meanwhile, Sullivan searched for the leak that had everyone talking. The National Baptist Publishing Board (NBPB), the publishing arm of the largest African American Baptist body, was among the first to respond regarding the *Becoming* episode. On November 3, 1971, the NBPB issued a statement supporting Twyla Wright and expressing its regrets that "the killing of the racial art text by the Southern Baptist Sunday School Board offers material to those who are against integration or Christian fellowship in any form."[38] Ironically, Sullivan first suspected the NBPB was responsible for the uproar. In a letter to W. A. Criswell dated November 29, 1971, and marked "Personal and Confidential," Sullivan thanked Criswell for his support and said, "Our dilemma in dealing with this particular matter is that the 'leak of confidential information' concerning the revision seems to have issued from one of the Negro publishing houses to whom courtesy across the years had been shown in their receiving galleys of our publications." Sullivan further claimed that the information had been deliberately distorted. "If we tell all the facts of this case," he said, "we will be working against our objective of trying to better racial relationships; therefore, we're keeping silent to let the storm blow through and let history do the correct interpretations."[39]

Sullivan was even more forthcoming in a confidential letter to Hershel Hobbs, pastor of First Baptist Church, Oklahoma City, Oklahoma. He blamed the National Baptist Convention for the incident and

---

[36] Ibid.

[37] Williams to Grayum, November 19, 1971 (19-16).

[38] National Baptist Publishing Board statement, November 3, 1971 (19-20).

[39] Sullivan to Criswell, November 29, 1971 (19-17).

accused them of wanting to resegregate for economic reasons. "You remember that the Boyd family actually maneuvered the publishing operation out of the hands of the Negro convention, and this is what split the Negro Baptists. The Boyd family profits off the publishing operation which they now head." If African American churches used SSB literature, the Boyd family lost money. Sullivan claimed the NBC was "trying to 'shoo' their own people back into their own camp and are seeking to use us as a scapegoat. In the process, they're coming out looking lily white, and are making us look like the scum of the earth."[40]

In time, Sullivan reached a different conclusion about who leaked the story to the media. In the meantime, he had bigger issues to address. The SSB was taking a beating from angry students, churches, and state conventions, much of which was fueled by the editors of state Baptist papers. Sullivan believed they were helping to blow the *Becoming* episode out of proportion. Worse, he believed they were operating from misinformation.

It was time for Sullivan to focus his attention on intra-agency housekeeping. Like it or not, he understood that the Sunday School Board depended on good will at all levels of SBC life, especially among its leaders within the denominational bureaucracy. Given the SSB's role, Sullivan knew that he shouldered the responsibility for engendering much of that good will. Not everyone approved of everything the SSB printed, and recent controversies left Sullivan on shaky ground. For instance, in 1961, Broadman Press published Ralph Elliott's *The Message of Genesis*. Elliott used a higher-critical approach in his exegesis of the creation narrative, and it did not sit well with the SBC's rank-and-file. As an imprint of the SSB, Broadman Press immediately came under fire for being out of step with Southern Baptists. Broadman pulled the book, but Elliott republished it with Bethany Press and lost his job at Midwestern Seminary.[41] Broadman Press came under fire again in 1969 when it launched *The Broadman Commentary*, an ambitious, multivolume commentary on the

---

[40] Sullivan to Hobbs, November 16, 1971 (19-14).

[41] Ralph Elliott, *The Message of Genesis: A Theological Interpretation* (Nashville, TN: Broadman Press, 1961) and *The Genesis Controversy and Continuity in Southern Baptist Chaos: A Eulogy for a Great Tradition* (Macon: Mercer University Press, 1992).

Bible. The first volume, *Genesis and Exodus*, was written by G. Henton Davies and sounded eerily similar to Elliott's *The Message of Genesis*. Under considerable pressure, Broadman pulled this volume and reassigned authorship to Clyde T. Francisco, professor of Old Testament at Southern Baptist Theological Seminary in Louisville. Francisco was a well-respected name among Southern Baptists, but by 1971, the SSB had little good will in reserve among many Southern Baptists.[42]

The SSB's determination to steer a middle course led to demands for clarity and biblical fidelity. Douglas Manning of Tulsa, Oklahoma, thundered, "Dr. Sullivan, we need the truth, not a consensus." Manning disagreed with the decision to pull the *Becoming* material, noting, "We need material that will lead us, not just agree with us. What difference does it make if the majority believes a certain way if that majority is wrong?"[43] Manning had a point, but truth and consensus were matters of perspective, and from Sullivan's vantage, W. A. Criswell's advice to steer a middle course was precisely the tack he intended to hold. But by the end of January 1972, the SSB had received 681 responses to the *Becoming* episode, with 476 unfavorable responses, compared with 205 favorable responses.[44] If the SSB's running tally of reader's responses was any indicator, Sullivan faced an uphill climb.

In Texas, Sullivan received support from state executive T. A. Patterson, but he faced withering criticism from the Baptist Student Union (BSU) at Baylor University in Waco. Baptist Student Unions served as gathering places for Baptist youth and other interested parties, and there were hundreds of BSUs on college and university campuses throughout America in the 1970s. Some sent letters of protest; others sent resolutions. None, however, were as vocal in their displeasure over the *Becoming* episode as the students at Baylor.

---

[42] Elliott, *Genesis Controversy*. This work details Elliott's perspective on the controversy that bears his name.

[43] Manning to Sullivan, November 2, 1971 (19-20).

[44] In-house tabulation, January 1972, James L. Sullivan Papers (19-18). The tally indicates total responses only and differentiates between positive and negative responses by month received. It also tracks the states that offered the most responses with Kentucky (111), Texas (100) Tennessee (64), North Carolina (57), Georgia (48), and Mississippi (33) leading the way.

A Reckoning on Ninth Avenue

On November 1, the vice president of Baylor's student government, Steve Fontaine, tried to empathize with Sullivan, but he had "no sympathy for those in the Convention who are still so racially biased that they cannot accept a picture of a black boy talking to two white girls."[45] Student government president Danny Pleitz was even more pointed in his criticism, accusing the Board of hypocrisy. "It often seems to me," he said, "that Baptists worship Colonel Sanders rather than Jesus Christ."[46] On November 23, 1971, the Baylor Student Government passed a strongly worded resolution condemning the Board's action while affirming Frank Grayum, the editor who resigned over the issue. In his cover letter, Fontaine said, "Your decision to recall was extremely disappointing and insulting. The action was, is, and will be interpreted as racist."[47] Sullivan responded with a brief note of thanks, adding, "We regret that you feel as you do concerning this action."[48]

North Carolina Baptists voiced their opposition to the *Becoming* episode in no uncertain terms. In a letter dated November 11, 1971, W. Harry Clarke offered his personal support. Clarke worked for the Baptist State Convention of North Carolina (BSCNC) as an associate in the Sunday School Department of the Convention. He praised Sullivan as a wise leader and summed up his sentiments with, "What I'm trying to say is—whether we always realize it or not, we need you, and we need this gift of God—The Board—more and more, and more."[49] Notwithstanding his kind words, Clarke may have known what lay ahead. On November 12, Nathan C. Brooks Jr., director of the Division of Church Programs, wrote a letter to Sullivan and included numerous press clippings from media outlets and a resolution passed by the North Carolina convention. He informed Sullivan that many North Carolina Baptists were outraged. As for himself, Brooks said, "I wouldn't hurt more if you had slapped me in the

---

[45] Fontaine to Sullivan, November 4, 1971 (19-19).
[46] Pleitz to Sullivan, November 5, 1971 (19-19).
[47] Fontaine to Sullivan, November 23, 1971 (19-17).
[48] Sullivan to Fontaine, December 1, 1971 (19-17).
[49] Clarke to Sullivan, November 11, 1971 (19-14).

face without warning. Jim, as you can see, I am hurt. I cannot understand it!!"[50]

Before Clarke or Brooks expressed themselves to Sullivan, W. Perry Crouch, general secretary-treasurer of the BSCNC, wrote to Sullivan and offered a measure of encouragement. He trusted Sullivan's judgment but noted that North Carolinians were reacting negatively, and he asked, "If this kind of censorship is necessary, can't it be placed at the planning [l]evel instead of the finished product where it becomes a big issue?" Crouch sympathized with Sullivan's plight, but he had his own problems in North Carolina. Crouch included a message he delivered before the General Baptist Convention (African American) on November 4 whereby he apologized for the pain the *Becoming* episode caused and assured attendees of his continued interest in better race relations.[51]

Doubtless, Crouch was sincere in his comments. He was, however, also playing the part of a good executive. He was trying to create peace and promote good will for the good of SBC work in general and his home state in particular. His correspondence is not lengthy, but it suggests a camaraderie born of shared experience and perspective. As an executive of the BSCNC, Crouch would be a good company man, and while he might question Sullivan privately, he would try to smooth things over publicly. That is, he would do his best to hold things together in North Carolina.

Nathan Brooks did not fare as well as Perry Crouch. In a letter marked "Personal and Confidential," Sullivan chided Brooks for buying into the media's malicious propaganda. Sullivan then referred to what can only be described as a creative reading of the parable of the Good Samaritan. A certain priest and Levite passed a wounded man, neither lending aid nor condemning the thieves who assaulted him. Sullivan asked, "Isn't this precisely what you are doing? They [media outlets] are the people who have done the wrong. Actions by state conventions would have been more in order if they dealt with the injustices of the public media. Unfortunately, some of them have fallen into the same trap which victimize the priest and Levite." Further, he assured Brooks that he knew things that he could not

---

[50] Brooks to Sullivan, November 12, 1971 (19-14).

[51] W. Perry Crouch, "Greetings—General Baptist Convention," November 4, 1971 (19-14).

A Reckoning on Ninth Avenue

share openly. But he assured him "our hearts are in the right place," and he urged him to trust the SSB's judgment.[52]

State Baptist newspaper editors were charged with keeping their readership informed of SBC affairs at the state and national level. In Kentucky, the editor of *The Western Recorder*, Chauncy R. Daley Jr., sent Sullivan a draft of an editorial he planned to run on *Becoming* in early November, and he requested corrections for any inaccuracies. Sullivan commended him for his courtesy and parts of his editorial. Daley missed several key issues, however, and Sullivan wanted him to know that in no way had the SSB "bowed to pressure" in revising the literature. He assured Daley that he and his staff all wanted racial reconciliation, but it would never happen by publishing an "accusatory editorial full of emotional overtones." Moreover, Sullivan claimed that revising the material was far better than leaving Southern Baptists with wrong impressions and ultimately ignoring the lesson altogether. Finally, Sullivan asked if Daley had studied the "four lessons on 'Bible Teachings on Race,' published in the <u>Adult Bible Study</u> quarterly." Those lessons included two interracial photographs and discussed "foundations of racial harmony, overcoming prejudice, race and Christian fellowship, and Christian love and race relations." Had Daley seen these lessons, Sullivan thought it was inconceivable that he would draft the editorial he did.[53]

Sullivan also crossed swords with James O. Duncan, editor of the *Capital Baptist* in Washington DC. On November 5, 1971, Duncan wrote to Sullivan and expressed his love and appreciation for him and the staff. Nonetheless, Duncan was baffled by the way Sullivan was handling the situation and suggested a review by the entire Sunday School Board.[54] On November 11, Duncan ran a front-page story on *Becoming* and an editorial denouncing Sullivan's actions as "Unchristian and Unwise." Moreover, Duncan claimed, "This is the most embarrassing thing to Southern Baptists in many years. It just makes me sick for such a small group to make

---

[52] Sullivan to Brooks, November 26, 1971 (19-17).

[53] Sullivan to Daley, November 3, 1971 (19-18). Daley's draft is missing from the Sullivan papers.

[54] Duncan to Sullivan, November 5, 1971 (19-14).

WHY STUDY BAPTISTS?

decisions that not only embarrass us all over the world, but will greatly affect our ministry."[55]

Sullivan responded on November 18 with a letter marked "Personal and Confidential Not for Publication." He was dismayed by what he saw as Duncan's duplicity. In the November 5 letter, Duncan professed love and admiration, but in the November editorial, he accused Sullivan and the SSB of jeopardizing ministry at home and abroad. "To whip me publicly," Sullivan said, "and commend me in private is the thing that offended Paul so, and I feel about the same way." Sullivan assured Duncan that in the end, the truth would come out, but until then, editors had to produce newsprint, even if it was wrong. Besides, writing without the facts was easier and it gave editors "so much more to write about."[56]

The contrast between public and private discourse left Sullivan dismayed. Some editors were casting the SSB in a negative light, which fueled opposition from rank-and-file Southern Baptists. Plus, Sullivan believed that Duncan and others did not have all the facts. Consequently, people were angry over misinformation. Worst of all, Duncan's private affirmations of love and respect did not help Sullivan in the public square, where he most needed support. Yet there was one thing upon which Sullivan and his critics could agree; namely, each believed the other undermined the other's work.

Sullivan was not the only SSB staff member answering editorial critics. Gomer Lesch wrote to Hudson Baggett, editor of *The Alabama Baptist*, to disagree with an opinion piece by Jack Brymer. As Lesch saw it, "Mr. Brymer's 'Personal Opinion' column entitled 'Don't Blame the Press' is, in my own opinion, almost a classic textbook example of why criticism comes to the press." He claimed that Brymer had perpetuated distortions and then spent three pages trying to straighten matters out. Lesch, however, agreed with Brymer on one thing: "A free press with all its errors is much better than a controlled press which is perfect. I work for an agency which

---

[55] *Capital Baptist*, "Sunday School Board Action Unchristian and Unwise," (November 11, 1971): 2.

[56] Sullivan to Duncan, November 18, 1971 (19-14). Presumably, Sullivan compared himself to the Apostle Paul in Acts 16.

24

has a controlled press—a press controlled by the Southern Baptist Convention. I wonder who controls the press for which Mr. Brymer works?"[57]

For Sullivan, another problem appeared to be with Baptist Press (BP) in general and Jim Newton in particular. Normally, BP supported SBC work, but in a memo to Gomer Lesch dated January 17, 1972, Sullivan had begun to wonder. The Religious News Service had been the first to address *Becoming* before a national audience, but the story failed to make it into its top 10 list for the year. Conversely, "our news writers and editors of state Baptist publications listed it as the No. 1 item of the year. I am led to ask whether this particular Episode was not manipulated into this position by Baptist Press and the irresponsible newspaper reporters who harped on it rather than the importance which it does not really deserve." If that was the case, Sullivan wondered about BP's ultimate purpose. In his mind, BP had not helped the SSB, and he planned to raise the issue at some point if the press did not alter its "approach." He did not specify what he meant by "approach," but he stated unequivocally, "At least we need to ask the question concerning our own Baptist Sunday School Board's relationship to it."[58]

James Newton was the BP correspondent who wrote the stories on *Becoming*. While Newton didn't break the story, in Sullivan's mind, he kept the fire burning, and Gomer Lesch agreed. In an internal memo dated March 23, 1973, Lesch noted that Newton insinuated himself into the situation on November 8, 1971, by essentially circumventing the SSB altogether. According to Lesch, Newton told the state paper editors that he wanted to do a "round up story" in the coming days, and he asked them to send copies of any editorials they might write. When Lesch contacted Newton about this "round up story," Newton claimed it was necessary and ultimately wrote the story, but Lesch remained convinced that it was unnecessary.[59]

One day earlier, Lesch had compiled a list of stories regarding the *Becoming* episode. Under the heading "Baptist Press Handling of the

---

[57] Lesch to Baggett, December 3, 1971 (19-17). Brymer's column, "Don't Blame the Press," appeared in *The Alabama Baptist* (December 2, 1971): 5.

[58] Sullivan to Lesch, January 17, 1972 (19-18).

[59] Lesch to Sullivan, March 23, 1973 (19-18).

'Becoming' Incident," Lesch claimed that BP published seventeen stories on *Becoming* between October 28, 1971, and February 3, 1972. He thought the number of stories was justifiable "when you look at it from their perspective," but he questioned their judgment when it came to journalistic tone. Lesch complained that BP led with criticism of the decision over all else. He was especially critical of the way BP handled Frank Grayum's resignation. Lesch claimed that Newton talked to Grayum before he turned in his letter of resignation to his supervisor. "Newton talked to Grayum Wednesday night, and called him twice Thursday morning, trying to get the story." When Lesch asked him why he was interested, Newton responded that he was uncertain who should handle the story, and he was trying to help Frank Grayum. Nonplussed, Lesch noted, "This is the first uncertainty of this sort Jim has ever shown, in my experience.... What Jim really knows is that Baptist Press normally does not carry resignation stories. It is my opinion that his handling of this phase of the situation is highly questionable." He had other opinions, but he could not substantiate them, and he concluded by saying, "My own opinion is that we have justifiable criticism of Baptist Press in this matter, but they can defend much of their treatment of the situation."[60] As a denominational insider, it would have been nice to have Newton as an ally, but neither Sullivan nor Lesch saw him that way.

One can understand the SSB's frustration. True, the state editors might have had their own constituencies, but they traditionally sided (more or less) with denominational agencies. Now, some had broken ranks, and Sullivan could not count on them to follow usual protocol, however informal. Editors and state executives could argue the opposite point. Given the controversies surrounding the Sunday School Board over the past ten years or so, could the SSB still be trusted?

Sullivan attempted to restore calm on December 31, 1971, with a letter addressed to SSB trustees, agency heads, state executive secretaries, editors, presidents of Baptist colleges, and various workers in Baptist groups. In this letter, Sullivan compared his job to piloting a jet. Prior to takeoff, there were many decisions to make and little time to make them. He found himself in that position in October when he made the decision to redo the

---

[60] Lesch to Sullivan, March 22, 1973 (19-18).

Becoming material. He said, "I do think I owe you certain information in light of all that has been said," and he referred to a BP press release dated October 28, 1971. Most of the information had been distorted "through mishandling or misrepresentation." In the end, Sullivan said nothing new and seemed determined to stay with the October 28 press release to explain what happened.[61]

Agency heads might have struggled to identify with Sullivan's jet-pilot analogy, but they could sympathize with his plight. Editors of state papers, however, were another matter. The October 28 press release had not explained what happened, and they, along with the national news media, suspected that Sullivan was not entirely forthcoming. The *Becoming* episode, however, demonstrated that the Southern Baptist Convention had entered new and increasingly contentious territory. There had been negative reactions to earlier publications on race, but now one could see clear battle lines. If some SBC churches openly called for literature supporting racial segregation, others were just as vocal in calling for the SSB to be integration advocates. Full disclosure would spark another controversy, but by steering his middle way, James L. Sullivan and the Sunday School Board pleased no one. The SSB and the Convention's churches were in a bind, and 127 Ninth Avenue, Nashville, Tennessee, was ground zero.

Conclusion

James Lenox Sullivan served as president of the Baptist Sunday School Board from 1953 until his retirement in 1975. He then served one term as president of the Southern Baptist Convention in 1976. Before leaving the SSB, Sullivan wrote two books that offer a measure of insight on the *Becoming* episode, both published in 1974. He had seen a lot in his time with the SSB, and one book on Baptist polity, *Rope of Sand with Strength of Steel*, reflected his belief that many issues in the SBC could be solved by returning to the fundamentals of procedure. After all, the Grand Compromise hinged on cooperation among autonomous churches and denominational agencies. "This is the structure," Sullivan claimed, "our

---

[61] Sullivan to SBC Agency Heads, December 31, 1971 (19-18).

forefathers gave to our denomination to prevent us from gravitating toward a totalitarian system."[62] Unfortunately, the same system also created problems, including fragmentation, but Southern Baptists had a system that worked, and it would continue to work as long as everyone supported the programs and followed procedure. Sullivan warned, "It is dangerous for churches to feel that they and they alone are right and everyone else is wrong. People tend to feel that the way they do something is the only correct way and all other ways are wrong."[63] The SBC encouraged diversity, Sullivan claimed, but, he noted, "within diversity there must also be unity of purpose, fellowship among the brethren, and a unified movement toward the common goal of winning the world to Christ."[64]

In his memoir *God Is My Record*, James Sullivan reflected on his tenure at the Sunday School Board. Not surprisingly, the *Becoming* episode was still fresh in his memory, and he attributed the entire matter to social activists attempting to force the SSB to endorse their position on race. Additionally, he claimed that outside influences used the *Becoming* episode to advance their own agendas. As in his earlier explanations, Sullivan maintained that the Board existed to educate and would not be forced into advocacy. It had been a difficult time, but the SSB survived. It had not veered left just as it had not veered right in the mid-sixties. And Sullivan was proud that the SSB had stayed the middle course. "The Sunday School Board came through both of these episodes unscathed," he claimed, "although battered mercilessly for months. Still the Sunday School Board's volume of business continued to expand, so the purposes of the critics were not accomplished."[65]

The SSB's business may have expanded, but the *Becoming* episode revealed more than a few things about the SBC: Sullivan's rope of sand was fraying, and the Convention was fractured along cultural lines. Sullivan understood that the *Brown* decision created tremendous social, cultural,

---

[62] James Sullivan, *Rope of Sand with Strength of Steel: How Southern Baptists Function and Why* (Nashville, TN: Convention Press, 1974) 100–101.

[63] Ibid., 102.

[64] Ibid., 103.

[65] James L. Sullivan, *God Is My Record* (Nashville, TN: Broadman Press, 1974) 127.

A Reckoning on Ninth Avenue

and political changes, but the record indicates that racial tensions simmered beneath the surface throughout the twentieth century. Such racial tension coupled with socioeconomic upheaval set the backdrop for the *Becoming* episode. Some accepted, even welcomed that change; others resisted. But in attempting to maintain a middle way, Sullivan failed to appreciate fully the depth of change and rage the civil rights movement was generating. Neither could he appreciate the differences on the nature of Scripture or how to interpret it. These differences would trigger a revolt in the SBC that erupted in 1979 but had roots going back much further. As so-called Conservatives battled so-called Moderates for control of the SBC, one wonders if James Sullivan ultimately realized that the reckoning on Ninth Avenue was cultural change on the national level and polity alone could never fix it or adequately address it.

The Shantung Revival:
Baptists, Pentecostals, and Spirit-Led Experience

C. Douglas Weaver

When I earned my PhD under the mentorship of Dr. Bill J. Leonard, I wrote on William Marrion Branham, a mid-twentieth century independent Baptist who became a self-identified prophet in the subculture of Pentecostal divine healing revivalism.[1] I first learned about Branham while a master of divinity student in a class Bill taught on American revivalism. In recent years, I have returned to the broad topic of Baptist-Pentecostal interactions and written extensively on Baptists, the Holy Spirit, and the role of experience as a Baptist identity marker.[2] In this essay, I will focus on the Shantung (Shandong) Revival in eastern China (1927–1937) and how Baptist, Holiness, and especially Pentecostal identities interacted. In particular, I will examine how Baptist missionaries of the North China Mission placed Spirit-led experience at the heart of their Baptist identity yet denied being Pentecostal while involved in a revival saturated with practices associated with Pentecostalism.[3] Baptist-Pentecostal interaction broadens and refocuses the roles of the Spirit and experience in the Baptist story.

Contemporary scholars of Christianity in China emphasize the indigenous nature of revivalism in Shandong. Most emphasize that indigenous Christian movements, which had been attracted to Pentecostal practices like speaking in tongues, physically demonstrative worship, divine healing, and visions, spread a revival throughout the province, especially the rural areas, beginning in 1930. Historian Daniel Bays highlighted that

---

[1] C. Douglas Weaver, *The Healer-Prophet, William Marrion Branham: A Study of the Prophetic in American Pentecostalism* (Macon: Mercer University Press, 1987).

[2] C. Douglas Weaver, *Baptists and the Holy Spirit: The Contested History with the Holiness-Pentecostal-Charismatic Traditions* (Waco, TX: Baylor University Press, 2019).

[3] Shandong was called Shantung in the 1930s. I will use Shantung because it is used in all the missionary correspondence.

The Shantung Revival

a movement began with the preaching of a traveling Chinese Pentecostal revivalist from south China, which led several Chinese pastors (most from the Presbyterian Shandong mission) to embrace Pentecostal experience and form a loosely structured new group, the "Spiritual Gifts Society" (*Lingen hui*).[4] One scholarly approach, emphasized by Lian Xi, argues that the indigenous revivalism was anticolonial, a protest against the staid practices of the foreign mainstream denominations in favor of more ecstatic Pentecostal piety, which "bore an uncanny resemblance to spirit possession in popular religion." The circumvention of missionary authority became a "major catalyst" in catapulting Chinese Christian leaders into roles of spiritual leadership.[5] Most scholars acknowledge that there were parallel missionary-driven movements (Baptist, Pentecostal, and Presbyterian) that converged and interacted, sometimes awkwardly, with the dominant indigenous groups.[6] Some give the missionaries significant credit while not diminishing the indigenous role.[7] This essay, by highlighting missionary correspondence, will examine how the Baptist missionaries understood their participation in the Shantung Revival. They wholeheartedly agreed with missionary Charles Leonard, who wrote to Southern Baptists in

---

[4] Daniel H. Bays, "Christian Revival in China, 1900–1937," in *Modern Christian Revivals*, eds. Edith Blumhofer and Randall Balmer (Chicago: University of Illinois Press, 1993) 173.

[5] Lian Xi, *Redeemed by Fire: The Rise of Popular Christianity in Modern China* (New Haven, CT: Yale University Press, 2010) 9. See also 85–98, 105–106.

[6] Bays, "Christian Revival in China," 168–75. Daniel H. Bays, *A New History of Christianity in China* (Oxford: Wiley-Blackwell, 2012) 134–37. For a Presbyterian view at the time of the revival's origins, see "Indigenous Revivals in Shantung," *The Chinese Recorder* 52/12 (December 1931): 767–72.

[7] Wesley L. Handy, "An Historical Analysis of the North China Mission (SBC) and Keswick Sanctification in the Shandong Revival, 1927–1937," (PhD Diss., Southeastern Baptist Theological Seminary (October 26, 2020). R. G. Tiedemann, "Protestant Revivals in China with Particular Reference to Shandong Province," *Studies in World Christianity* 18/3 (2012): 213–26. See Handy and the other articles cited in this paragraph for a full description of the different indigenous groups forming at this time.

1935, "The present revival in North China is the greatest known in the history of missions in all China."[8]

Missionaries and Chinese Christian Workers

While the missionaries related the revival story through missionary eyes and activity, they had no hesitancy to cite key roles of Chinese leaders in the revival. Influential indigenous leader John Sung (Song Shangjie) and the Bethel Band were mentioned frequently. For example, Bertha Smith sought healing from Sung's ministry.[9] Spirit-filled Chinese preachers were applauded for their gifts of gospel witness and acknowledged as important speakers at revival meetings. Southern Baptists, not prone to accepting women preachers, cited several Chinese women favorably. Mrs. Yu Su Shan, according to I. V. Larson, preached effectively to both men and women. Wang Sue, said Martha Franks, "could preach more forcefully and beautifully than many men she knew." John Abernathy related how an illiterate seventy-three-year-old woman with poor eyesight had been saved, filled with the Spirit, and healed. She then learned to read the four Gospels and a church invited her to be their "shepherdess."[10]

Missionary reports were filled with names of Chinese workers, yet missionaries very rarely suggested that the Chinese were the driving force

---

[8] The missionary correspondence (letters, newsletters) is used by permission from the Southern Baptist Historical Library and Archives. Thanks to Taffy Hall for invaluable assistance. Charles A. Leonard Sr., "Questions Asked a Foreign Missionary on Furlough," *Biblical Recorder* (March 6, 1935): 10.

[9] Bertha Smith, *Go Home and Tell*, ed. Timothy George and Denise George (Nashville, TN: Broadman and Holman, 1995) 64–67. See also Eloise Glass Cauthen, *Higher Ground: Biography of Wiley B. Glass Missionary to China* (Nashville, TN: Broadman Press, 1978) 154.

[10] I. V. Larson to Jessie Ford, July 13, 1934. Larson served in Laiyang (1919–1926) and Laichow (1927–1935). His spouse, Edith, is not mentioned in revival narratives. Ford was the office assistant to Charles Maddry of the FMB. J. Donald McManus, *Martha Franks: One Link in God's Chain* (Lancaster, SC: Taxahaw Publications, 1990) 140. Martha Linda Franks, "Revival Fires," *Home and Foreign Fields* (July 1932): 31. John Abernathy Newsletter, October 26, 1932. John and Jewell Abernathy served in Tsinan in the 1930s.

The Shantung Revival

of the revival or that the missionary revival was dominated by a grassroots phenomenon. Exceptions were rare. Mary Crawford distinguished between the missionary revival efforts and those of a separate "wing," the "Ling En" (Spiritual Gifts Society), whom she said were responsible for the revival's emotional excesses.[11] Wiley Glass also acknowledged that the revival was "almost purely indigenous," but he emphasized indigenous efforts to jab theological opponents that the Chinese were attracted to evangelism and not to liberal Modernism. Glass more stereotypically indicated to critics that the revival's unusual practice of public confession of unspeakable sins was initiated by the Chinese believers.[12] Missionaries were not shy attributing emotional excesses to Chinese converts. Certainly, missionaries worked to train Chinese workers, and blatant condescension was absent from the extant missionary correspondence—which is not always the case in missionary reports, Baptists or otherwise. Still, the willingness of missionaries to shift leadership to Chinese Christians was often a slow process.[13]

Shantung Revival: Beginnings

When unrest from the Nationalist Revolution (Chiang Kai Shek) hit the Shandong area in 1927, two dozen Baptist missionaries from the North China Mission were evacuated to the port city of Chefoo. They engaged in intense prayer sessions for themselves and the swirling political situation which they believed needed revival to counter increasing anti-Christian sentiment. During one prayer session, Charles Culpepper (president of the North China Baptist Theological Seminary during the revival) asked Norwegian Lutheran missionary Maria Monsen if she would pray for the healing of his spouse, Ola. Monsen's seemingly odd response was to ask Culpepper if he was filled with the Holy Spirit. Missionaries reported that Ola Culpepper was healed of an eye condition, and the story became known as the traditional Baptist story of the revival's origins. More importantly, missionary searching about the power of the Holy Spirit, already present

---

[11] Mary Crawford to Charles Maddry, December 6, 1933.

[12] Glass Cauthen, *Higher Ground*, 162.

[13] Alice Wells Hall, "Letter from Yangchow, China," *Biblical Recorder* (September 11, 1935): 5.

WHY STUDY BAPTISTS?

through reading of Holiness literature and hearing Holiness advocates at summer camps, would only increase.[14]

Missionaries were exuberant admirers of Monsen, a Keswick-influenced Holiness teacher (meaning she emphasized a post-conversion experience of being filled with the Spirit to empower gospel witnessing).[15] In 1929, with the missionaries back in Shantung, Chinese Christians, Monsen, and others, including Baptist missionary Jane Lide, spoke at a Chinese Christian worker's conference. The power of the Holy Spirit was a conference theme.[16] In 1930, the aura around Marie Monsen increased after she was captured by pirates but released unharmed.[17]

All the missionaries accepted, without hesitation, Monsen's method of direct, often confrontational questioning of each person about their spiritual condition. As one missionary described it, Monsen's message "caused sleepless nights and made food not good to many church members and evangelists."[18] Monsen asked each person in her audiences "are you born again?" The result was often that people who claimed to be Christian decided they were not, and, according to the missionaries, then had a new

---

[14] Smith, *Go Home*, 9–11, 37–45. Charles and Ola Culpepper served in Hwanghsien. Charles was the seminary's president from 1931 to 1942.

[15] Bays, *A New History*, 135. Bay assumed that Monsen had a Pentecostal experience. Monsen's autobiography and Baptist participants denied any ties to Pentecostalism. Marie Monsen, *The Awakening: Revival in China, 1927–1937* (Shoals, IN: Kingsley Press, [1959] 2011). Baptist testimonies identified Monsen more with other Keswick holiness teachers they read and heard at summer camps, such as R. A. Torrey, Ruth Paxson, and Charles Trumbull, all of whom highlighted the need for a post-conversion experience of the Holy Spirit.

[16] Lide had an encounter with Pentecostals two years earlier in California. While opposing Pentecostal ideas, Lide contributed to the Baptist interest in Spirit-led experience. Lide, "Chinese Christian Worker's Conference," 50/10 *The Chinese Recorder* (October 1929): 671–73.

[17] Most stories and analyses of the revival discuss Monsen. For example, see Gustav Carlberg, *China in Revival* (Rock Island, IL: Augustana Book Concern, 1936) 67–69. Jesse C. Fletcher, *Living Sacrifices: A Missionary Odyssey* (Nashville, TN: Broadman Press, 1974) 48–50. Lian Xi said that Monsen's influence and that of other missionaries was soon eclipsed and spread at the grassroots level, out of the missionaries' control. Lian Xi, *Redeemed by Fire*, 98.

[18] "From Katie Murray," *Biblical Recorder* (March 2, 1932): 13.

34

The Shantung Revival

authentic salvation experience. If salvation was secure, Monsen pressed to hear if a person had been filled or baptized in the Spirit, and, according to missionary reports, many received the gift of spiritual power.[19] While missionaries honored Monsen for her pioneering Spirit-led role, they insisted that the eruption of revival was tied to years of prior prayer and then ongoing revival prayer, which included all-night and all-day prayer sessions.[20] Monsen, in her later reflections, affirmed the Baptist story's focus on prayer. She described the Baptist missionaries as "godly warmhearted missionaries" and affirmed that the Baptist prayers had made revival success in her work easier: "It was like coming to a vast field fully ripe for harvesting."[21]

Revival Growth

In 1931, reports of widespread miraculous revival began to flourish. Baptist newspapers stateside began to share updates. Missionary reports described a revival where many missionaries received the baptism of the Holy Spirit and hundreds of Chinese were converted, filled with the Holy Spirit, and miraculously healed of illnesses.[22] Missionaries noted that revival first occurred among Presbyterians but emphasized that Baptists followed close behind with revival in Pintgu and Laiyang. I. V. Larson wrote excitedly that when revival hit Laiyang, "the fire of the Holy Spirit fell" and the "spiritual temperature rose."[23] In his newsletter sent back to mission supporters stateside, Larson described a nine-day "regular old-fashioned Holy Ghost revival" with multiple instances of confession of sins and conversions, but he also spoke of Spirit-led visions. In particular, he shared the

---

[19] Bonnie Ray to Maddry, November 3, 1933. Glass Cauthen, *Higher Ground*, 149. Mary K. Crawford, *The Shantung Revival* (Shanghai, China: China Baptist Publication Society, 1934) 23, 39–40, 45, 54–55, 66, 105.

[20] Katie Murray, "The Secret of Revival in China," *Biblical Recorder* (December 9, 1936): 1. McManus, *Martha Franks*, 103–104.

[21] Monsen, *Revival in China*, 62.

[22] "Report of Southern Baptist Convention," *Biblical Recorder* (May 20, 1931): 3. Wesley Handy analyzed annual reports of the SBC. They mentioned revival four times in 1927, but a turning point occurred in 1931 when revival was mentioned thirteen times. See Handy, "An Historical Analysis," 19.

[23] Larson to T. B. Ray, January 6, 1932.

WHY STUDY BAPTISTS?

vision of a seventeen-year-old woman who, in her two-hour trance-state, was transported to heaven and spoke to Jesus. "Her face took upon it a heavenly transparency and looked like an angel's," Larson wrote. Prior to this "epochal" nine-day event, Larson thought the revival spirit had primarily been among missionaries in his region, but now the Chinese had caught the revival fires and were going to be "flaming evangels."[24]

As revival spread, missionaries insisted that the typical focus on conversions was at the heart of the movement, but at the same time, their reports of miracles and healings proliferated. These included reported instances of speaking in tongues and being slain in the Spirit (compelled by the Spirit to fall prostrate to the ground). John Abernathy spoke of the revival as being like the days of miraculous signs and wonders and the exorcism of demons in the Book of Acts.[25] In 1933, Mary Crawford published a book about the Shantung Revival that included an extensive amount of unsigned missionary letters. The revival was a "great work of the Holy Spirit,"[26] Crawford believed, and she did not hesitate to describe conversions, testimonies of being baptized in the Spirit, healings, visions, and demon exorcisms. According to Crawford, at least twenty-four missionaries from 1930 to 1932, including herself, claimed the Holy Spirit baptism.[27] Missionary correspondence continued unabated in defense of the revival until its end in 1937 when missionaries evacuated China amid war, but a vigorous defense was necessary because not all Baptists were convinced that the Shantung Revival was very divine or very Baptist.

---

[24] Larson Material Newsletter, 1931.

[25] J. A. Abernathy, "Interesting Letter from China," *Biblical Recorder* (January 15, 1930): 11. Abernathy to Maddry, December 19, 1932.

[26] Crawford to Maddry, March 15, 1932. Crawford, *Shantung Revival*.

[27] Crawford, *Shantung Revival*, 23. I have focused extensively on Crawford's book and her role in the revival in an article published through the International Conference of Baptist Studies. Crawford served in Tsining (1922–1930) and Tsinan (1930–1941). See "Mary Crawford, the Shantung Revival (1927–1937), and Its Gendered Legacy," in *Baptists and Gender, Papers for the Ninth International Conference on Baptist Studies*, eds. Melody Maxwell and T. Laine Scales (Macon, GA: Mercer University Press, 2023).

Defense of Revival: Its Effects

Baptist missionaries insisted that the Shantung Revival was a movement of the Holy Spirit. They provided several proofs, or revival effects. Naturally, they applauded evangelistic success. In 1933, John and Jewell Abernathy exclaimed that they had seen more conversions in the last three years than they had in all the previous ten years they had been missionaries in China. For the Abernathys, such success was proof that the revival was Spirit-led and "according to God's Word."[28] The revival ignited continuous public confessions of sin, a practice emphasized by Keswick Holiness teachers, and missionaries declared that genuine confession of sin led inevitably to Spirit-led revival success. Missionaries confessing their sins was important, as Bonnie Jean Ray noted, "It is sad beyond words for the Chinese to feel a missionary lacks life."[29]

Revival success, according to the missionaries, was surely seen in extraordinary miracles such as healings and demon exorcisms. They knew Baptists stateside were uncomfortable with such testimonies, but missionaries never denied that they witnessed miraculous events;[30] they were not cessationist regarding any gifts of the Spirit.[31] While they decried excessive emotion and equated it with the distortions of Pentecostal evangelists, ultimately, the missionaries viewed emotion as part of the proof of the revival's success. Bonnie Ray admitted some of the emotion was probably fake, but she was confident most of it was real. As Wiley Glass assessed, the excesses "were but the foam in the eddies of a great and mighty tide that swept out the old channels and brought life and beauty to the whole field."[32] Or, acknowledged more practically, if the missionaries had not

---

[28] John and Jewell Abernathy to Maddry, November 17, 1933.

[29] Ray to T. B. Ray, November 16, 1931. Ray served in Pingtu (1919–1940).

[30] Oliver and Sadie Lawton, "From Chengchow and Kaifeng, Honan," *Biblical Recorder* (February 8, 1933): 15. John Abernathy Newsletter, December 10, 1934.

[31] Cessationism is the belief that miracles ceased after the era of the New Testament. Miracles were to help birth the church and were no longer needed.

[32] Glass Cauthen, *Higher Ground*, 162–64. Ray to Maddry, November 3, 1933. For another defense of emotion, see Alice Huey, "The Revival in North China," *Biblical Recorder* (September 5, 1934): 12.

seen the power of God in the revival testimonies of miracles, the Chinese converts were willing to leave them for those who were more affirming.

Proofs demonstrating a Spirit-led revival included a variety of practical signs. In years past, I. V. Larson noted, missionaries had to employ creative or flashy means like blaring phonographs to attract the Chinese to mission work. During the revival, he asserted, "people are being attracted through the power of the Holy spirit."[33] Missionaries affirmed that the salutary effects on the Chinese were proof of the revival's success. The Chinese had a hunger for the Bible that had intensified from the revival fires, and many responded to God's call to attend seminary for ministry preparation.[34] Some Chinese had left their businesses for a year in order to do evangelism, and, according to Charles Culpepper, "were filled with such a zeal for winning the lost as we had hardly dared hope before."[35] Revival participants also offered financial restitution to offended parties because of past sins, back tithes to the church, and school diplomas returned because of cheating. Even Bonnie Ray paid tithes she had failed to give before she was a missionary.[36] Missionaries were convinced that transformed lives were indisputable proof of a Spirit-led revival. Wiley Glass commented that he saw "too many sorry Christians become radiant witnesses to deny it."[37]

One proof of the revival was the genuine salvation of people who had previously been converted to Christianity rather than to Christ. The missionary perspective was certainly an assent to Marie Monsen's controversial method of asking each person she preached to if he or she had truly been born again. One missionary explained that the irony of unsaved church members was a cause of humility for the missionaries. They knew that something was wrong—the mission churches were stagnant and had failed the test of faithfulness during the political upheavals of 1927—and

---

[33] Larson to Ford, October 8, 1934.

[34] Larson to Maddry, November 29, 1933.

[35] Charles Culpepper to Maddry, November 20, 1933.

[36] W. B. Glass, "A Glorious Revival in Hwanghsien," *Home and Foreign Fields* (July 1932): 31. Charles A. Leonard Sr., "A Personal Missionary Letter Telling of the Revival in the North China Mission," *Biblical Recorder* (October 5, 1932): 13. Ray to Maddry, November 3, 1933.

[37] Glass Cauthen, *Higher Ground*, 154.

The Shantung Revival

the revival made them realize it was not simply ignorance of the Bible or lack of mission funds, but rather a "lack of any life."[38] Such a striking perspective was why missionaries were ebullient in their praise for missionary Lucy Wright, who claimed salvation during the revival. In Chinese culture, the missionaries noted, such an admission could mean "losing face," or losing the respect of peers. But Wright (as anyone should) responded to the Holy Spirit. As a result, Bonnie Ray exclaimed, "Lucy Wright is a wonder now.... Her testimony is powerful! Not all would want to lose face and come out as a lost, condemned sinner saved by grace after reaching the field. Where there is life, there is power."[39] Ray's further assessment of the current state of the local Chinese churches revealed how missionaries became convinced Monsen's revival methods were needed. "The real trouble there," Ray said, "is that the churches have too many unregenerated members in them."[40] Bertha Smith condescendingly blamed the Chinese evangelists for creating such a state. According to Smith, they were so eager to get the Chinese converted, they offered them an easy "only believe" gospel.[41]

Most reports of revival proofs were of extravagant Spirit-led success. A few stories, however, told a fuller story. Missionaries emphasized the results they thought proved the miraculous, in part, because they still experienced hardships. Six missionary children had diphtheria and one missionary had tuberculosis during the revival. The missionary setting—thirty missionaries were kept in the United States for periods of time during the revival, mostly for financial reasons, and no furloughs were granted for a whole year (1933)—made them marvel at the revival effects that did occur.[42] After the revival's initial fervor, missionaries noted in typical fashion that some converts had lost their zeal.[43] Bertha Smith's letters reveal that not all the missionaries in China worked under the constant glow of revival. Describing a trip into the Chinese country land in 1933, she

---

[38] "From Katie Murray," *Biblical Recorder* (March 2, 1932): 13. Katie Murray, "The Secret of Revival in China," *Biblical Recorder* (December 9, 1936): 1.

[39] Ray to T. B. Ray, November 16, 1931.

[40] Ibid.

[41] Bertha Smith Newsletter, May 4, 1933.

[42] Glass Cauthen, *Higher Ground*, 159.

[43] Mary Crawford Newsletter, November 30, 1935.

lamented, "Here where no one wants to talk on my subject and it is too cold to stay up or get up when the sun is out of sight. My nights are so long that I have split the canvas on my cot. This is my birthday but what does it matter to any one here that I was born! Would that the fact that I was born a second time might interest them but the news which I am spending a week here to bring seems to make no difference."[44] Ironically, Smith's description was consistent with the typical missionary response that the Shantung Revival was authentic because it was led by the Holy Spirit in response to prayer. She commented, "But is not Shantung the province from where the great revivals are being reported? Yes, but the revivals are in sections where there has been, in most cases, years of mission work. There must still be great sections of China where the people are as blind to the truth and as dead in sin as they are in this country, and there must first be the teaching of the truth to enlighten the mind before the Holy Spirit can use it to change the heart."[45] Despite her rationale for the lack of success, Smith still pined for more conversions like other missionaries were reporting.[46]

Defense of the Revival: Missionary Experience

A fundamental element of the revival's success—and the missionaries' defense of it—was their own personal experience. Being a missionary in a faraway land fraught with severe political stresses sent them searching for divine help. Specifically, or in theological terms, they desired more experience of God, or the baptism of the Holy Spirit. They refused to call the experience the "second blessing," a controversial term associated with Holiness and Pentecostal theology, but it was the power for witness, service, and intimacy with God that they cherished.

A sampling of the testimonies reveals the missionary mindset. Bonnie Ray, Mary Crawford, and Ola Culpepper all agreed that they did not have adequate spiritual power to be missionaries in a foreign land. Crawford related that it was impossible to serve on "past experience alone." Culpepper said Southern Baptists thought people called to the mission field were

---

[44] Bertha Smith Newsletter, November 1933.
[45] Smith Newsletter, November 1933.
[46] Bertha Smith Newsletter, January 1935.

40

The Shantung Revival

"fully surrendered to the Lord," but, learning from the Holiness call for victory over sin, she realized that she was in desperate spiritual need. Bonnie Ray said that as she observed the ministry of Marie Monsen, "a deeper hunger came into my heart for spiritual power that I knew I did not have as she did."[47] Jewell and John Abernathy said that because they felt spiritually empty amid the challenges of the mission field, they spent hours in prayer seeking the fullness of the Holy Spirit. Jewell especially desired the experience after learning that Mary Crawford had experienced it. "I am so hungry for God's Spirit that I ache all over," she confessed. Her husband, John, had the experience two weeks later after seeing the spiritual change in his wife. Both said that they participated in all-night prayer meetings. The key was confessing sins—even things she was not sure were sins, according to Jewell—and the contrite heart led to an "empty vessel [which] then received an outpouring of God's Spirit."[48]

Missionaries naturally said that the revival triggered their increased attention to what the Bible said about the power of the Holy Spirit. I. V. Larson declared, "As I studied the Word I found that Christ promised POWER to His disciples. I realized that there was a sad lack in my own life, and the lives of our native Christians. I found that I had not appropriated this power myself, and that I was powerless to give the Message to the Lost."[49] Charles Culpepper said that he "longed for a closer walk with God" as promised in Scripture, and in doing so, affirmed typical Holiness theology that there was a post-conversion experience that believers had failed to request from God—which he received during the revival.[50] Missionaries also commonly emphasized that they read Holiness literature that deepened their spiritual experience. The life story of Charles Finney and the writings of R. A. Torrey on the Holy Spirit were regularly cited as building desire for the Spirit's empowerment. As Pearl Caldwell said,

---

[47] Crawford to Maddry, December 6, 1933. Ola Culpepper to Maddry, November 20, 1933. Ray to Maddry, November 3, 1933. Ray to T. B. Ray, November 16, 1931.

[48] Fletcher, *Living Sacrifices,* 52–53. Abernathys to Maddry, November 17, 1933. See also Culpepper to Maddry, November 20, 1933.

[49] Larson to Maddry, February 29, 1936.

[50] Culpepper to Maddry, November 20, 1933.

"Like Dr. Torrey I believe not only in the 'second blessing' but in the three hundredth and on and on."[51]

In good Keswick fashion, the experience of being filled with the Spirit translated into passion for evangelism, but the identification of being Spirit-filled with spiritual intimacy had no set expression. Ola Culpepper's testimony, however, demonstrated how missionaries could express their experience in mystical terms while nevertheless insisting that they were not guilty of excessive emotion, as critics lampooned. Echoing Holiness and Pentecostal imagery, Culpepper wrote, "I haven't words to express to you what happened in my soul then. The joy that filled my soul just rolled over me in waves and waves.... I was utterly lost in the ocean of God's love. A spirit of intercession came over me as I had never known. My heart seemed melted in love to God and every person that I knew. The praise just poured out of my heart." Declaring that she had never heard a Pentecostal preach at the time of her Spirit baptism (1932), she added that she experienced holy laughter, a laughter that shocked her until she later realized that Scripture spoke of laughter in encounters with God.[52]

Revival Conflict: 1933

In January 1933, Charles Maddry, executive-secretary of the Foreign Mission Board (FMB) of the Southern Baptist Convention (SBC), wrote John Abernathy that he was pleased to hear of reports of genuine revival in China.[53] By the fall of 1933, however, Maddry wrote several missionaries stationed with the North China Mission (NCM) about reported doctrinal and behavioral excesses in the Shantung Revival. He forwarded a resolution that the FMB had adopted which asked that the missionaries be questioned about their involvement in the revival, specifically in relation to their "religious activities." While the resolution was not specific, Maddry was concerned that stories were circulating in Baptist newspapers that NCM missionaries had fallen away from their Baptist identity and New

---

[51] Pearl Caldwell to Maddry, December 23, 1933. Ray to Maddry, November 3, 1933. Abernathys to Maddry, November 17, 1933.

[52] Culpepper emphasized that Abraham laughed when God gave him the miracle of a child. Ola Culpepper to Maddry, November 20, 1933.

[53] Maddry to John Abernathy, January 16, 1933.

The Shantung Revival

Testament teachings—which were, of course, assumed to be the same—and had adopted Pentecostal practices such as speaking in tongues, bodily manifestations, falling allegedly under the Holy Spirit's guidance, and excessive emotionalism. Missionaries were also being accused of allowing Pentecostal ministers to preach at Baptist services. Maddry affirmed that the FMB wanted to move slowly and carefully, and that the agency was not assuming the accusations were accurate. He admitted, however, that economic factors were driving his concern. Reported revival successes notwithstanding, with the crushing debt of the Great Depression wreaking havoc on mission support, Maddry believed that the distractions of the Shantung Revival would only worsen the financial instability of the entire foreign-mission enterprise.[54]

The accusations initially came primarily from an independent Baptist missionary in China, T. L. Blalock, whose Landmarkist Baptist ministry, the China Direct Mission, was followed sympathetically by many Southern Baptists, especially those in his home state of North Carolina. Blalock had successfully recruited a Southern Baptist pastor from Tennessee, G. L. Winstead, to help spread accusations of Pentecostal heresy. Blalock no doubt had an axe to grind. In 1916, he had written about his disgust with the fledgling ten-year-old Pentecostal movement. According to Blalock, Pentecostal practices—"The biggest fraud I have ever heard of being palmed off on the public in the name of mission work"—were worse than those experienced by the Corinthian church in the New Testament. The Corinthian trouble was due to the immaturity of new converts, but the attack on his China mission was by his own missionaries, who disrupted the mission and then became Pentecostals.[55] Blalock claimed that his mission lost around three hundred Chinese converts to Pentecostalism. Two of the missionaries reportedly involved in the Pentecostal excesses of the Shantung Revival, John and Jewell Abernathy, had been part of Blalock's missionary team in the early 1920s (Blalock had performed their marriage ceremony) before they aligned with the SBC. Their extensive participation

---

[54] Maddry to Ray, October 18, 1933. The same letter was sent to I. V. Larson, Mary Crawford, the Abernathys, and the Culpeppers.

[55] "'Pentecostal Tongues' in China," *Biblical Recorder* (March 1, 1916): 5.

WHY STUDY BAPTISTS?

in the revival no doubt burned the cessationist fires and fueled the accusations of their former missionary supervisor.[56]

Revival Defense: Anti-Pentecostal

Baptists, at home and abroad, acted as if identification with Pentecostalism was a fate worse than death—well, almost. Pentecostals were considered of a different socioeconomic class (lower than the Baptists who had climbed the ladder), and their literal biblical restorationism of church practices from the New Testament's Book of Acts was a threat to Baptist claims that they were the most genuine embodiment of the New Testament church. Correspondence between Charles Maddry and NCM missionaries reflected the tensions that circled Pentecostal identity.

Baptist missionaries offered Maddry written explanations regarding a variety of so-called Pentecostal issues, especially in the context of whether they were expressions of excessive emotionalism. The Abernathys affirmed that the Shantung experience included emotion, but they strongly denied that the revival was marred by excessive emotion. Blalock's accusations that missionaries were jumping or dancing in the Spirit were wrong, they insisted. The Abernathys denied Blalock's charge that they "became blank or oblivious to what was going on around us."[57] They further denied that the missionaries were adopting the Pentecostal practice of "tarrying" for the Spirit for periods of two consecutive days and nights. They contended that some of the Chinese converts had at times "give[n] place to the flesh," but missionaries had worked hard to pull them back to correct biblical practices. The Abernathys told Maddry that the authentic emotions which characterized the revival were expressions of happiness. Examples included people shouting hallelujah—Abernathy himself was witnessed shouting praises—or sometimes "moaning under their terrible burden of sin." According to the Abernathys, Maddry should consider the Shantung miracle

---

[56] T. L. Blalock, *Experiences of a Baptist Faith Missionary for 56 Years in China* (Fort Worth, TX: Manney Printing Company, 1949) 199. In 1949, Blalock blustered, "Their modern miracles are like the morning dew which disappears before the rising sun."

[57] Fletcher, *Living Sacrifices*, 62.

The Shantung Revival

"an old fashioned revival," a biblical Pentecost, not Pentecostalism, and surely the "revival fires" should keep burning.[58]

Several missionaries, even before 1933, spoke to the seeming confusion of audible communal prayer practiced by the Chinese. The practice no doubt sounded like an environment where speaking in tongues flourished, and suspicious missionaries saw parallels with the "clanging" symbols of 1 Corinthians 13, where the Apostle Paul derogatorily described chaotic worship. Wiley Glass admitted that the first time he heard simultaneous "concert prayer," he thought it was "bedlam." Still, he eventually hoped to pray "with the same fervor."[59] While the practice did not originate with the revival, Charles Culpepper told Maddry that the revival did intensify the practice. With discomfort, he attributed the practice to Chinese culture: "It seems to me the Chinese almost think aloud. Chinese students study their lessons aloud, and it seems quite natural to them to pray aloud."[60] Culpepper did not enthusiastically affirm the Chinese Christians, but he concluded that Scripture did not forbid the practice and that Baptist history included stories of group audible praying when the Spirit was powerfully present in congregations. Missionaries were united that the audible congregational prayer was a sign of the revival's genuine Spirit-led power.[61]

While missionaries agreed some emotional excesses had occurred in the revival, they offered additional pushback to being associated with Pentecostalism. Missionaries countered that they tried to calm the excesses while working with the Chinese believers who were practicing them. I. V. Larson said that an outright harsh rejection of the experiences of the revival converts was counterproductive and lost the Chinese to other pro-revival groups. In contrast, Larson said that the missionaries "tried to

---

[58] Abernathys to Maddry, November 17, 1933.

[59] Glass Cauthen, *Higher Ground*, 154.

[60] Culpepper to Maddry, November 20, 1933. See also Franks, "Revival Fires," 31.

[61] In 1935, Charles Leonard, while not opposing the revival or the group prayer, suggested that the apostles in Acts 2, rather than exhibiting ecstatic speech (speaking in tongues), most likely prayed audibly at the same time in different languages. Charles Leonard, "A Bible Conference and a Revival," *Biblical Recorder* (December 18, 1935): 12.

WHY STUDY BAPTISTS?

sympathetically and tactfully deal with them" and were able to teach the Bible and Baptist principles, thus correcting error and sustaining missionary success.[62] More positively, Mary Crawford and Bonnie Ray were convinced that the transformed lives and active faith of the Chinese converts revealed the importance of the revival amid any excesses. Crawford agreed the indigenous Spiritual Gifts Society could be blamed for emotional excess, but she refused to judge them because they had brought life to spiritually dead churches. Ray thought Southern Baptists could learn from the Chinese. She wanted Southern Baptists to practice what they preached if they were going to criticize revival excesses. While she was grateful that some Southern Baptists were Spirit-led, she told Maddry that the SBC needed the spiritual power of revival to solve their problems.[63] Wiley Glass added that missionaries encouraged the Chinese converts to move away from emotional excess. For example, he told seminary students where he taught that they didn't need to jump up and down and shout hallelujah and cautioned, "Don't keep airing your sins. When God forgives, he forgets. You should too." Missionaries paternalistically hoped and asserted that with correct instruction, revival excesses gradually diminished. At the same time, Glass was pragmatic and agreed with Larson: missionaries needed to cooperate with the Chinese and affirm them, or else they would just leave the Baptists and do revival without them.[64]

One of the major complaints that Maddry worried about was whether Baptist missionaries were inviting Pentecostal missionaries to preach in Baptist settings. Baptists did not affirm "union" work, though the boogeyman, most Southern Baptists thought, was flirtation with Modernism by some missionaries.[65] The Shantung Revival revealed a starkly different manifestation of anti-union or anti-cooperative sentiment: association

---

[62] Larson to Maddry, November 29, 1933.

[63] Crawford to Maddry, October 13, 1933. Ray to Maddry, June 6, 1934.

[64] W. B. Gloss (Glass), "A Remarkable Revival in Shantung," *Home and Foreign Fields* (May 1932): 15–16. Glass Cauthen, *Higher Ground*, 154.

[65] Bertha Smith said that Shantung Christian University was modernistic and Baptist missionaries were not involved there because they did not do union work. Bertha Smith Newsletter, September 21, 1935. For reported Liberalism at Shanghai among Northern Baptists, see Charles Culpepper's letter to Maddry, September 12, 1934.

The Shantung Revival

with evangelistic Pentecostals might weaken the Baptist witness. While associating with Holiness teachers was stretching some Baptist comfort zones, consorting with Pentecostals went too far and was regarded as unwanted, unbiblical, and undesirable competition that might produce fallen, strayed Baptists. One of the charges leveled against the missionaries was not simply that they had cooperated with Pentecostals, but rather that the revival was Pentecostal-initiated and Baptists had compromised themselves by participating in such ill-advised distortions. While contemporaries (Presbyterian missionaries) noted, with criticism, that Pentecostalism was part of the revival's origins, Baptist missionaries adamantly opposed the suggestion. I. V. Larson said that the revival "at Laichow and Laiyang [where he served] was not brought in from without, but was the direct work of the Holy Spirit, in answer to our prayers."[66]

The real issue of compromising "union" work was with the former Free Will Baptist-turned-Pentecostal evangelist George Kelley. Had the missionaries allowed Kelley to invade Baptist work with Pentecostal heresy? Pentecostal magazines certainly asserted that Kelley was a successful evangelist in the Shantung Revival.[67] Pentecostals also testified that Kelley had significant interaction and success with Baptists on the mission field. When he preached at Baptist mission sites, Chinese participants were converted and/or baptized in the Spirit. One report said that in 1928—during the days that Baptists were fervently praying for revival—Kelley spoke to three hundred Chinese preachers and Bible women who were at a convention in the Baptist church.[68] At 1931 meetings with Southern Baptists, Margaret Kelley reported, "We had a wonderful outpouring of the Spirit there. Never have I witnessed such a hunger for God and His Word, and the Lord poured out His Spirit like on Cornelius's

---

[66] Larson to Maddry, November 29, 1933.

[67] "China," *The Bridegroom's Messenger* (August–October 1927): 4. Margaret Kelley, "Hong Kong, South China," *The Bridegroom's Messenger* (August–October 1927): 3. Margaret Kelley was also effective in healing. See "Many Chinese Healed by Great Physician," *Foursquare Crusader* (February 27, 1929): 16.

[68] Margaret Kelley, "China's Open Door," *Pentecostal Evangel* (July 7, 1928): 15. George M. Kelley, "Open Doors in China," *The Bridegroom's Messenger* 22 (July–September 1929): 13. Margaret Kelley, *"Sainam," Pentecostal Evangel* (January 8, 1927): 10.

household. The whole congregation stood with uplifted hands, either weeping over their sins or praising and magnifying God. Two Baptist missionaries received the Holy Ghost baptism, and also Chinese pastors, evangelists, teachers, and Bible women."[69] Like his Baptist counterparts, George Kelley declared that Shantung was experiencing a "Holy Ghost revival," though he also used the language of "the latter rain," a biblical concept used by Pentecostals to indicate that the Shantung phenomenon was evidence of an end-time harvest of souls before the imminent return of Jesus.[70]

Whereas I. V. Larson had denied any personal compromises with Pentecostal evangelists and promised there would be none, other Baptists were more vulnerable.[71] Bonnie Ray acknowledged that George Kelley had participated in revival services, but she said the Chinese Christians invited him. Still, she affirmed that the Chinese had experienced the Spirit in Kelley's meetings.[72] Charles Culpepper's response about Kelley was similar to Ray's but laced with criticism. Culpepper said that he and other Baptists at Hsanghsien had heard of Kelley's revivalistic success but declined to invite him to speak at their mission. Chinese converts, however, invited him, over the protest of some missionaries. Culpepper insisted that Kelley's Pentecostal view on speaking in tongues as *the sign* of the Holy Spirit baptism made no inroads among the Baptists, and he personally told Kelley not to mention his "extreme" doctrine when he preached where Baptists were present.[73]

Like I. V. Larson, the Abernathys denied that any missionary work they were involved with had ever initiated involvement with Pentecostals, but their caveat was revealing. They acknowledged that George Kelley was "out of courtesy" invited to preach as he passed through their Baptist

---

[69] Margaret Kelley, "Holy Ghost Revival in North China," *The Latter Rain Evangel* (December 1931): 22. Kelley says they also ministered with Swedish Baptist missionaries. George M. Kelley, "Where the Flaming Torch Is Lifted High," *The Latter Rain Evangel* (April 1932): 19.

[70] Kelley, "Holy Ghost Revival in North China," 22.

[71] Larson to Maddry, November 29, 1933. Maddry to Larson, January 2, 1934.

[72] Ray to Maddry, November 3, 1933.

[73] Culpepper to Maddry, November 20, 1933.

The Shantung Revival

missionary compound. The Abernathys, however, said "nothing came of his speaking" and they also told Kelley that they disagreed with his views on speaking in tongues. In addition, the Abernathys mentioned another Pentecostal not described in other Baptist correspondence, a Miss Botolfsen, but they emphasized that she had only stayed in their home for two weeks while her "Bible woman" was in the hospital in the area and had not spoken in Baptist meetings. The Abernathys found refuge in noting that Botolfsen was not associated with Aimee Semple McPherson, the Pentecostal leader whose female leadership and popularity scandalized Baptist Fundamentalists. The Abernathys' defense argued for distance from Pentecostalism, but Baptist interaction with Pentecostal missionaries was more extensive than the denial acknowledged.[74]

Charles Maddry's chief concern was the practice of speaking in tongues. Beyond the attacks leveled by T. L. Blalock, missionary W. C. Newton, who was reported to be sympathetic to the exercise of spiritual gifts in the revival, had written Maddry privately about the topic.[75] Additionally, reports had circulated in Baptist newspapers of events that sounded like speaking in tongues, even though not named that. For example, in 1932, in the missionary magazine *The Home and Foreign Fields*, Wiley Glass wrote about the "remarkable revival" in Shantung that was "full of power." He described a worship experience in language begging for rational explanation by hesitant readers. According to Glass, Mary Crawford was kneeling near the pulpit when she "stood up, stretching out her arms toward heaven and seemed to be transfigured. Her lips were moving, but her voice was not audible to me, for everyone was praying, some in a very loud voice. This went on for a long time. I was at a loss to know how to bring the meeting to a close."[76] With ambiguous evidence, however, Maddry did not press Crawford on the issue, and she only affirmed an experience of being Spirit-filled.[77]

---

[74] Abernathys to Maddry, November 17, 1933. Mary Crawford defended the Abernathys regarding both Kelley and Botolfsen. Crawford to Maddry, October 18, 1933.

[75] Handy, "An Historical Analysis," 19.

[76] Gloss (Glass), "A Remarkable Revival," 15–16.

[77] Crawford to Maddry, December 6, 1933. Maddry to Crawford, January 3, 1934.

49

WHY STUDY BAPTISTS?

Some missionaries, such as I. V. Larson and John Abernathy, testified that they had never spoken in tongues—the answer that Maddry demanded, given he equated the gift with Pentecostalism and its excesses—but they chose different ways to respond to their boss. Larson told Maddry he had never believed in or taught the doctrines of the "tongues movement," even though opponents such as T. L. Blalock had accused him of being slain in the Spirit. John and Jewell Abernathy and Ola and Charles Culpepper also told Maddry that they had not spoken in tongues. Like most missionaries, however, they were willing to say that they were not cessationists. They admitted speaking in tongues was a spiritual gift, but they emphasized that the experience was not *the* necessary sign of the Spirit baptism, as most American Pentecostals advocated. In arguing that the revival was genuine despite the presence of speaking in tongues, the Abernathys attributed excesses to the work of the Devil, who always did everything he could to stop the work of the Spirit. While the Abernathys did not call Pentecostals children of the Devil, they implied that devilish excesses were associated with Pentecostals.[78]

The extensive correspondence between Charles Maddry and Bonnie Ray best illustrates the way speaking in tongues was a topic loathed, or, at best, danced around, in Baptist circles.[79] In her first response to Maddry's 1933 letter questioning her "religious activities," Ray described her desire for more spiritual power, but she avoided answering the question about whether she had participated in Pentecostal practices. Maddry, however, wrote Ray again and insisted that the main information he sought was whether she and other missionaries were speaking in tongues. He asserted, "I feel certain that any missionary of the Southern Baptist Convention who has been swept away with this Pentecostal movement to such an extent that he or she is pretending to speak in tongues would raise a grave

---

[78] Abernathys to Maddry, November 17, 1933. Culpepper to Maddry, November 20, 1933.

[79] Pearl Caldwell to Maddry, December 23, 1933. Caldwell was also accused of speaking in tongues but for some reason was never required to appear before the board and never answered the charge.

question with the Foreign Mission Board as to whether such missionary really represented Southern Baptists in belief and practices."[80]

Maddry had not failed to reveal his agenda. If missionaries were speaking in tongues, they were "pretending" to do so. Such artificial, distorted faith could not be tolerated. In a follow-up letter, Ray finally answered Maddry, but carefully, and only after telling him that she would not be a "snitch" and that other missionaries could speak for themselves. She then described her experience in vivid terms:

> When I received my initial infilling I was filled with joy and peace. My Bible became new to me. I had such freedom in prayer and in witnessing. Later when in communion with the Father I was filled again and again, and did sometimes speak words I did not understand. I was sometimes under such a burden of prayer from some person that I spoke in a stammering tongue. It just seemed I was too full for utterance. This is called by some "unknown tongue." I did not "pretend", I assure you. I did not want to speak in tongues. But I did yield body, soul, and spirit to my Lord, and it isn't my wonder that He sometimes takes possession of real organs! (Experiences are sacred and hard to tell).[81]

Ray had rebuffed Maddry's contention that her experience was "pretending." She was conciliatory, however, in adding that she had not sought the experience, and she affirmed, against Pentecostal doctrine, that speaking in tongues was not the indispensable sign of Spirit baptism.[82]

Revival Defense: Pro-Baptist

If Charles Maddry was extremely concerned that missionaries were Pentecostal, he was equally concerned that their alleged Spirit-filled practices failed to represent the values of Southern Baptists who supported the entire SBC mission enterprise. In their responses to Maddry to justify their actions during the revival, the missionaries strongly affirmed their Baptist identity and even seemed aghast that Maddry would question it. Bonnie

---

[80] Maddry to Ray, November 13, 1933.
[81] Ray to Maddry, December 4, 1933.
[82] Ibid.

Ray said that if her revival experiences were not "real," or according to the New Testament, she "want[ed] His leading into the truth."[83] Ray told Maddry that even if the Board decided she could not remain a missionary, she would continue to pray for the mission work because she loved it and her Baptist identity.[84] I. V. Larson wrote Maddry that he was a "humble servant" who had "no intentions of doing other than standing on the foundations of the Bible and of Southern Baptists."[85] While all of the missionaries affirmed they had a Baptist commitment to the New Testament, Charles Culpepper defended his identity in the explicit language of biblical infallibility. He wrote, "So far as I know I hold to every historical Baptist position. I know I hold to the Bible as the unerring Word of God and in every instance make it the final guide and authority in teaching and practice, and would not for anything pervert its teachings." Culpepper added that his understanding of Pentecost—that is, that the Holy Spirit was given to believers once and for all at Pentecost—was the Baptist position.[86]

Missionaries argued that the revival turned Chinese believers toward the Bible and thus to Baptist identity. Bonnie Ray attested, "There is now a denominational consciousness as I haven't observed before. Many were Baptists because the missionaries were and they were receiving help from the [Foreign Mission] Board. They are Baptists now because they are studying their Bibles."[87] Both Ray and the Abernathys triumphantly insisted that the revival-flourishing of biblical truth meant Chinese Christians were leaving the falsehoods found in other Christian groups and becoming Baptists.[88] Despite his own Baptist identity under the microscope, John Abernathy confidently told Maddry that one couple on the Baptist mission field did not conform to Southern Baptist orthodoxy given their preference for "union" work with other denominations and their

---

[83] Ray to Maddry, November 3, 1933.

[84] Ray to Maddry, December 4, 1933.

[85] Larson to Maddry, November 29, 1933.

[86] Culpepper to Maddry, November 20, 1933.

[87] Ray to Maddry, December 4, 1933.

[88] Ray to Maddry, November 3, 1933. Abernathys to Maddry, November 17, 1933.

acceptance of open communion, in which non-Baptists were allowed to take the Lord's Supper in a Baptist setting.[89]

No missionary suggested that the revival led them away from Baptist identity. Bonnie Ray contended, "As a Baptist I stand on the New Testament.... I love my denomination."[90] John Abernathy wrote in similar fashion: "As to our leaving the Baptist faith and principles and going off into Pentecostalism, holy rollerism, etc. I am glad I can say that I was never a stronger Baptist in the real sense of the word than now. I have never spent more time teaching Baptist beliefs regarding the church and other important matters than since this revival has been on. I have never ceased to teach these truths to our Chinese Christians."[91] Mary Crawford put it succinctly: "We have been revived but that does not mean we are not Baptist."[92]

Revival Defense: A Temporary Respite

At the outset of 1934, Charles Maddry said he was satisfied with the answers to his questions about the "religious activities" of I. V. Larson, Mary Crawford, Ola and Charles Culpepper, and Jewell and John Abernathy, and required no more correspondence from them for the rest of the year.[93] For example, Maddry happily accepted Larson's denials of Pentecostalism at face value and was thankful that the missionary was standing for the "time honored Baptist position as outlined in the New Testament."[94] He was so impressed with Ola Culpepper's response that he expressed to her a longing for a similarly vibrant religious experience. Maddry's comments sounded as if Ola Culpepper had convinced him that the Shantung Revival was no longer an issue: "The Lord has certainly revealed Himself to you

---

[89] John Abernathy to Maddry, December 18, 1935. Maddry had asked Abernathy about a missionary couple.

[90] Ray to Maddry, November 3, 1933.

[91] Abernathys to Maddry, November 17, 1933.

[92] Crawford to Maddry, December 6, 1933.

[93] Maddry to Culpepper, December 19, 1933. Maddry to Abernathys, December 21, 1933. Maddry to Crawford, January 3, 1934.

[94] Larson to Maddry, November 29, 1933. Maddry to Larson, January 2, 1934.

and I believe to the other missionaries in a marvelous way. So far as I am concerned, I am ready to meet the criticism any and everywhere. Go on in this great work.... I myself want to get in this great revival and experience something of its marvelous blessing and power."[95]

Maddry's optimism with Ola Culpepper, however, dissipated. He was exasperated with Bonnie Ray's answers and continued to correspond with her throughout late 1933 and 1934 while she was on furlough concerning whether she would be allowed to return to China. Maddry asked Ray to not address speaking in tongues with anyone—"at least for the present"—in hopes that the controversy might blow over somehow. He fretted that with the prospect of impending financial disaster for the FMB, criticisms of her testimony would be even more than normal and adversely impact the Board.[96]

During 1934, Ray was not hesitant to tell Maddry of a story of a miraculous healing that Ola Culpepper had told her about. She pressed Maddry about returning to China. While she never apologized for speaking in tongues, she told Maddry that "I came under conditions that tested me as I had not been tested before." She also described other complications that created stress for her. Her furlough, scheduled in 1932, was delayed a year, and she was told when the time came that the FMB could not pay for her trip home. Yet she decided to trust God and return home anyway.[97] In his response, Maddry said questions persisted about letting her return to the mission field given she had admitted to speaking in tongues. He asked Ray for more information—"a frank statement"—that would assure the Board that she would avoid "the excesses, hysteria and extravagances that have gone along with this revival" and that she was "sound in the faith and in accord with the beliefs and practices of Baptists today." Ray never denied her experience but tried to soothe her boss's discomfort. She offered an olive branch that she hoped would prove her ill-fit for Pentecostal identity: "I do not like manifestations, not of the Holy Spirit any more than you

---

[95] Maddry to Ola Culpepper, January 3, 1934.
[96] Maddry to Ray, December 11, 1933.
[97] Ray to Maddry, March 9, 1934. Ray to Maddry, May 29, 1934.

The Shantung Revival

do."[98] At issue, of course, was what *was* the Holy Spirit? Maddry left Ray's fate up to a meeting with a special committee of the FMB. The summer meeting went well, and by fall she had returned to China.[99]

In early 1935, missionaries continued to tout and defend the Shantung Revival in Baptist publications. Sallie Jones told Southern Baptists that their lack of faith regarding revival miracles was like people in Nazareth who failed to believe in Jesus' power, and which led to Jesus not being able to do miracles where faith was not present.[100] John Abernathy wrote that much of the early "superficiality" had diminished. Charles Leonard, a missionary in Manchuria, told Southern Baptists that he had an unbiased view of the revival from his post, and he defended it, including its healings and episodes of speaking in tongues, asserting that the missionaries were attempting to deal with emotional excesses from Chinese Christians.[101] Clearly hoping to defuse concerns about the revival's suspicion of being Pentecostal, SBC president M. E. Dodd traveled to China. His report was glowing. In January 1935, he wrote that he wanted to see the revival with his own eyes. Once he did, he was not disappointed: "The spiritual atmosphere was electric, dynamic." At an I. V. Larson meeting, he saw the "worst type of sinners," like murderers and opium addicts, saved, and he was not shy about affirming some practices that raised the eyebrows of Southern Baptists. The sick were healed and demons were exorcised, Dodd asserted. Southern Baptists could affirm the revival, he concluded, because the stories came from "trustworthy Christian men and women."[102]

In January 1935, Charles Maddry traveled internationally to survey the state of missions. Despite his ongoing correspondence with missionaries, he was still concerned about pentecostalized missions in Shantung, particularly from a report from missionary John Lowe. Maddry expressed

---

[98] Ray to Maddry, June 6, 1934. Maddry to Ray, May 31, 1934. Maddry to Ray, June 8, 1934.

[99] Ray to Ford, July 19, 1934.

[100] Sallie Bailey Jones, "Sure Word of Promise," *Biblical Recorder* (April 4, 1934): 3.

[101] John Abernathy Newsletter, February 12, 1935. Leonard, "Questions Asked," 10.

[102] M. E. Dodd, "The Shantung and Honan Revival," *Biblical Recorder* (January 30, 1935): 13.

the intensity of his dilemma in a February letter to his office assistant at the FMB, Jessie Ford. Accepting Lowe's concern, Maddry wrote that "the Newtons are badly off color from the Baptist position." He privately instructed Ford to do whatever she could to keep the Newtons stateside on furlough without giving them reason for any delay of their return to China. He suggested that the medical doctor could assist the delay: "Tell Dr. Loving to look well to their health and not let them leave before I return." He then named names of problematic missionaries he believed had left Baptist identity for Pentecostalism: "Mary Crawford, Jane Lide, Miss Franks, Larson, both the Abernathys, and others are Pentecostals. Lowe says they have completely gone away from us."[103] Maddry's exasperation was seen in his closing remarks to his assistant, "I certainly have a 'mess' ahead of me. This is a blue Monday I suppose but frankly I never dreamed our work had so degenerated as it has." The strain was palpable on Maddry, and he told Ford that he needed a rest before he dealt with the North China Mission face-to-face.[104]

Surprisingly, Maddry's visit to the NCM in late May 1935 changed his mind dramatically. In a personal letter to Bonnie Ray, Maddry mentioned how he and his wife enjoyed being with her, and he added the commendation that "the evangelistic work around Pingtu is some of the finest we have in the world."[105] Missionaries expressed appreciation for his visit.[106] This renewed sense of cooperation resulted in Maddry offering a strong public endorsement to his Southern Baptist constituency regarding the Shantung Revival in subsequent mission reports. That August, he wrote Southern Baptists that the work in China needed more missionaries. He noted how older, faithful missionaries had "broken under the strain of the last few hectic years" and needed help to continue the work.[107] Maddry now praised the revival with picturesque revivalistic language: "The revival is still going like a prairie fire." He expressed pleasure that mission churches were growing and that the Baptist seminary was booming with

---

[103] Maddry to Ford, February 26, 1935.

[104] Maddry to Ford, May 13, 1935.

[105] Maddry to Ray, August 24, 1935.

[106] Culpepper to Maddry, November 14, 1936.

[107] Maddry, "Recruits Needed," *Biblical Recorder* (August 21, 1935): 5.

140 students, an increase of 115 in enrollment since the revival's beginning.[108]

In October 1935, Maddry published "A Day of Good Tidings" in *The Home and Foreign Fields*. The report functioned as a "state of the China mission." He assured the Southern Baptist masses that the ongoing Shantung Revival was an evangelistic success and that they could cease worrying about alleged Pentecostal excesses. He opened with a general declaration that during his eleven-month trip to various countries, he had seen "New Testament Christianity...confront heathenism and superstition that is appalling in its degradation and hopeless in its outlook." The focus of his report was the missionary work in China. Missionaries, he assured, were "worthy, devoted and sacrificial...sound in the faith, loyal to Jesus Christ, and true to the time-honored beliefs and practices of our Baptist fathers." He acknowledged that the Shantung Revival had included "some excesses and hysteria," but such elements were rapidly in decline and missionaries were building Baptist churches "modeled after the New Testament pattern." Leaning on the Southern Baptist romantic mythology regarding Chinese missions, Maddry triumphantly said that current missionaries were building on the "solid rock" of Jesus Christ and on the work of earlier "martyrs and heroes." Maddry concluded his approval of the Shantung Revival with classic evangelistic fervor:

> A glorious revival is sweeping Northern and Interior China, such as we have not seen in America in a hundred years. We have seen it and felt its power. It is a revival of fire and burning. Sin is being burned out of broken lives.... Satan has held sway and dominion over China for unnumbered and weary centuries. His kingdom is suddenly being challenged and broken by the power of a risen and enthroned Christ.[109]

---

[108] Maddry, "From Dr. Maddry's Note Book, "*Biblical Recorder* (August 21, 1935): 5.

[109] Charles E. Maddry, "A Day of Good Tidings," *Home and Foreign Field* (October 1935): 1, 6.

WHY STUDY BAPTISTS?

One of the sources of discontent about revival excesses was evidently pleased with Maddry's report: John Lowe wrote to Southern Baptists, "The great revival in North China, in spite of some excesses, has brought immeasurable spiritual blessings to all our churches. There has been a revival of prayer, preaching, Bible study, consciousness of sin, soul winning, and stewardship. For many long years we have prayed with the Chinese Christians: Lord send a revival and let it begin in me."[110]

In 1936, Maddry offered some additional public remarks that illuminated his views. He continued to applaud the revival in Shantung, calling it the "great revival," which had lasted for five years and showed no signs of "abatement." At the same time, when evaluating Southern Baptist missionary work to FMB officials, Maddry called the prior decade "the lean years" of the Great Depression era and other adverse factors: "The decade of 1924–1934 was a period of arrested development, and sad and tragic retreat in all of our foreign mission work. Very few new missionary recruits were sent out during those terrible years...many of our stations are undermanned and some have been abandoned. We have lost a total of 150 missionaries during these years of retreat."[111]

Revival: Continued Stress

Charles Maddry's public profession of support for the Shantung Revival was not the end of the story. In 1936, he again confronted Southern Baptist angst about missionaries turning Pentecostal. Trigger events included widespread criticism of Mary Crawford's book on the revival and the exuberance of John Abernathy and I. V. Larson about the revival while giving testimonies stateside on furlough.

On the same day (December 27, 1935), both Maddry and M. T. Rankin, Foreign Mission Board regional leader in Asia, wrote Abernathy to complain about his stateside activities. The FMB leaders were irritated that the head of the Oklahoma Baptist Convention had complained. According to Rankin, several critics said that the Pentecostal leaning of the missionaries was "more insidious and more dangerous" than Modernism,

---

[110] John Lowe, "Pastors—Urgent," *Biblical Recorder* (November 13, 1935): 10.

[111] Charles Maddry, undated 1936 report to FMB.

The Shantung Revival

and Maddry also referenced liberal theology, an issue that the FMB had opposed in some missionaries. He declared that Baptists were neither Modernists nor extreme Fundamentalists and certainly not Pentecostals. Southern Baptists "are just plain old fashioned New Testament Baptists and we are trying to stay in the middle of the road," Maddry insisted. Pushing the labels even further, Maddry said both Modernism and Pentecostalism were distasteful to him, but Pentecostalism was a greater threat to stability on the mission field in China.[112]

Rankin added that Abernathy surely must admit that Pentecostal evangelists were welcome among the Baptists in the North China Mission and that such activity was damaging Baptist convictions—a point that Maddry had harped on between 1933 and 1934, before publicly supporting the revival. Rankin seemingly pulled a power play when he said that he knew Abernathy believed he was ministering under the guidance of the Holy Spirit, but that the mission leaders asserting their convictions were also Spirit-led. On their side, however, was the fact that Abernathy gave "expression to opinions" out of harmony with other Southern Baptists.[113]

Rankin and Maddry were also irritated that Mary Crawford's book on the revival continued to produce damaging accusations from Baptists all over the convention, and they felt they must listen to their constituents.[114] Maddry complained about Crawford to his male missionary colleagues. He told Abernathy that the Crawford book on the Shantung Revival should be "suppressed," commenting, "It is just about the most intense Pentecostal treatise I have read in many years." He further lamented that Crawford had returned to China from her furlough without the conflict being resolved; it was his intention that she "clear her skirts as to this doctrinal matter."[115] Gendered insults were a matter of course.

Abernathy responded quickly to the serious letters he received from the leaders of the FMB. Even though he had responded to criticism in 1933, he said he was shocked by accusations that he was a Pentecostal. He

---

[112] Maddry to John Abernathy, December 27, 1935. M. T. Rankin to John Abernathy, December 27, 1935.

[113] Rankin to Abernathy, December 27, 1935.

[114] Ibid.

[115] Maddry to Abernathy, December 27, 1935.

WHY STUDY BAPTISTS?

suggested that critics were a small minority since most Baptists told him how much his testimony inspired them. He admitted, however, that he had been questioned by Baptist ministers in Oklahoma and Louisiana about his views on miracles and spiritual gifts. He had consequently begun to share less about the revival's miraculous details. Abernathy also noted that while phrases such as "baptism of the Holy Spirit" and "being filled with the Spirit" were biblical terms, his usage might have confused listeners not familiar with them. At the same time, he reiterated to Maddry and Rankin that he was not Pentecostal and had never talked about a second blessing, or speaking in tongues, as *the only* sign of the Spirit baptism. He acknowledged that he had used Mary Crawford's book in some stateside mission study courses and apologized for the conflicts the book had caused and promised not to use it anymore. Abernathy also apologized for being careless and promised a renewed focus on only allowing "real Baptists" to speak in future mission services.[116]

I. V. Larson wrote Charles Maddry a similarly lengthy response a few weeks after Abernathy. He repeated what he had written two years earlier to Maddry—that he had never had Pentecostal workers participate in his mission revivals, and that the revival was the result of prayer, not from Pentecostalism. In this response, however, he elaborated on the accusations that T. L. Blalock had levied against him. He said that the occurrences of speaking in tongues in revival meetings had surprised him and his colleagues, and, he added, "I have never advocated the speaking in 'tongues' whether to individuals or to groups. Not only have I not advocated this but I have suppressed it more than once. I have never been unconscious, gone into trances, or had 'spells,' Mr. Blalock to the contrary!" In contrast to Abernathy, Larson declared he was careful to avoid controversial phrases such as "baptism of the Holy Spirit." Like Abernathy, Larson said some of his language had been misunderstood.[117]

Abernathy and Larson reiterated their orthodox Baptist identity. Larson apologized for causing heartache, but insisted, "I protest that I have wanted to be, and still want to be, a loyal and true Baptist."[118] Abernathy

---

[116] John Abernathy to Maddry and M. T. Rankin, January 2, 1936.
[117] Larson to Maddry, February 29, 1936.
[118] Ibid.

The Shantung Revival

wrote Maddry and Rankin that he was sorry for the troubles he had caused and said that he would almost prefer to be classified as a despised Modernist than a Pentecostal, but "he was certainly neither." He insisted again that he was "a New Testament Baptist and have never been anything else." Abernathy identified principles that he thought finally would secure his Baptist identity: he affirmed closed communion for the Lord's Supper and eternal security over against apostasy. To attempt a distinction between Pentecostal practices and his Baptist participation in the revival, he affirmed that he believed in divine healing, "but only as Baptists have always believed, viz, praying for the sick, sending for the doctor, taking medicine he prescribes and asking the Lord to bless these means." Abernathy's conclusions about the revival and Baptist identity did, in his own triumphalistic way, confess some error. He lamented that they had allowed some people who were not "real Baptists" to preach, which allowed for doctrinal distortions, but if allowed to return to the mission field, his commitment to Baptist principles would be stronger than ever.[119]

Charles Maddry penned a separate letter to Mary Crawford on the same day he wrote letters to her male counterparts. Their exchange was the feistiest of all. With exasperation, he criticized the revival's intense emotionalism and urged her to cease using non-Baptists in meetings so that Baptists could build "denominational conscience" in China.[120] Crawford retorted that the guest speaker in question was an "immersed Presbyterian," but she recognized that Maddry's "thundering" against her was because of her alleged Pentecostalism.[121] Crawford offered an impassioned plea in support of her Baptist identity. She reminded Maddry of her long Baptist family tree (her grandfather had been president of Mercer University). She strongly denied any Pentecostal identity and then asked how Maddry defined Baptist identity, given how Baptist churches allowed Methodist bishops to preach and tell jokes from Baptist pulpits and Baptist bookstores sold books authored by Liberal Harry Emerson Fosdick.[122]

---

[119] Abernathy to Maddry and Rankin, January 2, 1936.
[120] Maddry to Crawford, December 27, 1935.
[121] Crawford to Maddry, February 10, 1936.
[122] Ibid.

Maddry did not let Crawford's defense go unanswered. He said her book had done more damage than anything associated with the Shantung Revival and that she was being criticized severely all over the Southern Baptist Convention. The book's contents were the best proof that she had become Pentecostal and strayed from her family's Baptist beliefs. Her criticisms of Modernism and Fosdick were red herrings and offered no explanation for her Pentecostal positions. Bookstores had one purpose—to sell books. Maddry ended his letter hoping he could calm the storms of criticism, but her book still stood in his way.[123]

Remarkably, all the missionaries still under fire in 1936 were approved to return to China. Meetings with regional FMB representatives went well.[124] The Chinese political situation worsened in 1937. The second Sino-Japanese War restricted travel for the few missionaries that remained. Many were evacuated. Heroic stories of faith followed missionaries such as John Abernathy, who interpreted the war as a sign of the imminent second coming of Jesus, but evacuations and war turmoil, according to the missionaries, brought the revival to a halt.[125] Baptist newspapers continued to cite the Shantung Revival as a sign of worldwide evangelization during the next decade.[126]

A private footnote to the revival's conclusion is a fascinating 1939 letter from Charles Maddry to Mary Crawford in which he apologized for his "over severe" past letters to her. He sought forgiveness for his "condemnation" of her and her methods and "any injury" he caused. Maddry had come to realize that the missionaries had been faithful in difficult circumstances, especially during the last two years of military conflict. He hoped to "put away" past difficulties and affirmed, ironically, "the Holy Spirit, I hope, has been at work in my heart and given me a larger and

---

[123] Maddry to Crawford, March 13, 1936.

[124] Maddry to Larson, May 5, 1936. Maddry to John Abernathy, April 13, 1936.

[125] John and Jewell Abernathy Newsletter, September 7, 1937.

[126] For example, see John R. Sampey, "An Old Man Dreams," *Biblical Recorder* (May 19, 1937): 4, 10. L. R. Scarborough, "Our Convention Speaks with a Challenge," *Biblical Recorder* (June 1, 1938): 4. "Editorial Outlook," *Biblical Recorder* (August 8, 1945): 3.

more tolerant view of things."[127] Crawford never spoke about the apology, but her future letters were conciliatory. Toleration had the last word, at least for a few decades.

Conclusion

In recent decades, the Shantung Revival became part of the mythical lore of Southern Baptist revivalism. As the charismatic movement erupted in the middle of the twentieth century, Southern Baptist charismatics, including those in Brazil, touted the revival's Spirit-led experience as evidence for their cause.[128] Others cited the revival with some revisionist twists. In 1971, Charles Culpepper published a memoir of the revival to spur evangelistic success among Texas Baptists.[129] His version did not deny some of the extraordinary reports of miracles, but it clearly focused on the goal of evangelism. Biographical memoirs of various missionaries like John Abernathy dotted the popular publishing scene. Perhaps most influential were the memoirs that highlighted the life and ministry of Bertha Smith, who became an icon for aspiring Spirit-filled, but anti-charismatic, Southern Baptists who participated in the "Conservative Resurgence" to reset the direction of the Southern Baptist Convention in the 1980s.

The legacy of the Shantung Revival (to note again, Shandong Revival, in today's literature) is manifold for Baptist identity. Throughout the revival, Baptists were consistently called, but denied, being Pentecostals. I have written elsewhere how Baptists who climbed the social ladder of respectability vocally distanced themselves from their Pentecostal neighbors who were attempting to climb that same ladder. Baptists and Pentecostals employed the same biblical hermeneutic, but Pentecostals applied it to the

---

[127] Maddry to Crawford, February 18, 1939.

[128] Joao B. Chaves, *The Global Mission of the Jim Crow South: Southern Baptist Missionaries and the Shaping of Latin American Evangelicalism* (Macon: Mercer University Press, 2022) 186. Southern Baptist missionary, Rosalee Appleby, known as the leading pioneer of the charismatic movement to Brazilian Baptists, cited the Shantung Revival in support of her promotion of Spirit-led revival. FMB leaders expressed displeasure with Appleby's ministry.

[129] C. L. Culpepper, *The Shantung Revival* (Dallas, TX: Crescendo Publications, 1971).

WHY STUDY BAPTISTS?

miraculous passages in the Book of Acts, whereas many Baptists were cessationists, or at least functionally cessationist, meaning any reports of divine healing or speaking in tongues were outside their theological or sociological comfort zone. Baptist missionaries, however, reflected the wider fact in Baptist life that some Baptists were open to explicit manifestations of modern-day miracles and spiritual gifts. Thus, the ongoing tension.

I have described Baptist openness to the Spirit as an example of what should be a dominant way of understanding Baptist identity—the focus on experience. More formally stated, Baptist identity reveals the interplay of Word-Spirit-Experience, and this triangular interaction never automatically follows one chronological pattern. Sometimes it is the Word that explains the experience, and sometimes the experience calls for a new understanding of the Word. Spirit-led experience and Spirit-inspired Word interact in Baptist life, and the Shantung Revival, as described by the missionary participants, is a vivid reminder of how people respond negatively and positively—but respond they do because the triangular interaction is not absent.

Were the Baptists who participated in the Shantung Revival Pentecostals? In classical definition, no. As most of American Pentecostalism developed during the early twentieth century, speaking in tongues became the required "initial evidence" of the baptism of the Holy Spirit. The missionaries in Shantung knew this definition—calling Pentecostalism the "tongues movement"—and rested their case that they were not Pentecostal. Technically, the missionaries can be called Keswick, radical Holiness-influenced Baptists. In other literature, scholars, including myself, have elaborated on this definition. In short, in late nineteenth-century radical Holiness circles, there was an emphasis on a post-conversion religious experience of grace that was called the baptism of the Holy Spirit. Adherents, which included some influential individuals such as Boston Baptist minister A. J. Gordon, said this second experience was a Pentecostal experience that empowered believers for witness and service in imitation of what the earliest Christian disciples experienced in Acts 1 and 2. Speaking in tongues was not the sign of such an experience—that definition came later with the eruption of what is called Pentecostalism in the twentieth-century's first decade. The Keswick tradition was popularized in the

64

writings of Charles Trumbull, R. A. Torrey, and others who spoke often about the need to be Spirit-filled.[130]

By the 1930s, however, as Pentecostalism spread, making clear distinctions, especially on a mission field, between radical Holiness faith and growing Pentecostal practices was difficult. In Shantung, Keswick books were being read, and speaking in tongues was flourishing. Demon exorcisms and divine healings were being touted—both of which could be placed under radical Holiness or Pentecostal beliefs. Pentecostal and Baptist evangelists were interacting together, and Westernized Baptist missionaries unsurprisingly undersold and underemphasized the influence of pentecostalized indigenous Chinese movements. While the Baptists frequently mentioned the indigenous players in the revival, the colonized sense was always that the Chinese participants were under the guidance of missionary supervision except when they exhibited emotional excesses. In reality, the Chinese evangelists and converts practiced Pentecostal gifts (evidently similar to practices they had before becoming Christian), and to make fine distinctions about whether or not they were Holiness or Pentecostal is ill-advised. The same should be said for the Baptist missionaries. They might have professed anti-Pentecostal theology, but their practices were Pentecostal. To use a contemporary term, the missionaries were "bapticostal."

The interaction of Spirit-Experience-Word in a Baptist/Holiness/Pentecostal setting illustrates how, in the global scene of world Christianity, neat so-called distinctions are not always helpful. American Pentecostalism that defines itself via speaking in tongues as the sign of the Holy Spirit baptism was never as rigidly defined in global Pentecostalism.[131] Even in the United States, boundaries were never as inflexible as denominational statements made them seem, although the focus on speaking in tongues certainly characterizes much of the North American story.

---

[130] The goal of Wesley Handy's dissertation was to demonstrate that the missionaries were Keswick holiness and not Pentecostal. He surveys much good material but in one line acknowledges that "their practice went further." Handy does not investigate the story past Charles Maddry's 1935 trip to China. Handy, "An Historical Analysis," 157.

[131] See Allan Anderson, *Introduction to Pentecostalism* (New York: Cambridge, 2014).

WHY STUDY BAPTISTS?

At the same time, traditional Baptist narratives that say Pentecostal practices negate Baptist identity also fail to find support. Most Baptists are cessationists, but that is hardly the full story.

The Shantung Revival story, then, pushes us to consider that Baptists participated in a charismatic,[132] bapticostal Christianity much earlier than the 1960s, when the label of charismatic began to take hold for Christians who practiced Pentecostal gifts but stayed in their non-Pentecostal denominations. Other denominations have stories of charismatic, or, if we desire, proto-charismatic stories prior to any official acknowledgement of such events. Charismatic Christianity has never been accepted by most Baptists, but the story of Shantung reminds us that it had never been absent. In essence, whenever such events are interpreted and evaluated, they add to the conclusion that unless you highlight the experiential in the Baptist story, you have missed a telling Baptist identity marker. Baptists have insisted upon their doctrinal 1,000s, but they have practiced with their hearts their experiential 10,000s.

---

[132] Seeking the experience of spiritual gifts (e.g., speaking in tongues or healing) for full salvation.

A Baptist on Capitol Hill:
The Progressive Evangelicalism of Mark O. Hatfield

Randall Balmer

On July 27, 1994, the senior senator from Oregon, a Republican, asked to address the United States Senate. "I must say very frankly that I oppose all prescriptive prayer of any kind in public schools," he began. "Does that mean that I am against prayer? No, it does not mean that at all. I am very strong in my belief in the efficacy of prayer."[1]

The issue at hand was an amendment offered by Jesse Helms, Republican senator from North Carolina, that would have mandated prayer in public schools. Ever since the Supreme Court's *Engel v. Vitale* decision in 1962, which struck down prescribed prayers in public education, some Conservatives had been trying to reverse that ruling with legislation. The amendment to an appropriation bill offered by Helms was merely the most recent of such attempts.

Mark O. Hatfield, a Baptist, opposed the amendment, pointing out the obvious fact that prayer in public schools had never been outlawed. In fact, Hatfield argued, "there is no way that this body or the Constitution or the President or the courts could ever abolish prayer in the public schools." The senior senator then confessed to "having prayed my way through every math course examination I ever took." He continued: "All I am saying is that this can be very personal, and silent prayer is happening all the time." He concluded his remarks by asserting that "the simplest and best way to deal with this subject is to take no action relating to school prayer. Let students continue to pray as they do now, silently as an undeniable personal right."[2]

One of the peculiarities of the debate over the Helms amendment was that both men were—or claimed to be—Baptists, even though they

---

[1] Senator Hatfield, speaking on S. 1513, 103rd Cong., 2nd sess., *Congressional Record* 140 (July 27, 1994) S 18211.

[2] Senator Hatfield, speaking on S. 1513, 103rd Cong., 2nd sess., *Congressional Record* 140 (July 27, 1994) S 18211-18212.

took opposite sides on the issue of school prayer. Helms was a member and deacon in the Hayes-Barton Baptist Church in Raleigh, North Carolina, and part of the Southern Baptist Convention. Hatfield's mother reared her only child as a Baptist in Salem, Oregon (his father was Methodist). Their opposite positions on school prayer illustrate evolving Baptist attitudes about liberty of conscience as well as an index of Hatfield's longstanding estrangement from his fellow Evangelicals, especially those associated with the Religious Right.

Born in the small lumber mill town of Dallas, Oregon, on July 12, 1922, Mark Odom Hatfield moved with his family to Salem, the state capital, in 1931. The Hatfields attended First Baptist Church, where they quickly became fixtures in the congregation, although they did not share the typical Baptist scruples about motion pictures or dancing. A teenage Mark sometimes blew pipe smoke into his Sunday clothes so he could scandalize some of the stalwart members. An avid reader, Mark was a member of the Boy Scouts and played the clarinet in the school band. He attended Leslie Junior High and then Salem High School, graduating in 1940. By then his interest in politics was taking shape. He sometimes upbraided his fellow Baptists for being apolitical, and he secured a job as a docent leading tours of the new, Modernist-Art Deco state capitol on weekends and during the summer. He did odd jobs for the secretary of state, Earl Snell, and he sometimes used his pass key to recline in the governor's chair—a chair he would one day occupy as the duly elected (and reelected) governor of Oregon.

Hatfield wanted to remain in proximity to politics, and Willamette University, located across State Street from the state capitol in Salem, was the logical place to continue his education. Willamette, a Methodist school and the oldest university west of the Missouri, offered majors in history and political science and encouraged its students to become involved in the political system. By the beginning of his second year, Hatfield was president of the Republican Club, and over the course of his undergraduate years, he joined and led several student organizations. Doubtless because of his church affiliation and his evident piety, Hatfield was tapped to chair the Friday student chapels at Willamette, a position of considerable prominence and visibility. Serving in that role, he hosted distinguished visitors on campus, including African American musicians

Paul Robeson and Marian Anderson. Because Salem hotels would not accommodate African Americans, Hatfield was responsible for ferrying Robeson and Anderson to and from Portland. His disgust at the city's "No Coloreds" policy later prompted him, as a member of the Oregon House, to push for civil rights legislation in a state with a history as a stronghold of the Ku Klux Klan. "I gained arguably one of the great victories of my entire career," he recalled many years later of his legislative achievement. "During that session I helped pass one of the bills I remain most proud of throughout almost 50 years of public service."[3]

Following the bombing of Pearl Harbor on December 7, 1941, Hatfield enlisted in the navy, although the military allowed him to complete his college education before he deployed to the Pacific. There, Hatfield drew an assignment that would profoundly alter his thinking about war and shape his political views. In September 1945, one month after the atomic bomb fell on Hiroshima, Hatfield was among the first Americans to visit what remained of the city. He remembered a peculiar smell—and total silence. "The devastation lay indiscriminate and the people cowered at our arrival, garbed in patchwork clothes," Hatfield remembered, noting that well over one hundred thousand had been incinerated by a single American bomb.[4]

The survivors were wary, but they were also hungry. When one member of the crew broke out his sack lunch and shared it with those who, days before, were considered enemies, Hatfield and others did the same in a scene reminiscent of Holy Communion. "I lifted up a small Japanese child and was purged, spiritually renewed as hate flowed from my system," Hatfield remembered. "Here were people I dehumanized in my mind throughout the war, thinking of them as one vast, massive enemy, not human, not like any of us." In a moment of clarity, Hatfield saw otherwise. "They were exactly like us, suffering, afraid—human. Oh, so human. As the adults relaxed and smiled, as my lunch was completely given to children, my loathing vanished. I stood awash, clean in an epiphany which has never

---

[3] Richard W. Etulain, *Mark O. Hatfield: Oregon Statesman* (Norman: University of Oklahoma Press, 2021) 41–42.

[4] Mark O. Hatfield, with Diane N. Solomon, *Against the Grain: Reflections of a Rebel Republican* (Ashland, OR: White Cloud Press, 2001) 43–44.

deserted me. Hatred had gushed out, transmuted into the powerful balm of compassion."[5]

Upon his discharge and return to Salem, Hatfield enrolled in law school at Willamette. It did not go well. Hatfield never talked much about that experience other than to describe it as a "dismal year." He hinted that he dropped out of law school before being expelled on academic grounds. "I did my professors a great favor," he wrote. "I left before being asked to leave." He redirected his academic focus to a master's degree in political science at Stanford University, which he completed in 1948 with a thesis on Herbert Hoover, before returning once again to Salem and Willamette as associate professor of political science and dean of students.[6]

Hatfield never lost an election. He began his meteoric political career with election to the Oregon House of Representatives in 1950 at the age of twenty-eight. The administration at Willamette allowed him to continue as dean of students in part because of the easy commute—literally across State Street to the capitol. He was reelected two years later, and in 1954 won election to a single term in the Oregon Senate. His election as secretary of state in 1956 made him the youngest person to hold that office in Oregon history. Similarly, his election to the first of two terms as governor in 1958 made him the youngest governor in Oregon history. Hatfield ran for the United States Senate in 1966, winning the first of five consecutive terms before choosing not to run again in 1996. He is the longest-serving senator in the history of Oregon.

Hatfield began attracting national attention during his second term as governor because of his opposition to the war in Vietnam, which, in turn, was informed by his Evangelical faith and by what he had seen as a GI in Hiroshima. The National Governor's Association met in Minneapolis in 1965, and Lyndon Johnson, who had almost maniacally sought support for the war from organizations as diverse as the US Chamber of Commerce and the AFL-CIO, sought the approbation of the nation's governors. The president dispatched his vice president, Hubert Humphrey, to the meeting to rally support. Hatfield had long expressed skepticism about the administration's "domino theory" argument that the "fall" of

---

[5] Ibid., 44.
[6] Ibid., 51.

Vietnam to the Communists would lead to the capture of other nations—Cambodia, Burma, Thailand, and eventually the United States—by the Communists. "Even if dominoes dropped, skipped, and jumped, the Vietnamese couldn't take up arms against us," Hatfield recalled. "They had no air force, no navy, and here we were, bombing the hell out of them—civilians and soldiers alike. They were peasants, pure and simple, strangled by centuries of tribal wars."[7]

In the run-up to the vote, several governors privately expressed their reservations about the war and the resolution of support Johnson was seeking, but Hatfield knew that he "absolutely could not support" the resolution. The "ayes" were resounding, so much so that the chair almost forgot to ask if anyone opposed. "Undeterred, in a clear voice," Hatfield recounted, "I called out my solid, 'No!'" During the ensuing press scrum, James Byrnes, governor of Florida, interrupted the questioning. "You, Mark Hatfield," he scolded his younger colleague, "have done a grave disservice to your country."[8]

By the time the next governor's conference rolled around, Hatfield was the Republican nominee for Senate, and 76 percent of Oregonians supported the war. The vote of the governors was the same 49–1 in support of the Vietnam War. Once again, Hatfield was undeterred. "Even if every person in Oregon was on the other side," he recalled later, "I'd vote my convictions." On the war in particular, Hatfield was adamant. "Vietnam was the issue that called me to the Senate," he wrote, "and Vietnam would haunt me for a long, long time to come."[9]

Hatfield prevailed over a pro-war Democratic opponent in 1966, but he quickly ran afoul of Republicans as well as Democrats. He marshalled opposition to the neutron bomb during Jimmy Carter's presidency, and he was the sole dissenting vote in the Senate, 96–1, to Ronald Reagan's first defense budget. One of the great ironies of Hatfield's career is that, at the behest of Billy Graham and others, he very nearly was chosen as Richard

---

[7] Ibid., 96.

[8] Ibid., 97–98; Etulain, *Hatfield*, 133. These two sources quote the Florida governor slightly differently.

[9] Hatfield, *Against the Grain*, 102–103; "Door Interview: Mark Hatfield," *Wittenburg Door*, 8.

WHY STUDY BAPTISTS?

Nixon's running mate in 1968; in time, however, Hatfield was named to Nixon's infamous enemies list.[10]

Hatfield's relationship with Nixon was not always contentious; despite policy differences, the two men and their wives remained relatively cordial. On July 20, 1969, for instance, the president invited Hatfield to the White House worship service to offer a prayer for the astronauts about to walk on the moon, and even then, the senator managed to press his case for peace and for the care of those less fortunate. "Even as our astronauts go to the moon in the name of peace, our world aches from the pain of wars," the senator prayed. "Excite our imaginations to transfer this genius of cooperation and spirit of teamwork to our many other needs," he continued, "lest our success on the moon mock our failures on the earth."[11]

More than likely, what set Hatfield on course for Nixon's enemies list was the McGovern-Hatfield Amendment to end the war in Vietnam. Hatfield had been introducing Senate resolutions against funding the war for some time but to little effect. Joining forces with George S. McGovern, a Democratic senator from South Dakota who had grown up in a Wesleyan Methodist parsonage and had studied for the ministry at Garrett Theological Seminary, gave the antiwar legislation the stamp of bipartisanship. Yet another Evangelical, Harold E. Hughes, a Democratic senator from Iowa, added his support to the McGovern-Hatfield Amendment, which was attached to an appropriations bill in the Senate in 1970. The amendment mandated the cessation of US military actions in Vietnam by December 31, 1970, and a complete withdrawal of American forces by the middle of the following year.

"Every senator in this chamber is partly responsible for sending 50,000 young Americans to an early grave," McGovern declared in a floor speech before the vote. "This chamber reeks of blood. Every Senator here is partly responsible for that human wreckage at Walter Reed and Bethesda Naval and all across our land—young men without legs, or arms, or genitals, or faces or hopes." The Nixon administration opposed the

---

[10] "The Peace Politics of Mark Hatfield," *Arms Control Today* 17 (April 1987): 32.

[11] Mark O. Hatfield, *Conflict and Conscience* (Waco, TX: Word Books, 1971) 169–70.

A Baptist on Capitol Hill

amendment, and the measure failed 55–39. The McGovern-Hatfield amendment came up again the following year. "We cannot avoid the harsh reality that we, the elected members of this body, share in the responsibility for those who are wounded and who die in this war," Hatfield said, echoing McGovern, albeit in more measured tones. "We cannot pretend that we can abdicate this responsibility." The amendment garnered three more votes in 1971, but it was defeated again 55–42.[12]

Hatfield's most public break with Nixon (and his many followers) occurred on February 1, 1973, at the National Prayer Breakfast held at the Washington Hilton. Nixon was riding high. The Watergate scandal had yet to metastasize, at least publicly, and Nixon had only days earlier taken his second oath of office as president, having vanquished George McGovern, the Democratic nominee, in the 1972 election. Nixon and his secretary of state, Henry Kissinger, had recently announced a negotiated settlement in Vietnam, which they characterized as "peace with honor." Hatfield was dubious. He enlisted the help of his legislative director, Wes Granberg-Michaelson, as well as Jim Wallis, the editor of a new alternative magazine, *The Post-American* (later *Sojourners*), to draft the senator's address. Hatfield walked decisively to the podium—Nixon seated on his right and Billy Graham on his left.

"As we gather at this prayer breakfast," the senator began, "let us beware of the real danger of misplaced allegiance, if not outright idolatry, to the extent we fail to distinguish between the god of an American civil religion and the God who reveals Himself in the Holy Scriptures and in Jesus Christ." Hatfield, who worried that Americans believed "we had done no wrong" in Vietnam, went on to call Americans, and by inference the president, to account. "Today our prayers must begin with repentance," he said. "Individually, we must seek forgiveness for the exile of love from

---

[12] Quoted in "The Remarkable Life of George McGovern," *Milwaukee Journal Sentinel* (October 22, 2012); Joshua Rothman, "Watching George McGovern Run," *New Yorker* (October 21, 2012); John W. Finney "Senate, 55–42, Defeats McGovern-Hatfield Plan," *New York Times* (June 17, 1971) A1. The amendment was in many ways symbolic. It would never have passed the House of Representatives, and even if it had, Nixon would not have signed it.

73

our hearts. And corporately as a people, we must turn in repentance from the sin that scarred our national soul."[13]

At the conclusion of the prayer breakfast, Hatfield noticed that some of Nixon's associates were decidedly cool toward the senator and his wife, Antoinette. Several days later, Hatfield received a "My dear Mark" admonitory letter from Billy Graham lamenting "with deep concern that the press interpreted your remarks as political and as a rebuke to the President!" The evangelist, ever loyal to Nixon, castigated Hatfield for his criticism of Nixon and proposed a different course. "If I had any suggestion to make it would have been that you as a war critic could have turned to the President and commended him for his determination and perseverance in getting the cease-fire in Vietnam," Graham wrote. "This would have had a unifying effect that the Country desperately needs at this time."[14]

In many respects, as Graham's letter demonstrates, Hatfield's most persistent critics were fellow Evangelicals and fellow Baptists. Members of a Baptist men's camp in Oregon, where Hatfield had given a Sunday school lesson for more than a dozen years, threatened to walk out when their senator strode to the podium because of his opposition to the war in Vietnam.[15]

Nothing illustrates mainstream Evangelical ambivalence toward Hatfield better than a news release from the Mennonite Central Committee dated May 17, 1968—an ambivalence that bordered on hostility. The committee reported on the gathering of the National Association of Evangelicals (NAE) meeting that year in Philadelphia. The early part of the release quoted a Mennonite leader, presumably speaking for American Mennonites, protesting that "if they wanted to use the NAE for nationalistic purposes and treat Christianity as synonymous with the Republican party, they should count us out." But when the release reported on the keynote address from Mark Hatfield, the senator was described as "a favorite key-noter among evangelicals at least until this year." Brief portions

---

[13] Mark Hatfield, *Between a Rock and a Hard Place* (Waco, TX: Word Books, 1976) 92, 94. The senator's remarks received national attention; see, for example, "'Beware Misplaced Allegiance,'" *Washington Post* (February 2, 1973).

[14] Quoted in Hatfield, *Between a Rock and a Hard Place*, 99.

[15] Hatfield, *Against the Grain*, 146.

A Baptist on Capitol Hill

of his address were quoted, including his warning about the callous approach to enemy casualties. "We measure success on the basis of kill ratio and have become accustomed to the nomenclature of the slaughterhouse," Hatfield said. "In the eyes of God a Viet Cong is worth as much as an American." The release also reported on Hatfield's call "for a rechanneling of resources to meet human need both at home and abroad."[16] Although Hatfield's address received "generous applause" at the NAE meeting, many conferees registered their objections. According to the news release, the organization's Layman of the Year award went to a military man, John C. Broger, and "none of the conference resolutions reflected the Hatfield message."[17]

Invited to address the Southern Baptist Convention in 1967, Hatfield took aim at Evangelicalism's long preoccupation with evangelism, which he nevertheless affirmed as important, to the exclusion of social concern. "I believe that there has developed within the church a spirit of withdrawal from the world, a secure seclusion in noninvolvement," he said. "We should have great concern as Christians today for man's physical well-being." Hatfield's vision for Evangelical social engagement also had the salutary effect of limiting the reach of government, a principle he imbibed from his political hero, Herbert Hoover. "It is high time for the church to obey her Lord and assume the task of meeting the social needs of the world in the love and power of Christ," he exhorted his fellow Baptists.

> Let me give you an example of what could be done with a pressing domestic problem. The hard-core unemployable segment of our population in America totals about one million. We have in America today over 300,000 church congregations. If each congregation would take responsibility for three persons in this group of unemployables, we could see that a huge government welfare program for the unemployed would not be necessary."

---

[16] News release, "NAE Convention Hears Words on War, Poverty and Race," Mennonite Central Committee, May 17, 1968.

[17] News release, "NAE Convention," Mennonite Central Committee, May 17, 1968.

75

WHY STUDY BAPTISTS?

In another forum, Hatfield declared that if every church in America adopted one and a half children, we could abolish the federal Aid for Dependent Children program.[18]

Hatfield worried that the Christian doctrines of universal sin and fallen humanity had interfered with social reform, and on more than one occasion, the Baptist from Oregon felt compelled to educate fellow Evangelicals about fundamental Baptist principles, including the separation of church and state. "Even our separation of church and state comes to us not out of a desire to create a secular society, but through the effort to insure the integrity of religious expression," he told a conference at John Brown University. "Further, it not only prevented the state from enforcing religious belief, but it kept the church from giving religious sanction to the acts of the state."[19]

Hatfield's conscience on Vietnam and his opposition to war drew criticism not only from governors, presidents, and constituents, but also from his fellow Evangelicals. In a commencement address at Fuller Theological Seminary in 1970, Hatfield opened by quoting from some of the letters he had received from Evangelicals. "Dear Senator Hatfield," one began. "I thought you were the man for the job of senator because we need Christian men in vital places. But, when anyone chooses to go against the president of our United States the way you have, that's where my support ends." Another correspondent doubted the senator's faith because of his criticism of the military, and another asked, "Have you forgotten that God's way is to respect and honor those in authority? What higher power is there than President Nixon?" Still another letter suggested that Hatfield's support for antiwar demonstrations constituted treason. "I and a lot of other Christian people are extremely disappointed in your performance in the Senate, for you who claim to be a Christian and have access to our

---

[18] Hatfield, *Conflict and Conscience*, 54, 56, 59; "Sen. Mark Hatfield Talks About: His Nuclear Freeze Idea, Why He Thinks He Wasn't Wrong about Vietnam, and the Reason Churches Should be Taxed," *Conservative Digest* (June 1982): 17.

[19] Hatfield, *Conflict and Conscience*, 73, 67.

Almighty God should have a better understanding of human nature and the evil in the human heart."[20]

Hatfield typically responded to criticism with humility, acknowledging that his grasp of the faith was hardly infallible. But he was also prepared to counter such attacks from the perspective of evangelical conviction and Baptist principles. In the Fuller address, for instance, he invoked the separation of church and state, dating back to Roger Williams, founder of the Baptist tradition in America, as well as to Nixon's more recent declaration of a "silent majority" in American politics. "There is a theological 'silent majority' in our land," Hatfield declared, "who wrap their Bibles in the American flag, who believe that conservative politics is the necessary by-product of orthodox Christianity, who equate patriotism with the belief in national self-righteousness, and who regard political dissent as a mark of infidelity to the faith." Hatfield was careful to stipulate that Williams's "wall of separation" did not mean that people of faith were excused from political and social concerns, providing an implicit rebuke to the Evangelical apoliticism that had characterized the middle decades of the twentieth century. "We can no longer afford the supposed luxury of social withdrawal," he said, "but must find viable means to relate the Good News to the turmoil of our era."[21]

For Hatfield, however, the reflexive association of Conservative theology with Conservative politics must be called into question. So, too, "we must reevaluate the faith we as a people have placed in the office of the presidency." A healthy suspicion of authority was crucial. "As evangelical Christians, we should be particularly sensitive to the dangers presented by such an all-encompassing trust," he said.[22]

Hatfield's commitment to the sanctity of life, prompted by his military experiences and borne out by his opposition to the war in Vietnam, manifested itself in other policies, including his opposition to abortion. Here the senator from Oregon anticipated the "prolife" positions of fellow Evangelicals by nearly a decade. Evangelicals overwhelmingly considered abortion a Catholic issue until the late 1970s, to the extent they considered

---

[20] Ibid., 21–22.
[21] Ibid., 23, 25.
[22] Ibid., 26.

WHY STUDY BAPTISTS?

it at all. Both before and after the *Roe v. Wade* decision of January 22, 1973, Evangelicals were at best ambivalent about abortion, and several groups and individuals supported its legalization.

A 1968 conference convened by the Christian Medical Society and *Christianity Today*, the flagship magazine of Evangelicalism, for example, drew twenty-six heavyweight theologians from the Evangelical world to discuss the morality of abortion. At the conclusion of their deliberations, they acknowledged that they could not agree on any one position. "Whether the performance of an induced abortion is sinful we are not agreed," the statement read, "but about the necessity of it and the permissibility for it under [certain] circumstances we are in accord," citing "individual health, family welfare, and social responsibility" as reasonable justifications. In those cases, fetal life "may have to be abandoned to maintain full and secure family life."[23]

In the early 1970s, both the United Methodist Church and the Southern Baptist Convention passed resolutions calling for the legalization of abortion. The Southern Baptists, meeting in St. Louis during the summer of 1971, resolved to "work for legislation that would allow the possibility of abortion under such conditions as rape, incest, clear evidence of severe fetal deformity, and carefully ascertained evidence of the likelihood of damage to the emotional, mental, and physical health of the mother." Southern Baptist W. A. Criswell, pastor of First Baptist Church in Dallas and past president of the Southern Baptist Convention (1968–1970), applauded the *Roe v. Wade* decision. "I have always felt that it was only after a child was born and had a life separate from its mother that it became an individual person," Criswell declared, "and it has always, therefore, seemed to me that what is best for the mother and for the future should be allowed."[24]

---

[23] *Birth Control and the Christian: A Protestant Symposium on the Control of Human Reproduction*, eds. Walter O. Spitzer and Carlyle L. Saylor (Wheaton, IL: Tyndale House, 1969) 414, xxv–xxviii.

[24] *Annual of the Southern Baptist Convention, 1972* (Nashville, TN: Executive Committee, Southern Baptist Convention, 1972) 72; Criswell quoted in "What Price Abortion?" *Christianity Today* (March 2, 1973): 39. For additional evidence of evangelical indifference to abortion during the 1970s, see Randall Balmer, *Bad*

While Evangelicals were indifferent toward or dithering over abortion, while James Dobson acknowledged that "a developing embryo or fetus was not regarded as a full human being," before Southern Baptists affirmed and reaffirmed their calls for legalization measures, and years before Jerry Falwell preached his first antiabortion sermon, Mark Hatfield was having none of it. His commitment to the sanctity of life made him a "dove" on military matters, prompting some Evangelicals to dismiss him as a Liberal, but it also impelled Hatfield to defend those the antiabortion activists would later refer to as "the unborn." Taking the floor of the Senate on May 31, 1973, barely four months after the *Roe* decision, Hatfield acknowledged that he had wrestled with the issue "morally, legally, biologically, and theologically," concluding that "how society regards this question directly relates to whether we can choose to nourish and enhance all life for the development of its full humanity, or whether we shall make quiet compromises about the sacredness of life, until the fundamental worth of any life becomes subject to society's discretion, rather than guaranteed by that life's being."[25]

Hatfield conceded that the abortion question would be simpler if it could be construed as merely a "personal" matter, but "the belief in life's fundamental right to be has inevitable corporate consequences." He drew a direct link to his opposition to war. "In opposing our intervention in Indochina, for example, I did not merely believe it would be wrong for me, as an individual, to fight there," he said. "I believed that no American should fight there, which compelled me to propose legislation expressing that conviction." The senator acknowledged that not everyone agreed on the "certainty of where personhood begins," but he urged erring "on the side of being too liberal about the definition of human life" and argued

---

Faith: Race and the Rise of the Religious Right (Grand Rapids, MI: Eerdmans, 2021), chapter 5.

[25] Dobson quoted in Letha Scanzoni, *Sex Is a Parent Affair: Help for Parents in Teaching Their Children about Sex* (Colorado Springs, CO: Regal Books, 1973) 147; Senator Hatfield, speaking on Protection of the Unborn—Introduction of a Joint Resolution, 93rd Cong., 1st sess., *Congressional Record* 119 (May 31, 1973) 17557. Falwell, by his own admission, did not preach his first anti-abortion sermon until February 26, 1978, more than five years after the *Roe v. Wade* ruling.

WHY STUDY BAPTISTS?

that the "burden of proof lies with those who would advocate abortion to demonstrate conclusively that they are not taking human life."[26]

It would be years before Evangelicals caught up to Hatfield's thinking on the question of abortion, and it is probably significant that following his address on the Senate floor, another Evangelical, political Liberal, and cosponsor of the resolution, Harold Hughes of Iowa, rose to concur with Hatfield, affirming his own "deep feeling that abortion is the taking of human life." But, although the Religious Right eventually came around to Hatfield's convictions on the abortion issue, they did so without taking into account the senator's broader perspective. "Women have suffered deeply and even been dehumanized by society's discrimination of them, and the socially enforced stereotypes every woman has been expected to fulfill," Hatfield acknowledged. "A review of our country's lamentable history in granting to women the very same right we have been discussing—full personhood under the law—makes us realize how tragically we have contradicted our ideals about human rights as far as women are concerned." Such sentiments, however, would later be very much at odds with those of Phyllis Schlafly, Beverly LaHaye, and other leaders of the Religious Right, especially as they mobilized to defeat the proposed Equal Rights Amendment to the Constitution.[27]

Hatfield also acknowledged that a position opposed to abortion carried with it certain obligations, some of which would inevitably be borne by the state. "Every unborn life has a birthright," he said, "for life that is unwanted by unwed parents, society must ensure that right." Such a holistic approach would include nutrition, health care, and perhaps financial assistance. "It means that adoption laws need substantial revision, so especially the mixed-blood or handicapped child will find the warmth and love of a family," he said. "Our whole approach to foster care must be humanized." Finally, he called for "widespread knowledge and availability of

---

[26] Hatfield, *Congressional Record* 119 (May 31, 1973) 17558.

[27] Senator Hughes, speaking on Protection of the Unborn—Introduction of a Joint Resolution, 93rd Cong., 1st sess., *Congressional Record* 119 (May 31, 1973) 17565; Hatfield, *Congressional Record* 119 (May 31, 1973) 17559.

contraceptive options" and "an uncompromising commitment to sex education and family planning services."[28]

"The reality we face is our reverence for life," Hatfield said in conclusion. "There is no single characteristic of our society that troubles my inner self more than the degradation, the cheapening, the dehumanization of life that we see all around us today." He cited capital punishment as one example, the arrogance of the state in depriving a citizen of the right to life. "Violence is no solution," Hatfield concluded, and one of the casualties of the war in Southeast Asia, he said, was the destruction of "all sensitivity to the sanctity of human life."[29]

Leaders of the Religious Right finally came around to Hatfield's thinking on abortion in advance of the 1980 presidential election, many years after the *Roe v. Wade* ruling. Sadly, these same Evangelical leaders ignored the senator's sentiments about violence more generally—the violence of war and capital punishment, the degrading struggle against poverty, and the persistence of women's inequality.

Where did Mark Hatfield derive his understanding of the faith and how it related to his responsibilities as an elected official? Surely his Baptist affiliation informed his views, although he became aware of the limitations of his Baptist congregation in Salem. "In my childhood exposure to Christianity and in the Baptist church I attended when I came home from the war, service of the country in the armed forces was a spiritually blessed duty and privilege," he wrote. "This was never posed to me as any basic conflict for the Christian." Both Hiroshima and Vietnam changed his thinking. "Vietnam fundamentally challenged the synthesis between faith and a nationalistic call to war," he wrote. "Partly because of my past experience in Indochina, I felt that the moral case against our involvement was overwhelming." As chair of the Appropriations Committee in the Senate during the Reagan years, Hatfield became convinced that not only was the prosecution of war wrong on moral grounds, but it also made no sense economically. "A defense dollar," he told *Conservative Digest* in 1982, "has the least multiplier impact on our economy as far as new jobs and new

---

[28] Hatfield, *Congressional Record* 119 (May 31, 1973) 17559.
[29] Ibid., 17560.

wealth are concerned than any dollar we spend in the federal government."[30]

Hatfield also confirmed the influence of James Dunn, longtime executive director of the Baptist Joint Committee, on his thinking. "James Dunn taught me in vivid terms about my Baptist heritage and tradition as he engaged in battles for religious liberty and the separation of church and state," the senator wrote in a tribute. "With a clearer perspective of Christian church history through its many eras and of Baptist history from the seventeenth century to the twenty-first, I came to better understand current church-state issues." Dunn's counsel, Hatfield said, helped him to appreciate the beauty of both pluralism and diversity as well as the "dynamic tension of the First Amendment." Referring to a famous atheist in the 1960s, Hatfield noted that "we have just as many rights in the Constitution for Madalyn Murray O'Hair—no more or no less—than we have for Billy Graham. And may it ever be so. I do not believe that the atheist or the agnostic should in any way be discriminated against." Elsewhere he affirmed that "no one group can enjoy freedom unless all groups can practice their faith and unless even the nonbeliever's conscience is protected."[31]

Dunn also warned the senator against the dangers of Christian nationalism. Hatfield took note, categorically rejecting the idea that the United States was "a Christian nation founded by great Christian leaders." In remarks on the Senate floor, on December 20, 1973, the senior senator from Oregon introduced a resolution for a National Day of Humiliation, Fasting and Prayer. "We tend to put our country out of reach of God's judgment," he said. "Our leaders solemnly invoke the name of God in their political speeches. We earnestly want to believe that ours is God's chosen land, that we are his chosen people, and that the leaders we have are divinely chosen and given special wisdom." Quoting Amos, the Hebrew prophet, Hatfield lamented Americans' faith in materialism as well as the

---

[30] Hatfield, *Between a Rock and a Hard Place*, 111; "Sen. Mark Hatfield Talks About," *Conservative Digest* (June 1982): 14.

[31] Mark O. Hatfield, "Mentor to a Senator," in *James Dunn: Champion for Religious Liberty*, ed. J. Brent Walker (Macon, GA: Smyth & Helwys, 1999) 43, 47. On Christian nationalism, see also "Sen. Mark Hatfield Talks About," *Conservative Digest* (June 1982): 18.

persistence of poverty and racism and the fearsome destructive capabilities of nuclear weapons. Far from anointing the United States as a Christian nation, Hatfield called for repentance. "There is hope for a land and a people who have the capacity to recognize their sins and their faults, and who turn from them." Hatfield carried the call to repentance from the realm of politics to the church. From the pulpit of National Presbyterian Church, in Washington, DC, he again enjoined his auditors to take stock of their arrogance, greed, and selfishness. Hatfield, *The Washington Post* reported, was someone "who is as much at home in a church as in a caucus room."[32]

In an interview for the student newspaper at Gordon College, an Evangelical school in Wenham, Massachusetts, Hatfield pressed his point, rejecting the notion that "God is somehow an American" or that the United States somehow had a divine destiny. "I see us taking false gods which is the sin most paramount in the national culture today," he said. "We have bowed down and worshipped the gods of materialism, the gods of prestige, gods of power, gods of possession." Echoing the sentiments of Charles Grandison Finney, the most influential Evangelical of the nineteenth century, Hatfield noted the paradox of IN GOD WE TRUST emblazoned on coins. "That is the very God of many people in America," he said, "the dollar, the symbol of our national wealth."[33]

Mark Hatfield's evangelical convictions undeniably shaped his policies and political positions, even when they clashed with the views of other Evangelicals. His understanding of Baptist principles, especially on liberty of conscience and the separation of church and state, helped him navigate the vicissitudes of a long and successful political career. He also tried to enlighten others. In a letter to the junior boys Sunday school class, in Shiloh, Ohio, dated October 20, 1970, the senator offered the following

---

[32] "Sen. Mark Hatfield Talks About," *Conservative Digest* (June 1982, 18); "Introduction of a Resolution for a National Day of Humiliation, Fasting and Prayer," News from Senator Mark O. Hatfield, December 20, 1973; Marjorie Hyer, "From Pulpit, Sen. Hatfield Calls on Nation to Repent," *Washington Post* (May 3, 1974).

[33] "Hatfield Says Civil Religion a Narcotic," *Christian Inquirer* (January 1974): 4. Regarding Finney, see Randall Balmer, "'An End to Unjust Inequality in the World': The Radical Tradition of Progressive Evangelicalism." *Church History and Religious Culture* 94 (2014): 505–30.

counsel. "There is nothing that would prevent a person from having a Bible in one's possession in the school room. In fact, the Bible is being made part of the curriculum in many places." He went on to lament that the Supreme Court's decision on school prayer was so widely misunderstood. "The important thing about your Sunday School class is the great opportunity to learn about Jesus Christ and build a relationship with Him," he concluded.[34]

Such a reminder would have been appropriate for Jesse Helms, Hatfield's Senate colleague and author of the Helms Amendment, some years later. Nothing in the Constitution or American law prohibits prayer or possession of a Bible in public school—or anywhere else, for that matter. The issue, in a pluralistic society, is the mandating of public prayer in public schools. Helms's denomination, the Southern Baptist Convention, in 1979 had abandoned its historic role of patrolling the wall of separation between church and state, opting instead to support posting the Ten Commandments in public places and using taxpayer funds to support religious schools. In so doing, Helms and other Southern Baptists turned their backs on Roger Williams, founder of the Baptist tradition in America, neglecting to recognize that Williams's principal concern was protecting the integrity of the faith—the *garden* of the church—from the corruptions of the state—the *wilderness* of the world.[35]

Over the course of a long and distinguished career, however, Mark Hatfield remained faithful to his Christian convictions and to his Baptist roots, even when that fidelity incurred the wrath of everyone from presidents to fellow believers.

---

[34] CN 459, Box 403: Fellowship Foundation, 1935–, Billy Graham Center Archives (Wheaton, IL).

[35] On the significance of Williams's "wall of separation" metaphor, see Randall Balmer, *Solemn Reverence: The Separation of Church and State in American Life* (Hanover, NH: Steerforth Press, 2021), chapter 1.

Evangelical Faith, Politics, and Race in Black and White, 1945–2020

Edward R. Crowther

Writing to the "churches in Galatia," the Apostle Paul reminded his readers that "you are all one in Christ Jesus," that earthly differences in social station, gender, and ethnicity yielded to the unity found through faith in Christ. Yet, in the long history of the United States, that self-evident truth of equality before Christ has too often crashed on the shoals of class, sex, and especially race. Most individual congregations and evangelical Christian denominations are racially identifiable; as Martin Luther King Jr. reminded his listeners, "eleven o'clock on Sunday morning is one of the most segregated hours, if not the most segregated hours, in Christian America." In the same way, political party preference and voting patterns represent a similar racialization. In the 2016 presidential election, 89 percent of African American voters supported the Democratic candidate, but nearly 60 percent of white voters supported the Republican. Religious identification seems to intensify racially partisan preferences. Some 80 percent of white Evangelicals voted for the Republican candidate. Although black and white evangelical Christians worship the same God, their racialized voting patterns appear more in keeping with racially identifiable secular concerns than with shared ethical precepts. This polarization has increased over time, especially since the 1960s.[1]

Although no race-free Eden ever existed in the United States, racialized voting according to political party has not been the only pattern for voting. First, few blacks voted between 1776 and 1867. States that had abolished slavery in the decades following the American Revolution often placed restrictions on black voting, even as they ended property

---

[1] Galatians 3:28; Martin Luther King Jr., "Interview on 'Meet the Press,'" in Clayborne Carson et al., *The Papers of Martin Luther King, Jr.: Threshold of a New Kingdom, January 1959–December 1960* (Berkeley: University of California Press, 2005) 435; "How Groups Votes in 2016," Roper Center, Cornell University. https://ropercenter.cornell.edu/how-groups-voted-2016.

WHY STUDY BAPTISTS?

qualifications for white voters. And the vast majority of the blacks in the United States—some 90 percent in 1860—lived in states whose laws rendered them enslaved property and not voting citizens in the eyes of the law. After the Civil War, African American voting and office holding soared under the aegis of congressional Reconstruction, especially through the Thirteenth, Fourteenth, and Fifteen Amendments. But flight of black voting was brought to earth and then crushed under the heels of white supremacy and privilege when congressional Reconstruction formally ended in 1877. The resurgent white supremacy, termed "Redemption" by its supporters, resulted in state-level voting laws that all but eliminated African Americans as voters in the former slaveholding states, where 95 percent of all African Americans lived in 1880.

Suppressing the black vote took the form of writing new state constitutions containing requirements that were all but impossible for African Americans—and many poorer whites—to meet. When these rules failed to keep blacks from the polls, whites resorted to violence, including lynching. In part, elite whites feared that poor whites and African Americans might form a permanent, interracial voting bloc, with numerical majorities favoring policies that would raise taxes on land and profit. During the 1880s, common whites and African Americans had challenged elite whites for political control in states such as Georgia and North Carolina during the brief era of Alliance and Populist Party politics. White culture justified political suppression by demonizing black people either as childlike at best, or as beasts at worst, and championing the idea of white superiority culturally and even genetically. By 1900, these structures and practices resulted in a United States where most blacks were not voters.[2]

But that racially exclusive pattern did not persist, in no small part because African Americans continued to press for voting rights through organizations such as the National Association for the Advancement of

---

[2] See generally Martha S. Jones, *Birthright Citizens: A History of Race and Law in the Antebellum America* (New York: Cambridge University Press, 2018); W. E. B. Du Bois, *Black Reconstruction in America: An essay toward a history of the part which black folk played in the attempt to reconstruct democracy in America, 1860–1880* (New York: Harcourt, Brace, 1935) 3–4; Edward L. Ayers, *The Promise of the New South: Life After Reconstruction* (New York: Oxford University Press, 1992) 8–9, 147–48, 156–59, 288–90, 298–99, 304–309.

Colored People (NAACP) and by making hard claims for citizenship rights due to military participation in the Spanish American War and especially the First World War. However, the most visible changes in racial voting patterns came as a result of black people moving out of the South in large numbers between 1890 and 1940, an exodus referred to as the Black Migration. Often a reflection of the Egypt of the Southern states, the Promised Land of the North did not overflow with the milk and honey of racial equality, and African Americans experienced the constant threat of physical violence along with economic and housing discrimination because of their race. Still, opportunities seemed greater in the industrial North than the agriculturally depressed South. Ironically, because adult blacks could now vote in these Northern states and white racism concentrated African Americans into precincts in which blacks were a huge majority, African Americans began to elect blacks to Congress, including Oscar De Priest from Chicago's First Congressional District in 1929, and then William L. Dawson in 1943. Both men were Southern born, embodiments of the Great Migration, and in their early careers both men were Republican, reflecting the legacy of the Republican Party as the party of Lincoln and Emancipation.[3]

White voting patterns between 1870 and 1936 followed class, regional, and ethnic lines. Outside of the former Confederacy, where the Republican Party was anathema as the party of Reconstruction, and the Democratic Party was the bastion of white supremacy, well-to-do whites typically voted Republican. Working-class people often voted for Democratic candidates.[4]

This established pattern—Southern whites as overwhelmingly Democrats and non-Southerners voting along class lines—proved durable enough to incorporate other demographic changes in the United States

---

[3] Michael J. Klarman, *Unfinished Business: Racial Equality in American History* (New York: Oxford University Press, 2007) 75–110, 114–15; Isabell Wilkerson, *The Warmth of Other Suns: The Epic Story of America's Great Migration* (New York: Random House, 2010); Steven E. Lawson: *Running for Freedom: Civil Rights and Black Politics in America since 1941*, 3rd ed. (Maiden, MA: 2009) 36–37.

[4] Donald Critchlow, *American Political History: A Very Short Introduction* (New York: Oxford University Press, 2015) 74–104.

that occurred during its Gilded Age and Progressive Era. After the Civil War, and especially after 1890, immigration from southern and eastern Europe transformed large cities and industrial centers, where Italian, Polish, Russian, and German migrants came to establish new homes. These new arrivals typically became Democrats, in part because they were working-class, but also as a result of the history of the Republican Party. When it was established in 1854, the party had opposed the foreign born and was the champion of Protestantism and was no more welcoming of the torrent of Italian and Polish Catholics and Eastern-European Jews than it had been of Irish Catholics before the Civil War. Immigration and the political cultures of the two parties also created a rural-urban division among voters; many whites in the cities were Democrats, while the countryside, often the abode of US-born Protestants, was solidly Republican. Hence, while race was a central theme in United States history and affected the nation's voting practices, white voters did not vote solidly in one party against nonwhites in another party. And black voters during Reconstruction, and in many Northern cities afterward, often voted Republican.[5]

In the wake of the Great Depression, a massive political realignment occurred among voters as the Republican Party, seen as the party of big business and moneyed privilege, lost support among scores of white voters who rejected Herbert Hoover, the Republican presidential incumbent in 1932, and voted for Franklin Roosevelt. In 1936, Roosevelt won reelection, and voting patterns in this election can serve as a baseline for understanding voting trends in the United States, especially in the years after World War II. First, the Socialist and Communist Parties lost ground from 1932, indicating that voters preferred the two-party system and supported the reforms of banking and industry that were features of Roosevelt's New Deal, his experimental program to grapple with the collapse of the US economy. Roosevelt took more than 60 percent of the popular vote and all but eight of the electoral votes. Second, in this election, Southern whites continued their support of Roosevelt and the Democratic Party, but were joined by intellectuals, labor unions and laboring people, college-

---

[5] Ibid.; Eric Foner, *Free Soil, Free Labor, Free Men: The Ideology of the Republican Party Before the Civil War* (New York: Oxford University Press, 1970) 237–246.

educated whites, and most African Americans to form what political scientists call the Roosevelt coalition. The rise and subsequent unraveling of the Roosevelt coalition provided a spine for understanding the social, political, and racial history of the United States for the next half century.[6]

During the remaining years of the Depression, World War II, and well into the 1960s, this coalition persisted in many elections. Its unraveling, especially observable in the presidential elections of 1968, 1984, and 2016, resulted in the seemingly durable racialized voting that exists in the United States today. While many whites vote for Democratic candidates, a growing number of white voters, especially those who identify as Evangelicals and those who live in the former Confederacy—whose great-grandparents were staunch Democrats (historians refer to the Southern white support for the Democratic Party as the "Solid South" for the years 1876 to 1968)—now vote Republican. Although a few African Americans have persisted in the Republican Party, the vast majority consistently vote for Democratic candidates, and this pattern has hardened since 1980, in part because the Republican Party has proven to be a safe haven for white supremacy and white privilege.

Historians and political scientists have offered compelling explanations for this realignment. The first component of the shift is a function of the unnatural nature of the coalition in the first place. Only the dire reality of the Great Depression temporarily lessened the antipathy between Southern whites and blacks rooted in years of violent suppression of African American demands for equality. Indeed, African Americans in the South did not vote in large numbers prior to 1965, and during the Depression and World War II, the Roosevelt administration permitted a number of concessions to white interests. For instance, to assuage Southern white Democrats, the Social Security Act of 1935 did not provide coverage to

---

[6] William E. Leuchtenburg, *In the Shadow of FDR: From Harry Truman to Ronald Reagan* (Ithica, NY: Cornell University Press, 1983) ix–x., 184, 243. The Depression created unnatural partnerships across racial, ethnic, regional, and class lines. The relationship between corporate Liberals—managerial elites—and traditional patriarchal leaders illustrates both the power of economic dislocation and fears of international threat to create a tenuous cooperation. See Richard E. Holl, *From the Board Room to the War Room: America's Corporate Liberals and FDR's Preparedness Program* (Rochester, NY: University of Rochester Press, 2005).

agricultural and domestic workers, most of whom were black. Similarly, the National Housing Act of 1934 operated in ways that ensured that whites received most of the mortgage money and African American neighborhoods were deemed undesirable (the origin of the practice known as "redlining," which still has an impact on voting and education today in many cities). When African Americans demanded equality under the Fourteenth Amendment and better treatment in the labor market after World War II, the fragile fabric of the Roosevelt coalition began to unravel.[7]

Second, many business and banking leaders opposed the New Deal's regulatory apparatuses and loathed their replacement as the natural leaders of community with government experts and legislative programs. Beginning in the 1930s, business leaders made a concerted effort to undercut the New Deal State as un-American and ungodly. Business should be left to its own devices and churches, not the state, should be responsible for helping the poor. Moneyed interests and their ministerial allies framed their opposition to collective action to address social ills in religious terms, even when it was backed by the legislative process and ostensibly with voter support. Individuals were to make their own way in the world, in the same manner that individuals stood accountable to God for their sins.[8]

This same partnership of plutocrats and pulpits gained momentum with the ending of World War II and the onset of the dangerous world of Cold War. The United States, "under God," stood as a moral beacon of

---

[7] Jefferson Cowie, *The Great Exception: The New Deal & the Limits of American Politics* (Princeton, NJ: Princeton University Press, 2016) 179–207; Ira Katznelson, *When Affirmative Action Was White: An Untold History of Racial Inequality in Twentieth-Century America* (New York: W. W. Norton & Co., 2005) 43–48; Terry Gross, "A 'Forgotten History' of How the U.S. Government Segregated America" *N.P.R.*, May 3, 2017. https://www.npr.org/2017/05/03/526655831/a-forgotten-history-of-how-the-u-s-government-segregated-america.

[8] Leuchtenburge, *In the Shadow of FDR*, 123, 166; Kevin Kruse, *One Nation Under God: How Corporate America Invented Christian America* (New York: Basic Books, 2015) 3–66; Darren E. Grem, *The Blessings of Business: How Corporations Shaped Conservative Christianity* (New York: Oxford University Press, 2016) 13–120; Sarah Ruth Hammond, *God's Businessmen: Entrepreneurial Evangelicals in Depression and War* (Chicago: University of Chicago Press, 2017).

freedom and prosperity against the godless Communism of the Soviet Union. While many whites in the late eighteenth and throughout the nineteenth centuries had constructed the United States as an exceptional nation—a country seemingly immune from the laws and limitations of history—and as a Christian nation, founded by Christian people to do God's work in the world, the crucible of Cold War produced a robust and powerful alliance between Caesar's and God's kingdoms. Popular president Dwight Eisenhower, who had recently converted to Presbyterianism, captured this new religion well: "Our form of government makes no sense unless it is founded on a deeply felt religious belief." In 1956, Eisenhower signed into law a requirement that the national motto, "In God We Trust," had to appear on US currency. This was a powerful signal of the privileged position of Christianity and capitalism in the United States during the Cold War. For white people, this partnership was something to celebrate.[9]

But other Christians, especially African Americans, wondered how Christian the United States was in practice, as it was clear that economic justice, and especially racial justice, seemed to be lacking in practice across the nation. Examples of racial injury seemed ubiquitous. Returning by bus to his home in Georgia after serving in World War II, Isaac Woodard, an African American, was arrested and deliberately blinded by Lynwood Schull, the chief of police in Batesburg, South Carolina. An all-white federal jury subsequently and unanimously ruled that Schull's actions had not violated Woodard's civil rights. J. W. Milam and Roy Bryant, two adult white men, brutally beat, mutilated, and shot Emmett Till, a fourteen-year-old African American youth near Money, Mississippi, in 1955. An all-white jury quickly acquitted both men. Apart from the routine brutalities inflicted on black people, from sexual assault to murder, African Americans also endured countless acts of discrimination in housing, employment, and educational opportunity. They pondered how just was the economic order in the United States, where black families made just over

---

[9] John Fea, *Was America Founded as a Christian Nation?*, rev. ed. (Louisville, KY, Westminster John Knox Press, 2017) 3–56; Kruse, *One Nation Under God*, 67–125.

WHY STUDY BAPTISTS?

half of what white families earned. African American demands for racial and economic justice strained the seams of the Roosevelt coalition.[10]

One of the ironies of the Cold War is its understandable outward focus—competing with the Soviet Union for the allegiance of newly decolonized nations in Africa and Asia, for example—meant that the engines of the national government, including senators and congressmen outside of the former Confederate States, could not ignore completely the demands of African Americans for racial justice at home. Not only did the United States Supreme Court undo race-based assignment of students in public schools in 1954, Eisenhower sent the 101st Airborne Division to Little Rock, Arkansas, to enforce a district court order carrying out the Supreme Court's will. As the Vietnam War was beginning to escalate, President Johnson signed the Civil Rights Act of 1964, outlawing discrimination on the basis of race, color, religion, sex, or national origin, including discrimination on those grounds by businesses classified as public accommodations. In 1965, Johnson signed the Voting Rights Act of 1965, which outlawed racially discriminatory voter-registration practices, especially targeting Southern states where such practices kept African Americans from registering to vote. Under the provisions of these two federal laws, blacks could dine at white-owned restaurants and, more importantly, could register to vote. In the South, African Americans began to vote in

---

[10] *New York Times*, November 6, 1946, p. 36; Richard Gergel, *Unexampled Courage: The Blinding of Isaac Woodard and the Awakening of President Harry Truman and Judge J. Waites Waring* (New York: Sarah Crichton Books, 2019); Klarman, *Unfinished Business*, 160–182; Jeanne Theoharris, *The Rebellious Life of Mrs. Rosa Parks* (Boston: Beacon Press, 2013) 43. Danielle L. McGwire, *At the Dark End of the Street: Black Women, Rape, and Resistance—A New History of the Civil Rights Movement from Rosa Parks to the Rise of Black Power* (New York: Knopf Publishing Group, 2010). Martin Luther King Jr. noted that the all-white jury that acquitted Roy Bryant and J. W. "Big" Milam of murdering Till "worships Christ," but he compared their faith to that of the observant Pharisees who believed moral concern and action were less important than "the gushing smoke of emotional adoration and ceremonial piety" as a religious duty. See Martin Luther King Jr., "Pride Versus Humility: The Parable of the Pharisee and the Publican," Sermon at Dexter Avenue Baptist Church in *The Papers of Martin Luther King, Jr. Volume VI: Advocate of the Social Gospel, September 1948–March 1963*, eds. Clayborne Carson et al. (Berkeley: University of California Press, 2007) 232.

proportions not seen since Reconstruction and run for office as Democrats. In the wake of these statutes, Southern whites moved in droves from the Democratic Party to the Republican Party, beckoned by Republican politicians like presidential candidate Richard Nixon, whose "law and order" campaign appealed to whites who had loathed Martin Luther King Jr.'s nonviolent demonstrations and were even more frightened by images of racialized urban violence in the name of Black Power.[11]

Nixon's evocation of "law and order" and courting of what he called "the silent majority" resonated with many white voters in the wake of the dislocations in 1968, including the Tet Offensive in Vietnam, the assassinations of Martin Luther King Jr. (which triggered riots in more than one hundred US cities) and presidential candidate Robert F. Kennedy, and the demonstrations and police riots outside of the Democratic National Convention in Chicago. In the general election, many Southern white Christians actually voted for the openly white supremacist Alabamian George Corley Wallace. By 1972, however, the white voters in six Southern states who had voted for Wallace were in Nixon's camp. Changes in the delegate selection process for the Democratic Party's national nominating convention earned it support from Progressive whites and African Americans but cost it the support of non-Southern white working-class voters. The Democratic Party was becoming much more noticeably racially and ethnically diverse; the Republican Party was becoming whiter, especially with Southern whites becoming reliably Republican the way their ancestors had been reliably Democrat.[12]

During the 1970s, many white evangelical Christian voters seemed less disturbed by persistent racial issues than by other cultural issues, including the sexual revolution's celebration of premarital, extramarital, and homosexual sexual liberty. It was not that race had ceased to matter to

---

[11] James T. Patterson, *Grand Expectations: The United States, 1945–1974* (New York: Oxford University Press, 1996) 388–95, 542–45, 579–83; John David Skrentny, "The Effect of the Cold War on African-American Civil Rights: America and the World Audience, 1945–1968" *Theory and Society* 27 (April 1998): 237–85.

[12] Patterson, *Grand Expectations*, 457; 698–700; Earl Black and Merle Black, *Divided America: The Ferocious Power Struggle in American Politics* (New York: Simon and Schuster, 2007) 55, 61–92.

WHY STUDY BAPTISTS?

them; ironically, despite the important transformations wrought in the name of racial equality in the areas governed by law (voting, and, to a degree, federal and state government jobs), whites concerned about white supremacy had preserved core institutions—their congregations and their children's schools—from unwanted racial mixing mandated by government. Progressive whites could still send their children to integrated schools, but, beginning in response to *Brown v. Board of Education* and rapidly accelerating after 1969, when *Alexander v. Holmes County Board of Education* ended most practices designed to protect white-only public schools, Conservative whites elected to send their children to private academies, some operated by churches, some even by the White Citizens' Council, sometimes abetted by Christian Reconstructionists like Gary North—not a few Conservative Christian parents opted for home-schooling.[13]

Ostensibly, these schools protected children from humanistic influences, including Darwinian biology, but they also segregated students in the main from nonwhites. For the well-to-do parents, white flight to racially segregated suburbs became a preferred option, especially after the Supreme Court struck down interdistrict busing as a remedy to racial segregation in schools in *Milliken v. Bradley*. Congregations moved out of the central cities to the suburbs in the wake of white flight. The challenges some whites experienced with "pray ins" by African Americans and their white allies, which called attention to racially segregated worship during the 1960s, helped encourage white congregations to relocate but also resulted in the cessation of efforts to desegregate on the part of many blacks and their white allies. Racial partisanship increased as white churches increasingly engaged in voter-registration efforts and encouraged

---

[13] See "Gary North on the Homeschooling Advantage," http://www.ron paullibertyreport.com/archives/gary-north-on-the-homeschooling-advantage. Gary North was the son-in-law of R. J. Rushdoony and has spent the past fifty years working on a number of causes, including abolishing public schools.

94

congregants to vote for candidates who supported the political right's morally tinged issues.[14]

The primacy of race as a dividing line becomes especially evident among Christian voters, especially Evangelicals, in the 1970s and 1980s. Christian politics around moral issues ranged across the spectrum from debates over liberation theology and environmentalism to culture-war issues such as abortion, school prayer, gun rights, and homosexuality. Most African American and white Christians oppose abortion, for example, but increasingly the Republican Party abandoned its earlier nuanced position on abortion and worked with increased vigor to overturn *Roe v. Wade* at the national level while supporting state-level adoption of the most restrictive measures legislatures were willing to craft. Many white voters now saw their partisan identification as a reflection of their pro-life values; many African Americans, not a few of whom viewed abortion as a tactic to limit black population growth, still did not support the Republican Party because they viewed its policies on crime, drugs, and the social safety net as measures targeting African Americans. Protecting hard-won political and economic gains mattered more to erstwhile pro-life black voters than the substantive and symbolic cultural issues that often motivated white voters.[15]

Conservative white Christians increasingly struggled with a globalizing world in which whites, especially white Christians, were a minority. Earlier missionary thrusts rooted in the confidence of a sovereign God who would bless their efforts to win the world to Christ yielded to a new playbook wherein white Christian voters would support a presidential candidate who reflected their own values; this president would then appoint

---

[14] Edward H. Miller, *Nut Country: Right Wing Dallas and the Birth of the Southern Strategy* (Chicago: University of Chicago Press, 2015) 70–77; Kevin Kruse, *White Flight: Atlanta and the Making of Modern Conservatism* (Princeton, NJ: Princeton University Press, 2005) 132–160; "Inner City Churches on the Move," *Religion & Ethics Newsweekly*, February 6, 2004. http://www.pbs.org/wnet/religionandethics/2004/02/06/february-6-2004-inner-city-churches-on-the-move/12510/. Retrieved August 29, 2018.

[15] John Fea, *Believe Me: The Evangelical Road to Donald Trump* (Grand Rapids, MI: Eerdmans, 2018); Frances Fitzgerald, *The Evangelical: The Struggle to Shape America* (New York: Simon and Schuster, 2017) 55–60, 352–62.

judges to protect Christian interests. However, these judges often seemed more inclined to protect white interests that masqueraded as Christian interests. Since the late 1970s, overturning *Roe v. Wade*, ensuring religious-liberty exemptions from the Patient Protection and Affordable Care Act, and ensuring the rights of small businesses to refuse requests for services from gay and lesbian clients have dominated the public agenda for many white Christians. Although the sources of the myriad of issues that vex Conservative whites are legion, many first attacked the federal courts for overturning racial segregation and then lambasted their decisions outlawing state-sponsored school prayer and Bible reading, all while continuing to focus on their rulings permitting what they consider to be infanticide. The way to protect Christian values and religious liberty is to wield political power effectively.[16]

Lost in the typical litany describing the use of the political process to turn the United States back to God by controlling the federal court system is a central element in its founding narrative: in large part, the current concept of religious liberty grew out of efforts to maintain racially segregated private schools that were tax exempt. Moral Majority founders Jerry Falwell and Paul Weyrich, who also cofounded the Heritage Foundation, helped forge a racialized voting bloc for the Republican Party because they feared Democrat Jimmy Carter would appoint Liberal judges to the Supreme Court who would then overturn nascent efforts begun by Richard Nixon to tack the court to the right and affirm efforts by the federal government to use the federal tax code as a tool to compel tax-exempt entities to desegregate. As Weyrich recalled, the efforts of "the Internal Revenue Service...to deny tax exemption to private schools...more than any [other] single act brought the fundamentalists and evangelicals into the political

---

[16] Fitzgerald, *Evangelicals*, 291–318. See David Green, "Donald Trump is our only hope for a Supreme Court that will protect freedom of religion, *USA Today*, September 1, 2016. https://www.usatoday.com/story/opinion/2016/09/01/hobby-lobby-religious-freedom-liberty-obamacare-christian-david-green/89597214/. Green is the founder of Hobby Lobby, whose company sued for exemption from certain provisions of the Patient Protection and Affordable Health Care Act.

process."[17] First, Weyrich blamed Carter's administration for a decision to revoke the tax-exempt status of Bob Jones University, which was actually done by the Nixon administration. Then, in 1978, the Internal Revenue Service threatened to require private schools to demonstrate that they had a quota of minority students or that they operated on a nondiscriminatory basis, in effect shifting the burden of proof to the school that it was complying with federal guidelines. Feeling besieged, Evangelical leaders motivated their congregations to engage in the political process to protect their institutions from what they considered unwarranted and unconstitutional federal interference. Although the IRS never implemented its proposal, in part due to the 150,000 protest letters written by Evangelicals, its abortive action alerted Evangelicals to the potential threat of governmental regulation of their institutions. As Weyrich notes, "The federal government's moves against Christian schools" catalyzed many Evangelical leaders to engage in the political process, but it required a broader appeal to the range of moral concerns of Conservative Christians to create the Religious Right, whose first organizational expression was the Moral Majority in 1979.[18]

To reach a national audience, Weyrich and Falwell decried "secular humanism," a term they borrowed from Francis Schaeffer, who was rapidly becoming a mainstream figure in Conservative white Christianity in the United States. The term was broad enough to include opposition to governmental regulations challenging religious liberty, and it embraced a welter of moral issues, rather than highlighting racial discrimination. The centerpiece of secular humanism was abortion on demand, so opposition to *Roe v. Wade* could serve as the focus of the culture-wars politics that would shape the 1980s and 1990s. While white Christian voters mobilized around the big tent of opposing secular humanism and abortion, Ronald Reagan whistled to the racialized base of this emerging movement when he denounced the targeting of "independent schools" by the overreaching

---

[17] Paul Weyrich, "The Pro-Family Movement," *Conservative Digest* 6 (May–June 1980) 14.

[18] Weyrich, "Pro-Family Movement"; *No Longer Exiles: The Religious New Right in American Politics*, ed. Michael Cromartie (Washington, DC: Ethics and Public Policy Center, 1993) 26.

IRS during a speech before ten thousand Evangelicals in 1980 at the Reunion Arena in Dallas. Joining Reagan on the platform was none other than W. A. Criswell, long-time pastor of First Baptist Church, Dallas, and, until recently, an articulate defender of racial segregation on scriptural grounds. Religious liberty had become a broad mantra to protect Conservative Christians from civic obligations to which they objected; its origin as a political value grew out of an effort to preserve white racial privilege.[19]

By 1984, more than two-thirds of Southern white ministers preferred the Republican Party to the Democratic Party, a number that rose to 80 percent by 1996. Whereas theologically liberal whites had been the most politically active during the civil rights crusades in the 1950s, Conservative whites decried Liberal activism as a perversion of the true Christian gospel. By the 1990s, most Conservative white ministers espoused a "civic gospel" of political activity. It mixed the historically flawed concept that the United States had been founded as a Christian nation but had become apostate and that Christians must engage the secular world to protect their right to live and worship freely, to ensure public morality, and to limit the power of the national government to the Constitution as it was originally written. This civic gospel enjoys the succor of a powerful strand of libertarianism often associated with the western United States, which emphasizes individual rights against governmental regulation and xenophobic nationalism, which began to leaven the Republican Party, especially during the presidential campaign of Barry Goldwater in 1964. Decrying the New Deal state for fostering lethargy and dependence, loathing the threat of foreign immigration (especially after the Hart-Celler Act of 1965), and brandishing a Fundamentalist reading of Scripture to shoot down critics, the Conservative Republican political garment seemed racially neutral. It often reflected the particular concerns of upper-middle-class white women, "suburban warriors," who did the ongoing organizing work of

---

[19] Randall Balmer, "The Real Origins of the Religious Right," *Politico Magazine*, May 27, 2014. https://www.politico.com/magazine/story/2014/05/religious-right-real-origins-107133. See also, Curtis W. Freeman, "'Never Have I Been So Blind': W. A. Criswell's 'Change' on Racial Segregation," *Journal of Southern Religion* 10 (2007): 1–12.

politics that women did in the various churches in the United States. The result was an approach to politics and life that reflects a white view of history and the present: nonwhites and immigrants threaten national security, secularists wish to destroy the church, and feminism wishes to destroy the God-given privilege women enjoy in harmonious, traditional marriages.[20]

For African Americans, the political expression that comes from the lived experiences of whites has little relevance, even though many African Americans share with many whites a belief in traditional gender arrangements, the values of hard work, and national pride. But unlike the nostalgia that informs white Conservative Christian politics, there is little of the past that black people wish to reclaim: certainly not the chattel status and brutal torture that characterized slavery, the murderous barbarity of Jim Crow, or, more recently, the bitter gall of police-on-black violence, a lethal continuation of the carceral state that imprisons black men five times more frequently than white men. The slogan of Republican Party's current standard-bearer to "Make America Great Again," to black people, begs the question of when was America ever great? A typical retort, that the United States is now post-racial because of the election and reelection of Barack Hussein Obama, falls flat for many black listeners, who know too well the indisputable fact that the leader of the Republican Party embraced and propagated the false claim that Obama was not even a United States citizen, and his presidency was therefore illegitimate.

The fact that many Evangelical leaders endorsed a member of the Church of Jesus Christ of Latter-day Saints over Obama in 2012 furthered the sense that white voters valued a candidate's race more than his faith. The noxious paternalism of many whites who insist that their lifestyles and politics are both preferable and godly offends the senses of black people

---

[20] James L. Guth, "Southern Baptist Clergy, the Christian Right, and Political Activism," in *Politics and Religion in the White South*, ed. Glenn Feldman (Lexington: University of Kentucky Press, 2007) 199–200. For "suburban warriors," see Lisa McGirr, *Suburban Warriors: The Origins of the New American Right* (Princeton, NJ: Princeton University Press, 2001) 365. Women's roles in sustaining privilege have often placed them firmly on the side of resistance to egalitarian change. See Elisabeth Gillespie McRae, *Mothers of Massive Resistance: White Women and the Politics of White Supremacy* (New York: Oxford University Press, 2018).

who go to church regularly, who distinguish themselves as employers, employees, and, when possible, as neighbors because black people experience police harassment while driving and other reminders of their status as less than equals. Harvard professor Henry Louis Gates, an African American, was arrested for breaking into his own residence, a current enactment of the truth that fifteen-year-old Martin Luther King Jr. had said in 1944: "The finest Negro is at the mercy of the meanest white man."[21]

The two-party system in the United States reflects well the history of race and racism in the United States. Both parties are dominated by white interests, and only historical contingency explains how most black people came to identify with the Democratic Party: the creation of the Roosevelt coalition in 1936 and the exodus of **Southern** whites from the Democratic Party after the Voting Rights Act of 1965 was passed. African Americans have had an uneasy time in the Democratic Party, especially in the 1990s when, in an appeal to white centrist Democrats, President Bill Clinton signed the Personal Responsibility and Work Opportunity Reconciliation Act of 1996, a measure whose burdens fell most harshly on poor black women. Often accused of possessing an institutional plantation mentality, the Democratic Party has often taken the votes of black people for granted. Yet, at the same time, the Republican Party has been indifferent and seemingly hostile to black voters. Rather than confront the reality of historical contingency and the changing demography of the United States by reaching out to black people, the party continues to stand for policies—reduced Pell Grants, for example—that appear to harm African Americans. While so many Republicans embrace subtle or even overt racism, the party itself

---

[21] Fea, *Believe Me.* 153–60; Campbell Robertson, "A Quiet Exodus: Why Black Worshippers are Leaving White Evangelical Churches," *New York Times* (March 9, 2018). https://www.nytimes.com/2018/03/09/us/blacks-evangelical-churches.html; Michelle Alexander, *The New Jim Crow: Mass Incarceration in an Age of Colorblindness* (New York: The New Press, 2010); Ta-Nahisi Coates, "The Arrest of Henry Louis Gates," *The Atlantic* (August 12, 2010). https://www.theatlantic.com/national/archive/2010/08/the-arrest-of-henry-louis-gates/61365/; Martin Luther King Jr., "The Negro and the Constitution," in *The Papers of Martin Luther King, Jr. Volume I: Called to Serve, January 1929–June 1951*, eds. Clayborne Carson et al. (Berkeley: University of California Press, 1992) 110.

continues to provide safe haven for overt white supremacists. Party loyalty seems to matter more than racial justice. Many of its members support measures that have the effect of suppressing African American voting. The forty-fifth president, a Republican who enjoyed overwhelming support from white Southern Baptists in the 2016 presidential election, referred to those African American athletes who kneel during the playing of the "Star-Spangled Banner" to protest the real problem of police-on-black violence as "sons of bitches."[22]

The world of evangelical Christians in the United States, however, has never been monolithic. Consider the perspectives and experiences of contemporary Southern Baptists who, to outsiders, seem almost homogenous but who, along with the various sects of the Reformed tradition, form the religious core of the active core of the Republican Party. Southern Baptist expressions of diversity spring from many sources, including hallowed beliefs that allow individuals, rather than an established hierarchy, to interpret the meaning of the Bible and, hence, what duties Christians owe to one another, to the state, and to humanity. Congregational autonomy enables the ongoing tension between local practice and shared denominational label, allowing the denomination to weather secular centrifugal storms. Even among white Southern Baptists who identify as politically **Conservative**, an awareness that the perceived alignment of denomination with a single political party is harming its witness, and likely fueling a measurable decline in membership, led to objections to Vice President Mike Pence addressing the 2018 Southern Baptist Convention. Although Pence spoke to the Convention, a seeming continuation of the common identity between a majority white denomination and the political party most of its members prefer, the messengers composing it selected a Moderate **Conservative**, J. D. Greear, as Convention president. The SBC's decision to elect Greear suggested to many observers that the hard

---

[22] Jemar Tisby, *The Color of Compromise: The Truth about the American Church's Complicity in Racism* (Grand Rapids, MI: Zondervan, 2019) 185–191; Jason Kurtz, "Trump's 'SOB' Remark Moves NFL Players to Kneel During Anthem," CNN *Politics*, December 21, 2017. https://www.cnn.com/2017/09/25/politics/dolphins-tight-end-julius-thomas-national-anthem-kneel-erin-burnett-outfront-cnntv/index.html.

linkage between white Southern Baptists and the Republican Party was moderating, especially around issues regarding race and the treatment of women. These issues are especially salient features, both nationally and in Southern Baptist life.[23]

Internal division among Southern Baptists expresses itself in a variety of ways. The Conservative Baptist Network came to believe that the work of the Conservative Resurgence in the late twentieth century was incomplete, and seemed to advocate a further purging of the Southern Baptist Convention of Liberal "wokeness." Shocking reporting by the *Houston Chronicle* about congregations covering up sexual misconduct and revelations about Paige Patterson's counseling of a female sexual assault victim placed the issue of seeming-systemic sexual abuse of Baptist women before the convention in 2019. As the calendar turned to 2020, the COVID-19 pandemic led to quarantines, masks, and restrictions on public worship. Then, in the wake of George Floyd's murder in May 2020, racially charged protests against police violence erupted across the United States, including in Washington, DC. Southern Baptists engaged the noxious racial times, in part, by debating the compatibility of what Christopher Rufo defined as "critical race theory" with the *Baptist Faith and Message*, a proxy for whether it was a useful tool to help apply the Christian faith in a fallen world or the seed of a godless Marxism. Against this bewildering welter of earthly chaos, in the November presidential election, most white Southern Baptists voted for the Republican candidate while most African Americans voted for the Democrat. They watched with a range of differing perspectives as the Republican candidate denounced the results as fraudulent and his supporters, on January 6, 2021, stormed the Capitol to stop the

---

[23] Michelle Boorstein, "Why Southern Baptists Giving Mike Pence a Platform Is So Controversial," *Washington Post* (June 13, 2018). https://www.washingtonpost.com/news/acts-of-faith/wp/2018/06/13/why-southern-baptists-giving-mike-pence-a-platform-is-so-controversial/; Jonathan Merritt, "Southern Baptists Call Off the Culture War," *The Atlantic* (June 2018). https://www.theatlantic.com/ideas/archive/2018/06/southern-baptists-call-off-the-culture-war/563000/.

counting of electoral votes in a quixotic attempt to keep the incumbent Republican in power.[24]

Moderate white Southern Baptists likely agreed with their outgoing convention president, Greear, when he said, "Whenever the Church gets in bed with politics, the Church gets pregnant. And the offspring does not look like our Father in heaven."[25] But many others believed that their country was besieged by secular socialism and that they were living under an illegitimate government, and they understood that doubling down as Republicans was their duty, as Bible-believing citizens in a beleaguered Christian republic. Both factions of white Baptists believed that they were deploying a Bible-based perspective to "strengthen the SBC in an effort to fulfill the Great Commission and influence culture," in the plain wording of the purpose statement of the Conservative Baptist Network, a powerful phrase that Moderate and Conservative white Southern Baptists and scores of African American Southern Baptists would agree is the collective mission of all Southern Baptists.[26]

But this commonality does not unify ecclesiastically or politically, especially when one considers race. Marshal Ausberry, an African American and one-time SBC vice president, gave his own perspective: "Some will tout that the Bible is the only answer we need. If that were completely true, we would not have had slavery and racism in America! If that were true, we would not have sexual abuse in America or in churches! Because many of the perpetrators of slavery, racism, and sexual abuse have the Bible." In addition to the light of the Bible, he suggests the deployment of tools such as critical race theory and other here-and-now aids to

---

[24] Benjamin Wallace-Wells, "How a Conservative Activist Invented the Conflict over Critical Race Theory," *The New Yorker* (June 18, 2021). https://www.newyorker.com/news/annals-of-inquiry/how-a-conservative-activist-invented-the-conflict-over-critical-race-theory; "Abuse of Faith," *Houston Chronicle*, https://www.houstonchronicle.com/local/investigations/abuse-of-faith/.

[25] Brian Kaylor, "SBC Meeting opens with Patriotism, Drop Attempts to Decry Jan. 6," *Word & Way* (June 15, 2021). https://wordandway.org/2021/06/15/sbc-meeting-opens-with-patriotism-drops-attempt-to-decry-jan-6/.

[26] Purpose. Conservative Baptist Network. https://conservativebaptistnetwork.com/.

understand and, he hopes, eradicate the expressions of "sin," like white supremacy and the sexual abuse of women.[27] To borrow from Abraham Lincoln, black and white Evangelicals devour "the same Bible" and beseech "the same God" in their earthly sojourn, but their experiences living as individuals in a society with durable, long-standing racial constructions largely shapes how they interpret the Bible and, of course, how they vote.

Hence, in the short run at least, racial polarization in voting among black and white Christians is likely to continue, if not intensify, in the foreseeable future, even as Evangelicals continue to embrace the Bible as the only authoritative guide to faith and practice. The problem is not with a clear gospel, with which black and white Christians in principle agree, but on how to apply it in civic life in a constitutional republic. Lived experience, rather than a consistent and shared hermeneutic, seems to drive which political measures and parties to support, perpetuating the current pattern of racialized voting.

---

[27] Kelly Shellnut, "While Southern Baptists Debate Critical Race Theory, Black Pastors Keep Hoping for Change," *Christianity Today* (June 29, 2021). https://www.christianitytoday.com/news/2021/june/black-pastor-southern-baptist-naaf-frank-williams-crt-churc.html.

"The True Ekklesia and the Hope of the World": Martin Luther King Jr. and the Theo-Politics of Black Baptist Ecclesiology

Corey D. B. Walker

Is organized religion too inextricably bound to the status quo to save our nation and the world? Perhaps I must turn my faith to the inner spiritual church, the church within the church, as the true ekklesia and the hope of the world.

> —Martin Luther King Jr., "Letter from the Birmingham City Jail"

In "A Theology for Racism: Southern Fundamentalists and the Civil Rights Movement," Bill J. Leonard writes, "Underneath all the political, doctrinal, and biblical rhetoric, however, was a powerful racism shaped by the prevailing social, cultural, and racial foundations of the white, segregationist South."[1] Leonard does not mince words in underscoring the racist foundations that secured the cultural, ideological, and political dimensions of Southern Fundamentalism. For Leonard, racism was not merely incidental to the thoughts, actions, and beliefs of this powerful sect in American Christianity, it was constitutive of how they conceived of themselves, their world, their religion, and, ultimately, their God. In this way, their faith and their way of life necessitated a theological expression to support a racism that was integral to their cultural, political, and religious identity. Indeed, as Leonard so perceptively reminds us, Southern Fundamentalists understood that to be white was to be human and to be human was to be white. In turn, the divine implication is that to be human and to be made in the image of God is to be made white.

Leonard's considered and critical dedication to examining Baptist history, polity, and practice exemplifies a commitment to exposing this line of thinking that is constitutive of the Baptist experience in America.

---

[1] Bill J. Leonard, "A Theology for Racism: Southern Fundamentalists and the Civil Rights Movement," *Baptist Heritage and History* (Winter 1999): 52.

WHY STUDY BAPTISTS?

In many ways, this intellectual practice is both professional and confessional. Leonard is the consummate church historian preoccupied with both the historical experiences of Baptists and the implications for Baptist life in society. He is also a faithful member of the Baptist community and thus dedicated to living out the meaning of the gospel in life, thought, and practice. The professional and the confessional are not at odds for they reinforce a critical aspect of his scholarship—examining the contingencies and contradictions of Baptist history and experience in a political and religious context suffused by such contingencies and contradictions. Leonard's scholarly and vocational dedication to the community of the faithful, particularly as gathered in the local Baptist church, is exemplary in critically examining how the powerful forces that have shaped the modern world are lived out in the everyday lives of ordinary women and men of faith.

The depth of this intellectual and religious challenge was constitutive of a unique course Leonard and I cotaught in the summer of 2018 on Baptists and religious freedom. We were cognizant that the ideal of religious liberty could not evade the material reality of chattel slavery, and we sought to develop a critical pedagogy that facilitated a continual engagement with the principles and practices that underwrote religious liberty and slavery. Indeed, we led the seminar through the complex geography of Richmond, Virginia, that refused to see as separate the twin heritage trails that mark this distinctive Southern city—the Liberty Trail and the Slave Trail. Indeed, they were and are constitutive of one another as well as of the nation. We challenged our students as well as ourselves to develop a critical intellectual and faith practice that recognized the deep imbrications of liberty and slavery and race and religion in Baptist history and culture. In so doing, we may unfold a new horizon for reconstructing Baptist life and culture in ways that affirm the worth, value, and dignity of all humanity and begin to build new forms of life together.

Lewis V. Baldwin perceptively notes that the "continuing racial divide in the nation's ecclesiastical life suggests a certain timelessness about the kind of concerns King raised."[2] Baldwin's observation only gains in

---

[2] Lewis V. Baldwin, "Revisioning the Church: Martin Luther King Jr. as a Model for Reflection," *Theology Today* 65 (2008): 27.

106

importance as we continue to wrestle with the legacies of slavery and a virulent antiblack racism that continue well into the twenty-first century. In the wake of Baldwin's astute observation and in the scholarly spirit of Bill Leonard, this chapter explores the often-overlooked ecclesial aspect of Martin Luther King Jr.'s protean Baptist theology. King was first and foremost a Baptist pastor. As a seminarian, he would write, "In the quiet recesses of my heart, I am fundamentally a clergyman, a Baptist preacher. This is my being and my heritage, for I am also the son of a Baptist preacher, the grandson of a Baptist preacher, and the great grandson of a Baptist preacher."[3] This sense of vocation is a defining aspect of King's pastoral and public theology. As such, it provides an organizing principle of his political philosophy in a fundamental way. Shaped and formed by the culture, practices, and ideas of the black Baptist church, King developed a prophetic Baptist ecclesiology that thought through the antinomies of American Christianity in articulating an ideal of beloved community.

King's "Southern" Manifesto

On April 19, 1961, Martin Luther King Jr. delivered the Julius Brown Gay lecture at Southern Baptist Theological Seminary in Louisville, Kentucky.[4] King's visit to Southern occurred in the wake of the 1947 recommendation to the Southern Baptist Convention by the Committee on Race Relations—chaired by J. B. Weatherspoon (who had served on the faculty of the Southern Baptist Theological Seminary since 1929)—to "pursue an education program on race and race relations through editorials, study programs, and classes at Southern Baptist colleges."[5] It also occurred in the wake of the Southern Baptist Convention presidency of W. A. Criswell, who so impressed South Carolina governor George Timmerman with his presidential address haranguing the *Brown v. Board of Education* decision

---

[3] *The Papers of Martin Luther King, Jr. Volume I: Called to Serve January 1929– June 1951* (Berkeley: University of California Press, 1992).

[4] For a full treatment of King's visit, see Henlee Barnett, "The Southern Baptist Theological Seminary and the Civil Rights Movement: The Visit of Martin Luther King, Jr., Part Two," *Review and Expositor* 93 (1996): 77–125.

[5] Alan Scot Willis, *All According to God's Plan: Southern Baptist Missions and Race, 1945–1970* (Lexington: University Press of Kentucky, 2015) 3.

that "he was invited to address a joint session of the South Carolina legislature. Criswell enthusiastically accepted the invitation and reprised his uncivil rejection of the civil rights movement, the high court, and other Americans who supported the end of Jim Crow. 'Let them integrate,' he thundered, 'Let them sit up there in their dirty shirts and make all their fine speeches. But they are all a bunch of infidels, dying from the neck up.'"[6]

Taking as his theme "The Church on the Frontier of Racial Tension," King critically examined the role and function of the church in a desegregating society. His lecture occurred at a moment when the modern black freedom movement, which had such a propitious beginning with the Montgomery bus boycott, was buffeted by calls for direct action by the recently organized Student Nonviolent Coordinating Committee and a deeper commitment to a growing movement for desegregation in Albany, Georgia. Just as King was challenged by the strains and tensions in the black freedom movement, so too was Southern Baptist Theological Seminary. By extending an invitation to King to deliver one of the spring Gay Lectures, Southern would expose the tensions between a nominally liberal theological faculty and the recalcitrant administration and supporters who viewed King and the movement he symbolized as being fueled not so much by Christianity as by Communism and a deeply anti-American spirit.

King opened his lecture by noting his previous visit to Southern to attend the women's meetings of the National Baptist Convention, which were held on the seminary's campus. His mother served as the organist for the Women's Auxiliary, and King visited with her and the other members on the campus during the gathering. King's lecture then swiftly moved to fully engage the announced theme. "An old order is passing away," he declared,

> and a new order is coming into being. Now we are all familiar
> with this old order that is passing away because we have lived
> with it, and we have seen it in all its dimensions. We have seen
> the old order in Asia and Africa, in the form of colonialism and

---

[6] Andrew M. Manis, "'Dying from the Neck Up': Southern Baptist Resistance to the Civil Rights Movement," *Baptist History and Heritage* 34/1 (1999): 33–48.

imperialism.... So something is happening, a change is taking place—the old order of colonialism is passing away and the new order of freedom and human dignity is coming into being.[7]

After delineating the changing global order, King turned his attention to the United States and said,

We all know the long history of the old order in the United States. It had its beginnings in 1619, when the first slaves landed on the shores of this nation. And unlike the Pilgrim fathers who landed at Plymouth a year later, they were brought here against their wills, and throughout slavery the Negro was treated as a thing to be used, rather than a person to be respected. With the growth of slavery it became necessary to give some justification for it. It seems to be a fact of life that human beings cannot continue to do wrong without eventually reaching out for some thin rationalization to clothe an obvious wrong in the beautiful garments of righteousness.[8]

The world historical context which frames King's discourse is reminiscent of the statement by W. E. B. Du Bois in his 1903 classic *The Souls of Black Folk*: "The problem of the twentieth century is the problem of the color line—the relation of the darker to the lighter races of men in Asia and Africa, in America and the islands of the sea."[9] It was this text that would serve as a catalyst for the "Father of the Social Gospel," Washington Gladden, to revise his views on race. Gladden received a copy of this text from Du Bois after he delivered the 1903 baccalaureate sermon at Atlanta University. Indeed, Gladden was so transfixed by the book that the following Sunday he preached a sermon on "The Race Problem," with most information drawn from *Souls*.[10] However, unlike Du Bois, King did not

---

[7] Martin Luther King Jr., "Address Given by Dr. Martin Luther King, Jr.," Southern Baptist Theological Seminary, April 19, 1961, 1.

[8] King, "Address Given by Dr. Martin Luther King, Jr.," 1–2.

[9] W. E. B. Du Bois, *The Souls of Black Folk*, eds. Henry Louis Gates, Jr. and Terri Hume Oliver (New York: W. W. Norton & Company, [1903] 1999) 17.

[10] Ronald C. White Jr., *Liberty and Justice for All: Racial Reform and the Social Gospel 1877–1925* (Louisville, KY: Westminster John Knox Press, 1990) xiv. See

view this problem as one of wrong thinking; rather, it involved the issue of wrong being. That is, for King, the problem of global white supremacy and antiblack racism was a profoundly theological one that implicated the community of faith. King rehearsed the biblical and theological arguments used to justify the enslavement of Africans and the denial of the worth, value, and dignity of Africans and persons of African descent across the centuries. The contemporary crisis in postwar America was not simply a political one but was a deeply theological one that implicated the church. According to King, "Now whenever the crisis emerges in society, the church has a significant role to play. And certainly the church has a significant role to play in this period because the issue is not merely the political issue; it is a moral issue. Since the church has a moral responsibility of being the moral guardian of society, then it cannot evade its responsibility in this very tense period of transition."[11]

At Southern, King called on all members of the church to "rise above the narrow confines of their individualistic concerns to the broader concerns of all humanity." But the call to move to engage the concerns of all humanity was posited by way of rejecting a foundationally antiblack Christianity that negated humanity itself.

> Strangely enough, I can never be what I ought to be until you are what you ought to be, and you can never be what you ought to be until I am what I ought to be.... The church must get this over in every community, in every section of this nation, in every country of this world. And also the church must make it palatably clear that segregation is a moral evil which no Christian can accept.... And so the underlying philosophy of segregation is diametrically opposed to the underlying philosophy of Christianity, and democracy and all of the dialectics of the logician cannot make them lie down together. The church must make this very clear. The church also has a responsibility of getting to the ideational roots of racial prejudice.... Where there is segregation in any area the church must be willing to stand up with an action

---

also Gary Dorrien, *The New Abolition: W. E. B. Du Bois and the Black Social Gospel* (New Haven, CT: Yale University Press, 2015).

[11] King, "Address Given by Dr. Martin Luther King, Jr.," 3.

program. One of the best ways that the church can do this is to remove the yoke of segregation from its own body.[12]

King's "Southern Manifesto," if you will, served as a veritable call to arms for the church. The problem of race was not an isolated issue for it had distorted all aspects of human being and belonging in the world. In this, King was truly radical, since "for Baptists, racism was primarily a moral question, and moral questions were individual questions. Solving the race problem was, therefore, a matter of individual moral change, and that mandated evangelism.... The solution to the race problem lay in converting individuals—even, perhaps especially, those who may already be Christians—to the Christian view of race."[13] Not only was the church to combat white supremacy and antiblack racism, but it must rid itself of all vestiges of segregation within the community of the faithful. This called for nothing less than a desegregation of community as well as a desegregation of God. The church must undertake a radical revision of its polity and practice as well as its theology. A theology of apology or reconciliation would not be sufficient in light of King's diagnosis. Nothing less than a radicalization of the church was required. Such a radicalization implicates our theological visions and political imaginations about the possibilities of life together. One cannot leap out of history nor can we become paralyzed by pessimism. The church must be desegregated. It is this vision of a desegregated church—a truly redeemed community—that lies at the heart of King's compelling and all-encompassing vision of beloved community.

The Problem of Community

Martin Luther King Jr. is inextricably linked with the concept of "beloved community." King is part of a long and extensive tradition of African American social, political, and religious thought on the concept of community. African American church historian Lawrence N. Jones writes,

> Ever since blacks have been in America, they have been in search of the "beloved community," that is, that community which to paraphrase Martin Luther King, accepts a person on the basis of

---

[12] Ibid.

[13] Willis, *All According to God's Plan*, 4.

the "content of his or her character rather than upon the color of his or her skin...." Black Christians grounded their confidence in a theology of history. Their efforts were to actualize on earth the vision of the "beloved community" embodied in the Declaration of Independence and explicit in the Bible.[14]

While Jones advances a unique genealogy of the concept of beloved community in African American thought, he makes an explicit theo-political claim about it. Jones asserts that a particular set of relations of people and way of life are actualized in the everyday and properly reflect a theological warrant on human being and belonging. In many ways, his is a normative claim in search of a history and historiography to support this theological vision. Indeed, beloved community as a regulative Christian ideal is far from a dominant vision in African American social and political thought on community. Given the varieties of black ways of being, the notion of beloved community is not so much a given as an argument that must be posited, supported, and advocated. As Melissa V. Harris-Perry notes, "Understanding African American political attitudes requires an analysis of seemingly mundane interactions and ordinary circumstances of daily black life, because it is in these circumstances that African Americans often do the surprising and critical work of constructing meaningful political worldviews."[15]

The concept of beloved community, therefore, is a particular theo-political conception of human community produced within a context sufficiently saturated with moral *and* political overtones seeking to influence the normative dimensions of community. It does not act imperially in King's thinking as it is framed in a minimalist manner cognizant of Kant's second and third formulation of the categorical imperative—"all human beings must be treated as ends and never as mere means...[and]...act in accordance with the maxims of a member giving universal laws for a merely

---

[14] Lawrence N. Jones, "Black Christians in Antebellum America: In Quest of the Beloved Community," *The Journal of Religious Thought* 38/1 (1981): 12, 19.

[15] Melissa V. Harris-Perry, *Barbershops, Bibles, and BET: Everyday Talk and Black Political Thought* (Princeton, NJ: Princeton University Press, 2010) 2.

possible kingdom of ends."[16] But the concept of beloved community offers more than a mere regulatory ideal for human interaction or as an ethical norm of human community. It is a holistic vision of human existence and practice that requires systemic and institutional transformation. King's ideal recognizes the import of Ronald Walter's understanding of political change: "The political history of Blacks suggests that *political strategies designed to produce large changes should be system challenging.*"[17] Beloved community seeks to fundamentally transform American society and global humanity. It offers (and suffers with) a vision of human existence beyond the current configurations of our world. At its heart, it is a conceptual revolution that offers a new social and political horizon for human community.

In offering this understanding of beloved community, it may prove beneficial to revisit the thinking of an exemplary scholar of letters who provides a frame for this conceptual revolution. Former Virginia Union University professor and famed scholar of theology and literature Nathan A. Scott Jr. writes about the lasting power and claim Ralph Ellison's mid-twentieth century classic *Invisible Man* continues to exert over us. As one of "the great masters of this century," Ellison joins James Joyce, Thomas Mann, William Faulkner, and T. S. Eliot in attempting "to give a 'shape and...significance to the immense panorama of...anarchy which is contemporary history.'"[18] Through his unnamed narrator in *Invisible Man*, Ellison offers up a liminar, a marginal figure who exists on the fringes of society but whose existence is not a "merely negative state of privation: on the contrary...it can be and often is an enormously fruitful seedbed of spiritual creativity, for it is precisely amidst the troubling ambiguities of the

---

[16] Kipton Jensen and Preston King, "Beloved Community: Martin Luther King, Howard Thurman, and Josiah Royce," *AMITY: The Journal of Friendship Studies* 4/1 (2017): 18.

[17] As cited in Andra Gillespie, "A Modest Proposal: A Call for Leadership Specialization and the Recognition of Multiple Black Constituencies," in *What Has This Got to Do with the Liberation of Black People: The Impact of Ronald W. Walters on African American Thought and Leadership*, eds. Robert C. Smith, Cedric Johnson, and Robert G. Newby (Albany: State University of New York Press, 2014) 140, emphasis original.

[18] Nathan A. Scott Jr., "Ellison's Vision of *Communitas*," *Callaloo* 18/2 (1995): 310.

WHY STUDY BAPTISTS?

liminar's *déclassement* that there is born in him a profound hunger for *communitas*."[19] Scott continues,

> Ellison's essays are often being controlled by the same vision of *communitas* that guided *Invisible Man*. "The way home we seek," [Ellison] says, "is that condition of man's being at home in the world which is called love...." In short, he took it for granted that the regulative norm to which our social and cultural life are accountable is what the *koiné* Greek of the New Testament denominates as *agape*. But he had a clear sense of how infinitely difficult any full realization of this ultimate norm is.[20]

To be sure, the unnamed narrator in *Invisible Man* raises that most probing of questions, "Can politics ever be an expression of love?" Scott reminds us of the capacity of the liminar to be a prophetic harbinger of *communitas*—"the vision of an open society in which all the impulses and affections that are normally bound by social structures are liberated, so that every barrier between *I* and *Thou* is broken down and the wind of *communitas* may blow where it listeth."[21] Ellison's thinking of community and Scott's reflection on community via Ralph Ellison remind us of the singular place of this concept in the intellectual tradition of African American social, political, and religious thought and culture. In many ways, Scott enables a rethinking of community in King as the spirit of *communitas* that is bound up with his vision of beloved community. In other words, beloved community facilitates a critical *thinking* of community captured in King but moves along a logic that reimagines the human being and belonging not through dominant peoples, institutions, and ideas, but rather by the liminar who

> lift[s] *communitas* into the subjunctive mood:...dwelling on the edges of the established order [puncturing] "the clichés associated with status incumbency and role-playing" and [filling]...the open space of absolute futurity with a vision of what the theologians of Russian Orthodoxy call *sobornost*—which is nothing

---

[19] Ibid., 313.
[20] Ibid.
[21] Ibid.

other than that "catholicity," that "harmony," that "unanimity," that free "unity-in-diversity," which graces the human order when a people gives its suffrage to the "open morality" (as Bergson would have called it) of *agape*.[22]

A Theology of the Beloved Community

Political philosophers have recognized the unique dimensions of King's conception of beloved community as well as his political philosophy.[23] Kipton Jensen and Preston King write, "What King espoused then was not just any community, for community could be counterfeit. What he embraced in particular was beloved community, which was a society of friends, a colloquy of equals, a practice of concern, caring, giving—in which each person had standing, each stone in place, none rejected, in a rising tumult of aspiring mutuality."[24] Jensen and King recognize the critical political import of King's concept, fully appreciating the manner in which it contributes to the formation of political subjects and political community. Yet they hold in abeyance the theological dimensions of King's thinking, thereby attenuating the import of his lifelong grappling with this notion. Despite community being a "many *splendored* and *splintered* thing," to appropriate the words of ethicist Walter Fluker, the analytical and normative dimensions of this concept are not exhausted within the confines of a particular disciplinary lens.

King's understanding of community unfolds within his deep and evolving conception of beloved community. The intellectual and experiential roots of this concept are broad and complex. In this regard, Fluker's *They Looked for a City: A Comparative Analysis of the Ideal of Community in the Thought of Howard Thurman and Martin Luther King, Jr.* remains an

---

[22] Ibid., 313–14.

[23] See Hanes Walton Jr., *The Political Philosophy of Martin Luther King, Jr.* (New York: Praeger, 1971); Greg Moses, *Revolution of Conscience: Martin Luther King, Jr., and the Philosophy of Nonviolence* (New York: Guilford Press, 1997); and *To Shape a New World: Essays on the Political Philosophy of Martin Luther King, Jr.*, eds. Tommie Shelby and Brandon M. Terry (Cambridge, MA: Belknap Press of Harvard University Press, 2018).

[24] Jensen and King, "Beloved Community," 16.

indispensable source for understanding King's formation and thought.[25] To be sure, however, King's notion is deeply rooted in a genealogy of black Baptist thought and culture. More specifically, King's ecclesiology owing to the history, culture, and practices of the black Baptist church provides the architecture for his ideal of beloved community. The historical dimensions of this claim are not straight forward and require a revision of our methods of interrogating black Baptist thought and culture. Indeed, Baptist history in America is grounded in negotiating the dialectic of spiritual freedom and political unfreedom. Baptist history and identity are indeed one, shaped by the compromises—politically and theologically—of this dialectical relationship. Recently, John Saillant has offered a revision of black Baptist history that authorizes and supports a critical genealogy of a distinctive black Baptist theology of community as well as a revision of Baptist history more generally.

In his article "'This Week Black Paul Preach'd': Fragment and Method in Early African American Studies," Saillant argues that the limitations of black Baptists' access to print culture in the early Republic precludes a full textual analysis of black Baptist thought and culture. A revised method is necessary in order to fully explicate the distinctive thinking of black Baptists within the varieties of African American thought in this period. Saillant advocates exploiting fragments of black Baptists by analyzing them "through contrast, comparison, and contextualization, setting the records in unfamiliar as well as familiar contexts." Saillant continues:

> For black Baptists in particular and for black antislavery figures in general, the late colonial and early national periods should be understood in and of themselves, separate from the independent black denominations and immediatist abolitionism that succeeded them. Many early black public figures entered twentieth- and twenty-first-century scholarship mainly though nineteenth-century posthumous accounts that almost certainly reflected as least as much about the circumstances in which they were written as about their ostensible subject matter.... Unless scholars

---

[25] Walter E. Fluker, *They Looked for a City: A Comparative Analysis of the Ideal of Community in the Thought of Howard Thurman and Martin Luther King, Jr.* (Lanham, MD: University Press of America, 1989).

delineate methods for dealing with the textual fragments of early African American history, we shall be limited to a few figures who left an extensive documentary record or to figures as interpreted by their nineteenth-century commentators.[26]

Saillant correctly draws our attention to the method in which singular African American thinking has constituted all of African American thought. In an effort to begin to delineate the complexities of black Baptist thought without reducing it to a categorical logic, Saillant critically explores the thinking of early black Baptists Nathaniel and Benjamin Paul and the ways in which their thought from 1780 to 1805 "reveal both a deep connection to eighteenth-century Baptist theology and a sharp attraction to separate churches for African Americans."[27] The exploration of the Paul brothers enables scholars to revisit the ways in which "scholars and church apologists have long noted the popularity of Baptist churches among African Americans without considering their origins in Baptist theology."[28] The evangelical Calvinism of the Paul brothers creates an intertextual conversation with other black religionists such as the Huntingdonian Connexion minister John Marrant, the Congregationalist Lemuel Haynes, the Methodist George White, and the white Baptist Isaac Backus, particularly his 1782 *Doctrine of Universal Salvation Examined and Refuted*. Saillant reminds us that critical attention to black Baptist theology is vitally important to understanding black Baptist thought and culture and, by extension, American religious thought and culture.

This historiographical excursion in black Baptist history facilitates a critical thinking of how and in what ways Martin Luther King Jr. articulated a distinctive black Baptist conception of beloved community in twentieth-century America. King's formulation of beloved community often suffers from either simplistic reduction to the quest for the end of antiblack racism in American democracy while the practices and norms of democracy continue apace or it is rendered as an eschatological vision that is

---

[26] John Saillant, "'This Week Black Paul Preach'd': Fragment and Method in Early African American Studies," *Earl American Studies: An Interdisciplinary Journal* 14/1 (2016): 52.

[27] Ibid., 53.

[28] Ibid., 54.

untenable in light of the condition of society and humanity. In either formulation, what is missing is a full engagement with this ideal within King's black Baptist theology, more specifically how his ecclesial imagination was shaped by the promise and prospects of the beloved community ideal.

"One of the most perplexing problems in Black Theology," writes James H. Evans, "is that of ecclesiology."[29] Evans underscores the seeming paradox in black theological thinking. Within black theology, the idea of the Black Church is ubiquitous yet there are a paucity of robust theological treatments of ecclesiology in black theology. For Evans, there are two significant factors for this situation:

> The first is the heterogeneity of African American congregations.... The unique context and the array of traditions, customs, and styles within African American Christianity make the formulation of a black ecclesiology difficult. The second factor impeding the ecclesiological task is that the notion of community is so basic to African American religious experience that the normal doctrinal explanations for church formation are not sufficient. The Black church was not born primarily of doctrinal disputes and heresy trials, but rather emerged out of deep-seated cultural tendencies toward solidarity and association among African American Christians.[30]

Evans's factors direct our attention to two dominant trends in scholarly treatments of the Black Church. One is the advancement of categorical claims of the Black Church that evade the depth, complexity, and variety of black religious formations in the United States.[31] The second is the theological inelasticity of dominant theological categories and frameworks to account for the cultural, historical, and theological dimensions of black

---

[29] James H. Evans Jr. and Stephen G. Ray Jr., *We Have Been Believers: An African American Systematic Theology* (Minneapolis: Augsburg Fortress Publishers 2012) 139.

[30] Ibid., 140.

[31] On this point, see the provocative essay Eddie S. Glaude Jr., "The Black Church Is Dead," *Huffington Post* (April 26, 2010).

Christian institutional formation.[32] These trends have so captured the scholarship and thinking on the Black Church that instead of revising our methods of analysis, scholars have been preoccupied with a correspondence theory of knowledge.

To begin to think critically about Evans's statement is to begin to analyze how and in what ways African American religious thinkers in general, and King in particular, advance new frameworks drawn from critically *thinking* about the Black Church and the multiple meanings of black ecclesial practices and experience across space and time. Theologically, this means engaging black ecclesiology in a much more profound and nuanced sense. In the black Catholic tradition, for example, theologian Jamie T. Phelps argues that

> the central theme of the unity of the human community is the teleological focus of both Black liberation theology and communion ecclesiology. The synodal and papal documents on social justice promulgated following Vatican II were an elaboration of the churches' self-understanding of communion that linked the intraecclesial communion of the Christian churches with the extraecclesial communion of the human community. This unity of the human community is also an explicit central value of African traditional religions and the African American religious tradition.[33]

Phelps makes explicit the ecclesiological implications of African and African diasporic cultural and religious traditions by critically thinking through black religious practices. These practices are not ancillary to the theological enterprise. Indeed, for Phelps they are constitutive of a particularly Catholic notion of communion ecclesiology that links sacramental theology with the black ecclesial imagination. That is, ecclesiology matters to how we conceive of the institutional expressions of Christianity and African

---

[32] A recent corrective to this trend with respect to the dialogue between Black Theology and the Black Church is offered by Raphael G. Warnock, *The Divided Mind of the Black Church: Theology, Piety, and Public Witness* (New York: New York University Press, 2013).

[33] Jamie T. Phelps, "Communion Ecclesiology and Black Liberation Theology," *Theological Studies* 61 (2000): 672–73.

American Christianity. These institutional expressions remind us that ideas and institutions are not mutually exclusive.

In the formulation of King's unique conception of beloved community, Walter Fluker correctly reminds us that "from his early childhood until his death, there is a progression in [King's] personal and intellectual understanding of the nature and goal of human existence which he refers to as 'the beloved community.'"[34] Fluker recognizes the evolution of King's thinking in his personal, professional, and pastoral development. The concept of the beloved community was not a static ideal for King. It was a living phenomenon that responded to his continual thinking, practices, and relationships. His experiences with the black Baptist churches in Alabama, Georgia, and Pennsylvania informed him about the history and possibility of these unique communities of faith. And it was at Crozier Theological Seminary where King would encounter a theological space to inaugurate a process that would enable him to synthesize ethics, epistemology, and experience into an evolving and protean theo-political matrix of beloved community.

King's experiences at Morehouse College and Boston University have been justly highlighted. Entering Morehouse at the age of fifteen and graduating four years later, he encountered such figures as Samuel Williams, professor of philosophy; George D. Kelsey, professor of religion and philosophy; Gladstone L. Chandler, professor of English; and Walter Chivers, professor of sociology.[35] As the college's president, the Baptist theologian and educator Benjamin E. Mays had enormous influence in the lives of students. His influence culminated in his delivering the eulogy at his former student's funeral. At Boston University, Edgar Sheffield Brightman and L. Harold DeWolf helped guide and shape King's doctoral work in philosophical and theological studies. But it was Lucius M. Tobin, a 1923 graduate of Virginia Union University and professor of religion at Morehouse, who recommended a nineteen-year-old King to continue his

---

[34] Fluker, *They Looked for a City*, 81.
[35] Ibid., 87.

education at Crozer Theological Seminary "after trying to persuade him to enter Colgate-Rochester, my school."[36]

A Baptist Politics of Friendship

It was at Crozer that King encountered a space of theological exploration and practice in community that facilitated his ever-evolving synthesis of a distinctive black Baptist ecclesiology that grounded his concept of beloved community. While much has been written about King's distinctive encounter with Walter Rauschenbusch, it was a young Niebuhrian who would not only attenuate his zealous optimism of the social gospel but would also critically explore King's thought and publish one of the foundational texts on his ideal of beloved community.

Born on the eastern shore of Virginia near Exmore, Kenneth Lee "Snuffy" Smith entered the University of Richmond as a member of the class of 1945. At Richmond, Snuffy earned his BA while participating as a member of the Mu Sigma Rho Literary Society and the Ministerial Association. He continued his education at Crozer and received a bachelor of divinity degree in 1948 and went on to earn his PhD from Duke University. He returned to Crozer in 1950, where he taught ethics and theology and held a number of leadership positions including serving as dean of Crozer Theological Seminary at Colgate Rochester Divinity School/Bexley Hall/Crozer Theological Seminary. During King's final year at Crozer, Snuffy provided another mind for King to think with and against. An early biographer quotes King as stating, "Smith loved an intellectual quarrel with his students."[37] Recalling King's years at Crozer, Smith states, "When he came to Crozer, he was a biblical literalist.... He

---

[36] Letter from Lucius M. Tobin to Charles E. Batten, February 25, 1948, in Clayborne Carson, Ralph E. Luker, and Penny A. Russell, *The Papers of Martin Luther King, Jr., Volume I: Called to Serve, January 1929–June 1951* (Berkeley: University of California Press, 1992) 151. On the intellectual influence of Lucius Tobin on King's thought, see David J. Garrow, "The Intellectual Development of Martin Luther King, Jr.: Influences and Commentaries," *Union Seminary Quarterly Review* 40 (1986): 5–20.

[37] Patrick Parr, *The Seminarian: Martin Luther King, Jr. Comes of Age* (Chicago: Lawrence Hill Books, 2018) 198.

believed the Bible word-for-word. When he left Crozer, he could no longer believe that. It sort of shook him up. And a lot of other things at Crozer shook him up and he reoriented a whole pattern of thinking theologically as a result of the experience at Crozer."[38] King was far from a biblical literalist when he entered Crozer. Indeed, his decision to enter Crozer was as a result of his having moved from the Fundamentalism of his father and a desire to forge a distinctive path possibly leading to the professoriate. But Smith is correct in highlighting "a lot of other things at Crozer" that would shape King, including his intellectual maturation with the theologian George Davis; his mentoring relationship with J. Pious Barbour, pastor of Calvary Baptist Church in Chester; his deep friendship with fellow seminarian Walter McCall; and his interracial relationship with Betty Moitz. It was during his time at Crozer that King would confront the violence of white supremacy in the residence hall of Old Main, formally engage his first civil rights court case in New Jersey, and glimpse the prospects of an ecumenical outlook beyond a narrow Baptist provincialism.

Smith and King shared a complex relationship with one another at Crozer as pool-hall rivals, debate antagonists, and former and current boyfriends of Betty Moitz. But it was as professor and student that Smith and King would transform one another. Smith's two courses Christian Social Philosophy II and Christianity and Society, taught during King's final year at Crozer, facilitated King's critical weaving of theology, philosophy, history, and ethics to formulate his concept of beloved community. Christian Social Philosophy II "covered the ethical and social thought of the Church from New Testament times to the present. Its major purpose was to analyze and to assess the various historical 'strategies' which have characterized the relationship between Christ and culture."[39] Christianity and Society "focused specifically on present-day issues...[and]...delved into such topics as democracy, family concerns, the role of the United Nations, the strong influence of the labor movement, and nuclear warfare."[40] Smith recalled King's intellectual interest in these courses being focused on "the

---

[38] Ibid.
[39] Ibid.
[40] Ibid., 199.

strategies of the past as they provided insights for the development of a Christian social ethic adequate to meet the needs of contemporary society."[41] Smith's classes provided a critical forum for King to engage in debates over the various positions of Walter Rauschenbusch and Reinhold Niebuhr, with Smith later stating, "I must confess, I followed [Niebuhr] somewhat uncritically during those early days of my teaching."[42] (Smith's engagement with King left a lasting impact on the professor.) Smith eventually collaborated with Ira G. Zepp to publish *Search for the Beloved Community: The Thinking of Martin Luther King, Jr.*[43] Smith's classes and engagement with King offered the seminarian a valuable venue to thread his ideas into a unique concept of beloved community.

"The True Ekklesia and the Hope of the World"

While the idea of beloved community was first expressed in the philosophy of Josiah Royce, King's theology of beloved community shifted the grounds of Royce's project to a distinctly black Baptist foundation for his unique mid-century formulation. To be sure, Royce and King looked to the church as a model gathering for beloved community. According to M. L. Briody,

> Royce's notion of the invisible church is the closest he comes to being specific in his philosophy of religion. It is the notion of an ideal kingdom whose present reality (insofar as it has any present reality) is the closet possible human approximation to the perfect community which bears the label "beloved." As means for approaching this ideal, the Church is seen by Royce as the instrument through which he hopes ultimately to solve the "religious paradox."[44]

While Royce's ideal is inspired by the church, he is apprehensive to an all-encompassing intellectual commitment to doctrinal Christianity.

---

[41] Ibid.

[42] Ibid., 200.

[43] Kenneth L. Smith and Ira G. Zepp Jr., *Search for the Beloved Community: The Thinking of Martin Luther King, Jr.* (Valley Forge, PA: Judson Press, 1974).

[44] M. L. Briody, "Community in Royce: An Interpretation," *Transactions of the Charles S. Peirce Society* 5/4 (1969): 234.

Nevertheless, he recognizes the import of Liberal theological thinking in his two-volume *The Problem of Christianity* and incorporates that theological frame for his philosophical work. Indeed, Royce's philosophy owes a great deal to its theological underpinning. Briody comments,

> Although Royce generally speaks of...love in terms of loyalty, it is love which makes interpretation possible in the Community of Interpretation; it is love which makes existent the communal reality of Church; it is love which forms the basis of Royce's hope for a Great Community. Finally, it is Love personified which founds the reality of the Beloved Community. As Peter Fuss suggests, love thus becomes a fourth condition for community, one which Royce does not list as such, but which he presupposes in his exposition of the other three. Without love, or its universal form of loyalty, there is no community—whether as end or means.[45]

Whereas Royce is reticent regarding the theological infrastructure of his conception of beloved community, King's formulation is established on an explicitly theological architecture. If "Baptists began, and to a great extent continue," as noted Baptist historian Bill Leonard reminds us, "as a Christian communion grounded in a radical congregational polity," then black Baptists instantiate a dissenting community seeking to radicalize an ecclesial Christian vision of a communion that offers new modes of being, acting, and belonging in the world.[46] This vision lies at the heart of King's vision of beloved community.

While Smith and Zepp provide the first sustained attempt at analyzing King's thought, they fail to examine the black Baptist dimensions of King's thought in the development of beloved community. The black Baptist church is an ever-present reality of God's promise and love of creation. As with the cross and the church founded in its wake, King views the black Baptist church as a continuation of God's promise and desire for right community despite the loss of experience as a result of the Middle Passage,

---

[45] Ibid., 238.

[46] Bill J. Leonard, *The Challenge of Being Baptist* (Waco, TX: Baylor University Press, 2010) 39.

The True Ekklesia and the Hope of the World

chattel slavery, Jim Crow, and the arrested development of democracy.[47] The history of black Baptist church formation and development not only affirms the worth, value, and dignity of black humanity, it also instantiates the redemptive vision of Jesus for the marginal and the oppressed of society. The black Baptist church's history of affirmation and creation of a community that welcomes and practices a deep hospitality for all, particularly the oppressed, is the animation logic and *telos* of beloved community. As Walter Fluker writes, "The black church symbolized the authentic mission of the church in society through its redemptive suffering for injustice in the Civil Rights Movement."[48] King's ecclesial vision is evident at the beginning of his involvement in the black freedom struggle. Smith and Zepp add, "In one of his first articles he stated that the purpose of the Montgomery bus boycott 'is reconciliation; the end is redemption; the end is the creation of the beloved community.'"[49]

Prior to the Montgomery bus boycott, King's ecclesial understanding of the roots of beloved community was at work in his invitation to then Virginia Union president Samuel DeWitt Proctor to speak at Dexter Avenue Baptist Church on the topic "The Relevance of the New Testament to the Contemporary Situation" in 1955. Already echoing a theme that would resonate in his public theology and political activism, King sought to bring together Christianity and contemporary life in an attempt to challenge his congregation at Dexter to understand the meaning of Christian community. King's understanding of the black Baptist church was informed by his ecclesiology in that the black Baptist church inherits the mandate of the New Testament Church in witnessing to the redemptive event inaugurated by Jesus Christ. King's black Baptist vision is not grounded in the Baptist quest over church and state; rather, for King, "The church must be reminded that it is not the master or the servant of the state, but rather the conscience of the state. It must be the guide and the critic of the state, and never its tool. If the church does not recapture its

---

[47] Walter Lowe, *Theology and Difference: The Wound of Reason* (Indianapolis: Indiana University Press, 1993) ix.

[48] Fluker, *They Looked for a City*, 152.

[49] Smith and Zepp, *Search for the Beloved Community*, 130.

125

prophetic zeal, it will become an irrelevant social club without moral or spiritual authority."[50]

The suffering witness of the black Baptist church, past and present, authorizes and sustains King's vision of beloved community. Nonviolence as a way of life forms new subjects and a new humanity for the church and the world. "For never in Christian history," King argues, "within a Christian country, have Christian churches been on the receiving end of such naked brutality and violence as we are witnessing here in America today. Not since the days of the Christians in the catacombs has God's house, as a symbol, weathered such attack as the Negro churches." King's ecclesiology propels his notion of beloved community beyond a narrow and provincial Baptist in pushing beyond boundaries into new possibilities of human being and belonging in the world—a true beloved community.

For King, the church "demonstrate[s] in its fellowship the power of *agape* to create community. The moral failure of the church is that it has conformed to the mores and customs of society which work against community."[51] The *ekklesia* is the beloved community—a space set apart to inculcate, cultivate, nurture, and shape behaviors and practices cognizant of God's gift of human modes of being in the world.

> "Ekklesia" bears an etymology stemming from both ancient Athenian citizen assemblies and, later, early Christian churches; each was a local congregation gathered in the name of either the polis or the body of Christ, of the demos or of God.... Jean-Luc Nancy notes that the word *ekklesia* was "drawn from" or gestured to institutions of the Greek city yet marked the birth of a new mode of assembly distinct from the social or political, in that sense signaling at once the twin origin and "essential separation" of church and state.[52]

The beloved community, in this sense, is not the American dream, but rather a radical ecclesiology animated by the principle of love. "As

---

[50] Fluker, *They Looked for a City*, 151.

[51] Ibid., 152.

[52] Paul Christopher Johnson, Pamela E. Klassen, and Winnifred Fallers Sullivan, *Ekklesia: Three Inquiries in Church and State* (Chicago: University of Chicago Press, 2018) 1–2.

Christians," King writes, "we must never surrender our supreme loyalty to any time-bound custom or earth-bound idea, for at the heart of our universe is a higher reality—God and his kingdom of love—to which we must be conformed."[53] The community of the faithful, in its New Testament faith and black Baptist tradition, serves as the scaffold of King's beloved community, the "true *ekklesia* of Christ in the world."[54]

In *Baptists in America*, Bill J. Leonard writes, "Concerning the nature of the church (ecclesiology), black Baptists link worship and service, belief and practice in ways that distinguish 'faithfulness' as 'an incarnational issue not a doctrinal discussion.'"[55] Leonard accurately underscores the relational principle at the heart of black Baptist ecclesiology. The example of Martin Luther King Jr. is exemplary in this respect. King's theology of beloved community offers us a preeminent example of the distinctive Baptist ecclesiology born out of the unique witness and testimony of the black Baptist tradition. King's adept theological navigation of transcendence and history and Leonard's faithful scholarship provide us with a vision to embrace as we continue this righteous struggle, now and into the long future.

---

[53] Fluker, *They Looked for a City*, 150.

[54] Ibid., 152.

[55] Bill J. Leonard, *Baptists in America* (New York: Columbia University Press, 2005) 200.

"Bold Mission Thrust" and White Baptists in the South: Beyond the Offense of Objectification toward a Theology of Mutual Regard

Robert N. Nash Jr.

In 1976, Southern Baptists launched a mission campaign entitled "Bold Mission Thrust" with the goal of sharing the gospel of Jesus Christ with the entire world by the year 2000. Interestingly, the Southern Baptist Convention (SBC) undertook the campaign without issuing an invitation to any other Christian mission organization or denomination in the world to join the effort. Such heady confidence was shared across the Southern Baptist theological and political continuum as Conservatives, Moderates, and Liberals alike embraced the program. Few protestations were raised. At the time, most agencies and seminaries of the SBC were led by Moderate Southern Baptists who were as insular as the more Conservative leadership that would emerge in the mid- to late 1980s when the Convention split into two separate camps, with more Moderate Baptists aligning with the Cooperative Baptist Fellowship (CBF).

At the Foreign Mission Board (FMB) of the SBC, new strategic initiatives were undertaken after the adoption of Bold Mission Thrust to reach people in the 10-40 window, that portion of the world between the 10th and 40th parallels where the majority of "unreached people groups" lived. This region stretched across North Africa, the Middle East, India, China, Japan, and Southeast Asia and included a majority of the world's Muslims, Buddhists, Hindus, Taoists, and persons of other Eastern religious traditions. This swath of the world represented the religious "others" who remained outside the boundaries of the old centers of Christendom in Europe and the Americas and thus, in the minds of Southern Baptists, most in need of conversion to the Christian faith and least likely to offer any helpful perspective on ultimate truth or the nature of God.

Three realities about Bold Mission Thrust shed light on the history of Baptist engagement with otherness and difference when it comes to religion. The first is the fact that white Baptists in the South were convinced of their own ability to evangelize the world without assistance from any other group of Christians. The second is that Baptists in the region undertook the effort solely for the purpose of evangelism, with little attention to the interfaith cooperation and connection that might accomplish social and economic empowerment and transformation and lead Baptists themselves toward a deeper understanding of the divine. Finally, and perhaps of greatest concern, upon its founding in 1991, the Cooperative Baptist Fellowship (CBF), the new "Moderate" organization of white Baptists in the South, adopted the same strategies employed by the International Mission Board of the SBC, targeting persons in the "10-40 window" as the focus for its missionary efforts. Adopting this imported a model that rendered persons of other religions as objects to be witnessed to rather than as persons of religious faith who might offer something of value to the Baptist tradition.

This rather recent history of the Southern Baptist engagement with otherness and difference in terms of religion begs the following questions: How did the two major white Baptist denominations in the South (SBC and CBF) reach the conclusion that the sole reason for engaging and embracing other religions in the world was for the purpose of evangelism of the religious "other" and not for Baptists' own theological and spiritual benefit? Has this always been the perspective of white Baptists in the South? If so, where did such a perspective come from? If not, at what points in their history have these Baptists approached other religions differently?

In 2002, E. Luther Copeland, a retired professor of theology from Seinan Gakuin University in Japan and a former missionary of the Southern Baptist Convention, wrote a compelling book entitled *The Southern Baptist Convention and the Judgment of History: The Taint of an Original Sin.*[1] In its pages, he advances the provocative thesis that "if history adversely judged the institution [of slavery], it is a strange irony that a denomination [the SBC] which was born because of its support of slavery

---

[1] E. Luther Copeland, *The Southern Baptist Convention and the Judgment of History: The Taint of an Original Sin* (Lanham, MD: University Press of America, 2002).

129

nevertheless seems to have thought of itself as 'God's last and only hope' for world evangelization."[2]

Copeland's argument is that the SBC's defense of slavery and its determination to see slaveholders appointed as missionaries is the "original sin" that resulted in "our tenacious racism, our missionary paternalism and imperialism, our denominational arrogance, our depreciation of women and our theological restrictiveness."[3] To his litany of evils resulting from this original sin, I would add the sin of an exclusivist Baptist perspective toward other religious traditions that refuses to accept the deeper perspective on God and creation that is possible if the vast contributions of other religions to Baptist and Christian perspectives on God and creation are acknowledged. I would also argue that there is within the Baptist tradition a path toward such acceptance and acknowledgment that emerges from the very best theological foundations of the tradition, namely through the theological and missiological perspectives of Roger Williams and W. O. Carver, respectively.

The history of Southern Baptist engagement with otherness and difference is grounded in the missionary efforts of the tradition and in two periods of immigration in US history, the period from 1880 to 1920 and, most recently, the significant immigration that has occurred since the passing of the Immigration and Nationality Act of 1965 under the Johnson administration. While William Carey of England was neither a US American or a Southern Baptist, his successful plea to British Baptists to create a board for the purpose of sending missionaries to Asia had a profound impact upon the way Southern Baptists shaped their own missionary-sending efforts and on their rationale for such engagement. In addition, Carey's mapping of the world religious landscape set the foundation for the objectification of persons of other religions, and of Catholicism, in the minds of white Baptists in the US American South and beyond.

Fortunately for white Baptists in the South, the path forward to overcoming such objectification is possible through the theological lens of two

---

[2] Ibid., 3. Note that Copeland takes the phrase "God's last and only hope" from the title of Bill J. Leonard's book *God's Last and Only Hope* (Grand Rapids, MI: Eerdmans, 1990) p. vi, where Leonard cited Levi Elder Barton.

[3] Copeland, *The Southern Baptist Convention and the Judgment of History*, 4.

of their leading thinkers, namely Roger Williams, founder of the Rhode Island colony and of the First Baptist Church of Providence, Rhode Island, and William Owen Carver, a professor of missions at the Southern Baptist Theological Seminary in the first half of the twentieth century. Williams's highly Calvinistic perspective on the sovereignty of God led him to the conclusion that all religions should gain a hearing in the public arena. Carver encouraged a perspective on other religions infused with loving engagement, rather than impersonal objectification, by insisting that God had initiated an "intimate, supporting presence with each individual in the world"[4] that demanded "a friendly appraisal of all religions."[5]

In 1792, William Carey published his views in *An Enquiry into the Obligation of Christians to Use Means for the Conversion of the Heathen*. This publication would serve as the foundation for the theology and the organizational structure of the Protestant world mission in the modern world. The book was a remarkable apology for a Protestant and Baptist world mission, answering Calvinist arguments against such a mission predicated on the conviction that God should do the saving and not human beings. In it, Carey summarized the work of missions across nearly two thousand years of church history and then provided an analysis of the mission field itself by identifying the sizes and locations of the major religions of the world. For the next two centuries, most missionary-sending agencies followed Carey's model, which called for the establishment of a board to oversee the financing of the missionary movement, the selection and training of missionaries, and the oversight of their work.[6] This model for missionary work around the world on the part of English Baptists was ultimately adopted by most every Western missionary-sending denomination between 1800 and 2000.

Carey surveyed the locations and sizes of the various world religions in a chapter entitled "A Survey of the Present State of the World." This

---

[4] W. O. Carver, *Missions in the Plan of the Ages: Bible Studies in Missions* (New York: Fleming H. Revell Company, 1909) 34.

[5] W. O. Carver, *Christian Missions in Today's World* (New York: Harper and Brothers, 1942) 138.

[6] William Carey, *An Enquiry into the Obligations of Christians to Use Means for the Conversion of the Heathen* (Leicester, England: Ann Ireland and Others, 1792) 82–83.

chapter represents the nascent moment in which the objectification of other religions beyond the Abrahamic faiths was entrenched in white Baptist missionary efforts. Here Carey noted his intention to consider "countries, population, civilization and religion," with the focus on religion given over to "Christian, Jewish, Mahometan [sic] and pagan."[7] Note the designation Carey gave to the "pagan" traditions, which included, for him, Buddhism, Hinduism, and other Asian traditions such as Taoism and Confucianism as well as all First or tribal religions. He did include Europe in his assessment and provided a table of the Christian traditions that were prevalent in various European nations, though he used the term "Papists" to refer to Catholics and "Christians" to refer to Protestants, betraying his bias and also importing it into the white Baptist missionary perspective.

Carey's assessment of religion in Asia is instructive as it reflects his utter lack of knowledge of the religious traditions of the region beyond "Mahometan," or Islam. The mostly Christian nation of the Philippines, predominately Catholic since Spanish colonization in the sixteenth century, is divided into regions, with the predominately Muslim island of Mindanao labeled as "Papist" and "Mahometan," and other regions identified as either "Papist" or "Pagan."[8] New Zealand is lumped in with Asia and identified as "Pagan—1 or 2 ministers are there."[9] China is identified simply as "Pagan." India is listed as "Mahometan and Pagan."[10]

Carey's assessment of religion in Africa reflects the same tendency to recognize the Abrahamic religions and to utilize the term "Papist" rather than Christian when referring to Catholics. He identifies the region of Biledulgerid, a nation across the broad swath of North Africa, as composed mostly of "Mahometans, Christians and Jews," and he distinguishes between French colonies as either "Mostly French Papists" or "Mostly French Christians," obviously preferring the Protestant identity of the latter.[11]

---

[7] Ibid., 38.
[8] Ibid., 50.
[9] Ibid., 51.
[10] Ibid., 46 and 47, respectively.
[11] Ibid., 53 and 55, respectively.

"Bold Mission Thrust" and White Baptists in the South

The Americas seem to have presented a significant challenge in terms of religious identity for Carey. He departs from religious categories in describing inhabitants of certain portions of the Bahamas as "Half English and Half Slaves" and those of Curacao as "Dutch and Pagan Negroes."[12] The "States of America" are identified as "Christians, of Various Denominations," but areas like California, still outside the United States, are called "Pagan."[13] Significantly, most of South and Central America as well as Mexico are simply labeled "Papist" or "Pagan."[14]

Carey concludes that the world's population in 1792 is approximately 731 million, with 420 million "still in pagan darkness," 130 million Muslims, 100 million Catholics, 44 million Protestants, 30 million Orthodox, and 7 million Jews. An assessment of world religions in 1800 distributed recently by Gordon-Conwell Theological Seminary assessed the actual statistics at the time as 204 million Christians (roughly 30 million above Carey's estimate, when Catholics, Protestants, and Orthodox statistics are combined), 91 million Muslims (40 million below Carey's estimate), and 9 million Jews (2 million above Carey's estimate). The world's population in 1800 was approximately 885 million as assessed by Gordon-Conwell's research (150 million above Carey's estimate).[15] Both Carey's and Gordon-Conwell's assessments are in line with most recent estimates of the world's population in 1800 that put it at somewhere between 600 million to 1 billion people.

The influence of Carey's *Enquiry* upon the Baptist perspective on the world's religions cannot be exaggerated. First, he was remarkably accurate in his estimates despite the fact that he lumped together most of the religions of Asia, Africa, and the Americas into the category of "pagan." Second, this reduction of those religions into a single category is possibly the single greatest influence upon the general Baptist objectification of religions of the world. This objectification minimized religious differences among those Asian, African, and American traditions at the same time

---

[12] Ibid., 58.

[13] Ibid., 56.

[14] Ibid., 56.

[15] http://christianityinview.com/religion-statistics.html. Accessed April 15, 2022.

that it removed Catholics from the category of "Christian" in the minds of most Baptist Christians of the day. To be other than Protestant, Catholic, Orthodox Jewish, or Muslim was to be pagan, and to be pagan was to believe in false gods as opposed to believing in the God of the Judeo-Christian-Islamic tradition.

William Carey does not bear all the blame for the tendency of white Baptists in the South to objectify persons of other religious traditions. The concept of Anglo-Saxon supremacy—the belief that the white races possessed a superior intellect, religion, and civilization in comparison to the rest of the world—had a profound influence on the tradition. This idea was advanced by Josiah Strong in *Our Country*, published in 1885. In its pages, Strong advances the notion of "an Anglo-Saxon realm that would transform the whole world."[16] His ideas were eagerly embraced by many white Baptists in the US American South who feared the encroaching pluralism of the day brought on by immigration from Eastern Europe and elsewhere. Strong's book built upon the burgeoning notion of Manifest Destiny, which combined religious and political motivations for expansion under a single umbrella, nurturing the idea of an American civil religion that glorified the nation.

The influence of Strong's work reached deeply into the mindset of white Baptists in the South, especially when it came to global mission strategy, to the point that it became institutionalized within the mission work of the Foreign Mission Board of the SBC. Under the administration of James Franklin Love, who served from 1915 to 1928 as the corresponding secretary of the FMB of the SBC, Southern Baptists isolated themselves from the mainstream of the Protestant missionary movement with constant warnings of the perils of ecumenism as expressed in numerous tracts and books that defended SBC isolationism as a way to protect the purity of Scripture.[17] Such efforts offer proof of the veracity of Copeland's thesis concerning the taint of the original sin of slaveholding and its

---

[16] Josiah Strong, *Our Country: Its Possible Future and Its Present Crisis* (New York: Baker and Taylor, 1885) 29–43.

[17] See J. Franklin Love, *The Union Movement* (Nashville, TN: Sunday School Board of the Southern Baptist Convention, 1918) for an example of this isolationist rhetoric, pp. 7–18.

influence upon Southern Baptist missions. Bold Mission Thrust, launched in 1976, may have been the most radical expression of that isolationism and racist ideology as it was couched in antiseptic missionary terms that hid its white supremacist roots even as it called for global religious domination.

Under Love's administration, the basic premises of Anglo-Saxon supremacy were adopted with considerable intentionality as mission strategy. In an effort to encourage Baptist expansion into Europe, Love argued that world evangelization could be accomplished more quickly if the aggressive white races were evangelized first: "Let us not forget that to the white man God gave the instinct and talent to disseminate His ideals among other people and that he did not, to the same degree, give this instinct and talent to the yellow, brown or black race. The white race only has the genius to introduce Christianity into all lands and among all people."[18] Love added that "this is not a ground for spiritual pride nor of contempt for any colored race. It is a solemn fact."[19]

Love's theory of Anglo-Saxon supremacy was rooted in the idea that God had called Paul to go over into Europe rather than to continue his ministry in Asia. His plan was "first to evangelize the white Gentile world...to move toward the coming Anglo-Saxon civilization, and so get his hands on the mightiest national life of the world."[20] God recognized the superior talents and civilization of this new race: "Until then the Jews were the chosen race; since then the Anglo-Saxon race has been God's favored people."[21] In Love's estimation, "There is not a colored race in the world which could evangelize the white race.... If all of China were Christian, the Chinese race very probably could not evangelize a single American state. All of Africa could not evangelize one county of American white people."[22]

---

[18] James Franklin Love, *The Appeal of the Baptist Program for Europe* (Richmond, VA.: Foreign Mission Board of the Southern Baptist Convention, 1920) 14–15.

[19] Ibid., 15.

[20] J. Franklin Love, *The Mission of Our Nation* (New York: Fleming H. Revell, 1912) 18.

[21] Ibid., 21.

[22] Ibid., 64–65.

While Love focused his strategy primarily upon ethnicities rather than religions, it is not difficult to see how damaging such a perspective was upon Southern Baptist perspectives on other religions. Where Carey had objectified Islam with the term "Mahometan" and other Asian religious traditions with the term "pagan," Love elevated Anglo-Saxons above other ethnicities and enshrined white Christianity as the sole legitimate source of spiritual and theological truth. In the process, he denigrated Asians, Africans, and Latinos as incapable of offering such truth to the white races of the world. He institutionalized Carey's initial assessment of the other world religions in a pernicious doctrine that legitimated the perspective that other religions and ethnicities offered absolutely no value at all to the Christian faith.

After 1925, the borders of the United States were sealed to stave off the deleterious influence of immigrant populations from the rest of the world. The borders would not be reopened until the Johnson administration, in 1965, with the passage of the Immigration and Nationality Act. During that time, Southern Baptists sent out into the world the largest missionary force in the history of the Christian faith. Those missionaries carried with them perspectives on other peoples and religions that had been profoundly shaped by the global perspectives of William Carey and James Franklin Love.

Is there a path forward for white Baptists in the South to move beyond such objectification of otherness and difference and toward embrace in ways that are helpful both to those Baptists themselves and to those whom they have previously objectified? My conviction is that there is and that the path forward is grounded in the theological and missiological ideas of two significant Baptists, namely Roger Williams and W. O. Carver. Williams provides a powerful theological grounding that overcomes such objectification, and Carver affirms for white Baptists in the South the value of other religions of the world as the source of spiritual and divine truth.

Roger Williams, born around 1603 in London, was educated at Cambridge, where he studied theology and fell under the influence of Puritan Separatists. He then immigrated to New England in about 1631. To be a Separatist in the 1630s was to move beyond non-separating Puritans in an effort to "purify" the Anglican tradition of any Catholic practice. In time,

Williams's position was deemed too radical even for his non-Separatist Puritan brothers and sisters, and he was booted from the Massachusetts Bay colony and sent out into the "howling wilderness." There he eventually founded the Rhode Island colony and helped to start the first Baptist church in America in Providence.

Over the course of his life, Williams became increasingly convinced of the need to establish a "pure" church composed only of those persons who were among God's elect. One would assume that such a position would lead to a desire to establish a theocratic government on earth in which only the purest of persons could rule. In fact, though, for Williams, the very opposite occurred. Even as he became convinced of the need for a pure church, he became more convinced of the need for religious freedom and the separation of church and state as intrinsic foundations for every government. His theological perspective on this matter emerged from his Calvinist roots, which affirmed two realities: the absolute goodness and sovereignty of God and the absolute depravity and sinfulness of humanity. Taken together, these doctrines led him to the conclusion that there could be no theocratic government prior to the return of Christ to earth and that there could be no true church until that same event.[23]

Williams presents his theological framework in *The Bloudy Tenent of Persecution*, published in 1644 as a conversation between Truth and Peace.[24] The book was not widely read in the seventeenth century, but it came to have a remarkable influence upon religious liberty and the separation of church and state, particularly in the United States. Even if Williams did not take his argument to its logical conclusion, it does, in fact, hold the key to religious liberty in all forms of government, whether a democracy like the United States or a religious theocracy like Iran. One does not have to reside under a government in which religion and state are separate

---

[23] Edmund S. Morgan, *Roger Williams: The Church and State* (New York: Harcourt, Brace and World, 1967) 49.

[24] Roger Williams, *The Bloudy Tenent of Persecution, for cause of Conscience, discussed, in A Conference between Truth and Peace, Who, In all tender affection, present to the High Court of Parliament, (as the result of their Discourse) these, (amongst other Passages) of highest consideration*, ed. Richard Groves (Macon, GA: Mercer University Press, 2001. Originally printed in London, 1644).

WHY STUDY BAPTISTS?

in order to champion religious liberty in a way that is in line with the deepest convictions of one's faith.

Williams could not tolerate compulsion in religious belief, believing it tantamount to requiring "an unwilling spouse...to enter into a forced bed." He detested the fact that people who did not believe in God were forced to take public oaths in the name of God. Williams freed God from the human mind as much as any other human being, and certainly more than most any Baptist. Williams argued that as a sinful and fallible human being, he could not ultimately understand the mind of God, which meant neither he nor any other human being had the right to compel others to make any religious assertion about God. If he made such absolute statements, then he usurped the place of God, provided absolute proof of his own sinful state, and, in the process, violated one of the most foundational theological assertions of his own religious tradition.

In the first introductory piece to his work, Williams offers twelve theses that he intends to defend. Numbers six and eight are directly related to religious freedom. Number six argues that "it is the will and command of God that...a permission of the most paganish, Jewish, Turkish, or anti-Christian consciences and worships be granted to all men in all nations and countries."[25] He eschews any sort of religious warfare, insisting that battle should be done only with the word of God or Scripture in order to convince others of the truth. At the same time, he displays the same ignorance of Eastern religious traditions that William Carey would display some 160 years later, though Western knowledge of Asian religions is more easily forgivable in the early seventeenth century than in the late eighteenth century. In the eighth thesis, Williams points out that God requires no uniformity of religion "to be enacted and enforced in any civil state" because such conformity leads to civil war, persecution, and violence in the name of religion.[26]

The starting point of Williams's argument appears to be his radical notion that Almighty God does not seek or demand the utilization of violence in order to accomplish his purposes in the world. Williams insists that Jesus Christ himself had decreed that "the tares (or weeds) and the

---

[25] Ibid., 3.
[26] Ibid.

138

wheat...should be let alone in the world, and not plucked up until the harvest, which is the end of the world."[27] Jesus was so committed to this idea, Williams says, that he charged his disciple to be "so far from persecuting those that would not be of their religion that when they were persecuted they should pray (Matthew 5:44), when they were cursed, they should bless, etc."[28] Williams points out how often the tares become wheat and blasphemers and persecutors become faithful and idolaters become worshippers of God if their salvation is left up to God and not left to a sinful humanity that is fully incapable of understanding the truth. He also points out just how often those persecuted by the church (such as Jesus or John Wycliffe or Martin Luther) turned out to have been promoting a truth later embraced by the church. Williams warns in his own day

> of hundred thousands, men, women, children, fathers, mothers, husbands, wives, brothers, sisters, old and young, high and low, plundered, ravished, slaughtered, murdered, famished! And hence these cries [on the part of the religious power-holders], that men fling away the spiritual sword and spiritual artillery in spiritual and religious causes, and rather trust for the suppressing of each other's gods, conscience, and religion...to an arm of flesh and sword of steel.[29]

According to Williams, those who embraced the ways and teaching of Jesus ought to have faith and trust in God's power and ability to bring about God's purposes in the world and that no assistance was required from a sinful humanity except for its willingness to use the sword of the Spirit and the Word of God as its weapons. Indeed, whenever the church sought to use swords of steel, it often killed the wheat at least as much as it destroyed the tares. This was why Jesus had insisted that the wheat and tares should be allowed to grow up together.

Because of the dismal history of Christian persecution of even other Christians, and certainly of Jews and Muslims, it was Williams's conviction that human beings ought to leave it all to God and embrace the conviction that "a false religion out of the church will not hurt the church, no

---

[27] Ibid., 11.

[28] Ibid.

[29] Ibid., 32.

WHY STUDY BAPTISTS?

more than weeds in the wilderness hurt the enclosed garden, or poison hurt the body when it is not touched or taken."[30] He also insisted that "a false religion and worship will not hurt the civil state in case the worshippers break no civil law." False religion should be allowed to exist in the presence of both the church and the state, and it should be left to God to inhibit its progress and not to a sinful humanity to attempt to do so.

The key theological idea upon which Williams established his convictions about religious freedom and the separation of church and state was his belief in the huge gap between God and humanity—a gap that could never be overcome through any human effort, including the fashioning of a theocratic government. Sinfulness and the total depravity of humanity would always blind human beings and keep them from being able to ascertain the will and purposes of God. Williams did not seek religious freedom for its own sake; rather, he sought it "because it was the only way to reach the true God."[31] Force, in his estimation, only advanced false religion; it never advanced the truth. And, left to its own path, truth would win out in the end. Left to the whims of a sinful humanity, truth would inevitably be lost, and the purposes of God frustrated.

Roger Williams offers a perspective on religious freedom that should be embraced by white Baptists in the South precisely because it emerges from this absolute conviction in the sovereignty of God and the sinfulness of humanity, concepts generally affirmed by such Baptists. Williams's theological position affirms God's sovereignty as the basis for religious freedom in any government, whether it be a Liberal democracy, a Communist form of government, or an Islamic theocracy. For Williams, whatever the government (and he certainly preferred one in which church and state were separate), religious freedom should be protected for all because it is the only way to guarantee that God's truth emerges apart from contamination by human depravity and sin.

Embedded in Williams's theology is the foundation for acknowledging God's presence among persons of all other world religions. Most every white Baptist in the South would acknowledge that her or his knowledge of God is limited. God's ways are beyond human comprehension. No

---

[30] Ibid., 120.

[31] Morgan, *Roger Williams*, 141.

human being can dictate through whom or by whom God might speak to any other human being. For this reason, white Baptists in the South, by virtue of their own theological heritage, must be open to what a Muslim or Jew, Buddhist or Hindu, Taoist or Confucian person might say to them about God, creation, and truth. Failure to be open to the perspectives of these religious "others" is a violation of God's power and sovereignty in the world. His perspective encourages Christian people to approach persons of other religions with mutual regard and with open and listening hearts that do not discount other religious beliefs. Divine truth could be present in any such encounter.

Williams's call for openness to other religions lay dormant in Baptist life for some two hundred years after his death. In that time, European colonists destroyed or displaced entire Native American civilizations. Millions of Africans were enslaved and exported to the American colonies (later the United States) as free labor. White Puritan mythologies of "chosenness" and the "divine errand," appropriated from the Jewish tradition, legitimated white European subjugation of the North American continent and justified white Christian global domination. Bold Mission Thrust simply represented the late-twentieth-century iteration of such subjugation and domination.

William Owen Carver, born near Lebanon, Tennessee, in 1868, was the son of a Confederate veteran father and a devoted and pious mother who raised him in the Southern Baptist faith. He studied at Richmond College in Virginia, earning a master of arts degree. Later he enrolled at the Southern Baptist Theological Seminary in Louisville, Kentucky, which became his theological and spiritual home and where he served as a faculty member from 1898 until 1943, a period of forty-five years.[32]

Carver's most influential work was entitled *Missions in the Plan of the Ages*. Published first in 1909 and continuously until at least 1955, it rivaled Carey's *Enquiry* in its influence on white Southern Baptist missiology.[33] Carver is considered one of the first professors of missions in the United States and one of the first to teach a course on comparative religion and

---

[32] Hugo H. Culpepper, "The Legacy of William O. Carver," *International Bulletin of Missionary Research* (July 1981): 119.

[33] Ibid., 120.

missions.[34] His contributions extend far beyond the field of Christian missions in that he offered an uncompromising defense about their importance at a time when the scientific study of world religions at many universities delegitimized such work. Carver argued that the vitality of other religions of the world necessitated an expansion of the Christian understanding of the divine presence in all of creation.

Carver's genius rests in his integration of religious experience beyond the Christian faith as the source of divine revelation for persons of other religions while simultaneously insisting upon the supreme revelation of God in Jesus Christ as the means of salvation. He believed other religions emerged from a deep-seated human awareness of God that beckoned all persons toward the divine, and that dictated Christian missionaries should "seek to interpret, develop, supplement, or better include, the religion that a man has."[35] For this reason, converts to the Christian faith could retain many of the practices and beliefs of their former religion as those beliefs were integrated into their Christian perspective and understanding of the divine.

Again, even as Carver defended the presence of the divine in other religions and the validity of such religious experience, he was convinced that only the Christian faith offered a perspective on God that was sufficient for the spiritual needs of humanity. In one of his last books, *Christian Missions in Today's World*, Carver assessed several of the world's major religious traditions and critiqued each for its potential to serve all of humanity. Any such religion must have a "universal element." If such an element is not present, "there will be in the religion no universalizing drive, no compelling urge to meet the universal need and to seize the expanding opportunity" to meet the spiritual needs of the world.[36] To put it another way, Carver's assessment of each religion's value emerged specifically from the sense of mission or desire for converts that motivated it. Here, in his

---

[34] David W. Daily, "Between Province and World: Comparative Religion in the Missionary Apologetic of William Owen Carver," *Baptist History and Heritage* (January 1997): 48.

[35] W. O. Carver, *Missions and Modern Thought* (New York: Macmillan, 1910) 293.

[36] Carver, *Christian Missions*, 128.

estimation, Christianity had no significant competition, though its own efforts were severely flawed.

The first religion Carver considered in his critique was the religion of Zoroastrianism, which he credits with an early missionary universalism that existed purely as an ideal in the tradition. While it did reach India many centuries after its founding, it undertook no missionary efforts and now "exists in a respectable remnant so concerned for self-preservation of its hundred thousand devotees as to be so absolutely exclusive as not even to admit a convert."[37]

Carver points out that the Jewish religion never "accepted the prophetic universalism as either essential or fundamental," and, in fact, "persisted in subordinating the universal spirit to the ethnic consciousness," thus reducing "their missionary calling."[38] For this reason, Christianity "took over as a central the universal principle of prophetic Judaism and made it the core of its faith." Condemning the ethnic purity of the Jewish tradition, Carver argues that "if there is one God, he saves all races on the same plane, by the same process, into the common humanity."[39]

Of Islam, Carver notes its "universal aim grounded in universal sovereignty of the emphatically One Allah," but he insists that "the ethical love of Allah" did not "cause him to commend his own love to sinners or to urge his adherents to the ends of the earth." Instead, Carver argues, "in Allah sovereignty is ultimate and love is limited," while in Christianity "God achieves and maintains his sovereignty through love which is his essential quality." God's ultimate goal is "redemptive seeking," while Allah's ultimate goal is "avenging anger." Carver concludes that Islam's "success in India and among the Negroes of Africa offers no contradiction to the fact that the religion of the Arabian Prophet is not, as a religion, essentially universalistic or potentially universal." In the end, "its capacity for progress is inherently limited by its doctrines of God and of man, of justice and of mercy."[40]

---

[37] Ibid., 129.
[38] Ibid.
[39] Ibid.
[40] Ibid., 129–130.

WHY STUDY BAPTISTS?

The final religion Carver considered in his assessment of the universal element present in other faith traditions was Buddhism. He was convinced that "the principle of unity in Buddhism is negative, escape from the wheel of individual existence. Its complete success would be its complete destruction by the annihilation of personality." He condemns it for the fact that it only expanded after it became a state religion and "largely by reason of political patronage." In the final assessment, "Buddhism lacks necessary missionary urge and drive...attested by a thousand years during which it has advanced into no new territory."[41]

At this point, one anticipates from Carver an apologetic defense of Christianity as the one religion of the world that possessed the "universal element." Unexpectedly, though, he points to Christianity's deficiencies: "Christianity cannot become universal unless, and in the measure that, Christians are universal in spirit and committed in purpose and in personality and in possessions to mankind as a whole and to men in all relations."[42] This universality demands that all of its adherents be "intolerant of all injustice, all inhumanity, all divisiveness and segregation among the sons of God."[43] Such universality could only occur when "all who extend their Christian contacts—missionaries preeminently, but the rest of us no less truly...eliminate all race and place provincialism from our religion as we move into new environments."[44]

In Carver's assessment of various religions, including Christianity, we witness the emergence of an apologetic for the missionary witness of the Christian faith that takes local contexts and religions seriously and yet still insists upon the superiority of the revelation of God in Jesus Christ as the means of the salvation of all of humanity. "Actual religions," Carver insists, "because they are human, while divinely related and mediated, always have in them elements which have been determined by, and are suitable to, limited horizons and to group unities."[45] In other words, to be most effective in the United States, a religion must be "conditioned by the distinctive

---

[41] Ibid., 130–131.
[42] Ibid., 131.
[43] Ibid., 132.
[44] Ibid.
[45] Ibid., 133.

features of American life. So in every other country."[46] His conviction is that "only by being a 'local' religion with definite adaptation can a religion be realistic and effective."[47] This local identity, by definition, demands an integration of the religious experience that converts to the Christian faith bring with them from their previous religions.

We can certainly hold Carver accountable for his flawed perspective on the universalizing elements of such religions as Zoroastrianism, Judaism, Islam, and Buddhism. His critique exposes some of his own objectification, and, quite honestly, betrays his lack of relationship with persons from these traditions. His was the scholarship of books but not of experience. He had little opportunity to engage with adherents of other religions, and neither did he do much traveling outside of the United States.

Yet deeply embedded in his missiological perspective is a profound respect for religious experience outside the bounds of the Christian faith itself. He is among a very small group of white Baptists in the South in the first half of the twentieth century to wrestle with the challenges that other religions presented to the Christian faith. His missiological convictions integrate a profound respect for other religions and localized religious experience even while insisting that Christianity, properly understood and expressed, is the universal religion for all of humankind.

White Baptists in the American South would do well to consider the theological and missiological perspectives of Roger Williams and William O. Carver, respectively, as we reflect upon the future of Christian mission in a pluralistic world. Williams's theology, grounded in a profound respect for the sovereignty of God, demands of us the cultivation of a listening heart and spirit and the realization that divine truth is not limited to our own narrow Christian perspective. Carver's missiology builds upon Williams's work, reminding us that all of our experiences of the divine are local and contextualized, emerging from the religious understandings that we receive from those religions and worldviews into which we are born. For this reason, it behooves all of us to listen to the perspectives on the divine that we receive from our brothers and sisters of other religions.

---

[46] Ibid.
[47] Ibid., 132.

Perhaps there could have been a worse fate for the world in the late twentieth century than its total evangelization by white Baptists from the US American South, but I have trouble imagining it. Williams and Carver, two Baptist voices crying in the wilderness, remind us that, contrary to the spirit and intentions of Bold Mission Thrust, we have as much to learn as we have to teach and, quite frankly, are in as much need of conversion.

"There Is No Area of Religious Privilege Fenced Off for the Exclusive Use of Men"[1]: Baptist Preaching Women, 1630–2000

Pamela R. Durso

Women preachers have been, and sometimes still are, a conundrum for Baptists. For more than four hundred years, Baptist theology and polity have stressed the priesthood of believers and congregational autonomy. Baptists have taught equality for all people in the area of salvation, and Baptist churches have welcomed women to give voice to, or testify of, their conversion experiences, sometimes publicly and other times privately. For most of their history, however, Baptists have not invited women to use their voices as preachers. In most places and in most eras, Baptist women's preaching voices were carefully controlled or completely silenced. Yet Baptists since their earliest days have had women preachers. These women found ways and places to preach—on street corners, in their homes, in lecture halls, and behind pulpits. Because of the restrictions encountered, some did not embrace the label preacher, and some were hesitant to identify themselves as preachers. Some, in fact, denied that the use of their voices was, in fact, preaching. Yet given the content of these public addresses, their sermonic presentations of biblical insight, and their community's recognition of their public spiritual leadership, women have been preachers since the earliest days of the Baptist movement.

Until the last thirty or so years, little information has been available about Baptist preaching women. While this statement is true of all Baptist women preachers, for Baptist women of color there is even less information. What is known has been discovered in state Baptist histories, local church histories, associational minutes, church records, letters, autobiographies, journals, and diaries, all of which provide glimpses into the

---

[1] Helen Barrett Montgomery, "The New Opportunities for Baptist Women," in *Third Baptist World Congress, Stockholm, July 21–27, 1923*, ed. W. T. Whitley (London: Kingsgate Press, 1923) 99.

preaching of Baptist women. In more recent years, numerous books of Baptist women's sermons have been published, and new technologies have made possible easy access to listening to their sermons.

Following is an overview of Baptist preaching women, beginning with the earliest known preachers in the 1630s and tracing the growing number of Baptist women using their preaching voices. The overview concludes with the twentieth century, a time of expanded opportunities in some Baptist denominations and greater restriction in others. Seventeenth-, eighteenth-, and nineteenth-century women who were the first in their Baptist circles to be ordained or to gain access to the pulpit are highlighted, and because of the much larger number of Baptist women preaching in the twentieth century, the stories and sermons of a select few are included as representative of hundreds of other women who were preaching. The first names of women are used throughout to distinguish them from their spouses, who often were preachers too. Where possible, excerpts of the women's sermons are provided.

The Earliest Baptist Women Preachers, 1630–1800

Even in the early decades of the seventeenth century, as British Baptists first began organizing churches, women outnumbered the men, and "they played a more active role in Baptist life than did women in the Church of England."[2] These years were not easy ones for Baptists in England. The Anglican Church was a state-established church, and membership was not merely an expectation but a requirement. Participation in dissenting religious groups was forbidden as a violation of the law of the land, and those who refused to comply were subjected to spiritual sanctions as well as financial penalties. While the enforcement of sanctions and penalties varied from parish to parish, leaders of the Anglican church and the British government sought to "suppress ideas which might be used to undermine their political and religious legitimacy."[3] As a dissenting group, Baptists were

---

[2] *A Company of Women Preachers: Baptist Prophetesses in Seventeenth-Century England, A Reader*, ed. Curtis W. Freeman (Waco, TX: Baylor University Press, 2011) 2.

[3] Stephen Wright, *The Early English Baptists, 1603–1649* (Woodbridge, Suffolk, UK: Boydell Press, 2006) 3.

perceived as a threat to social and ecclesiastical order, and, as a result, they suffered much persecution and often were targeted for punishment.

Throughout most of the seventeenth century, British Baptist women experienced oppression and lived with the threat of persecution. Despite the hardship of membership and participation in this dissenting religious movement, many Baptist women held fast to their convictions and were faithful to their churches, and a few of them were preachers.

A document published in 1641 lists six women—Anne Hempstall, Mary Bilbrow, Joane Bauford, Susan May, Elizabeth Bancroft, and Arabella Thomas—and noted that they preached throughout England in the 1630s.[4] The women, who hailed from Middlesex, Kent, Cambridgeshire, and Salisbury, declared that they took up preaching because "there was a deficiency of good men, wherefore it was but fit that virtuous women should supply their places."[5] Anne Hempstall proclaimed that she received her calling during a vision of the biblical prophetess Anna, and her preaching astonished her listeners, not so much because of her content or even because she was a woman preaching; they were astonished that she preached such lengthy sermons. The author of the 1641 document wrote, "long did she preach, and longer I dare avouch than some of the audience were willing."[6]

Another early English Baptist women preacher, Mrs. Attaway, was a lace-maker and member of Bell-Alley Church, a General Baptist congregation in London. In the mid-1640s, Thomas Edwards, a Presbyterian minister and vehement opponent of Baptists, labeled Mrs. Attaway as the

---

[4] *A Discoverie of Six Women Preachers in Middlesex, Kent, Cambridgeshire and Salisbury* (n.p., 1641). Although the six women are not specifically identified as Baptists, Baptist scholars such as Edward Caryl Starr and William Thomas Whitley included this document in their bibliographies of Baptist writings, indicating that the women were Baptists. See Edward Caryl Starr, *A Baptist Bibliography: Being a Register of Printed Material By and About Baptists, Including Works Written Against the Baptists*, 25 vols. (Philadelphia: Judson Press, 1947–1976) and William Thomas Whitley, *A Baptist Bibliography: Being a Register of the Chief Materials for Baptist History, Whether in Manuscript or in Print, Preserved in England, Wales, and Ireland*, 2 vols. (London: Kingsgate Press, 1916–1922).

[5] *A Discoverie of Six Women Preachers*, 1.

[6] Ibid.

"mistress of all the she-preachers on Coleman Street."[7] This Baptist "she-preacher" began in 1645 speaking at sessions held on Tuesday afternoons at four o'clock. Her initial audience was comprised only of women, but in response to the influx of a huge crowd of people, including many men, Mrs. Attaway opened her meetings to all who would like to attend. Edwards noted that "there came a world of people, to the number of a thousand."[8]

During one gathering, Mrs. Attaway offered "a word of exhortation" from Acts 2, noting that the prophecy of Joel was now being fulfilled, for the Spirit of God was being poured out on handmaidens. After speaking, Mrs. Attaway led a lengthy prayer and then read John 14:15: "If you love me, keep my commandments." Edwards noted, "Analyzing the chapter as well she could, she then spoke upon the text, drawing her doctrine...for the space of some three quarters of an hour." She then opened the floor for discussion "for that was their custom to give liberty in that kind."[9] On some occasions, such liberty resulted in expressions of opposition. At one gathering, a woman member of the Bell-Alley congregation asked Mrs. Attaway "what warrant she had to preach in this manner." When questioned by what she meant by "what manner," the woman responded that Mrs. Attaway should only preach to the baptized. A heated discussion of infant baptism ensued, but in the course of the conversation, Mrs. Attaway noted that she was not preaching but was exercising her gifts in the manner set forth in 1 Peter 4:10–11, that she was fulfilling the Hebrews 10:25 command that Christians "exhort one another," and that she was obeying Malachi 3:16, which instructed, "Then they that feared the LORD spake often one to another: and the LORD hearkened, and heard it."[10]

---

[7] Quoted in Dorothy P. Ludlow, "Shaking Patriarchy's Foundations: Sectarian Women in England, 1641–1700," in *Triumph over Silence: Women in Protestant History*, Contributions to the Study of Religion, no. 15, ed. Richard L. Greaves (Westport, CT: Greenwood Press, 1985) 96.

[8] Thomas Edwards, *Gangraena: Or a Catalogue and Discovery of Many of the Errours, Heresies, Blasphemies, and Pernicious Practices of the Sectaries of This Time* (London: Printed for Ralph Smith, 1645) 1:31.

[9] Ibid., 1:30.

[10] Ibid., 1:31.

"There Is No Area of Religious Privilege Fenced Off for the Exclusive Use of Men"

Many twenty-first century readers would identify Mrs. Attaway as the preacher during these sessions, and some in attendance at her meetings clearly assigned her this title. Curtis W. Freeman, however, noted that seventeenth-century Baptists "recognized their preachers as valid if they were called by a gathered congregation,"[11] and Mrs. Attaway's Tuesday afternoon sessions were not sponsored by a church or understood to be official church services. Thus, because she had not received a congregational call, had not been officially recognized as a minister, and did not serve a local congregation, she understood her role as that of an exhorter, not as a preacher. In addition, Edwards, in describing Mrs. Attaway as a preacher, certainly did not intend it as a compliment or as a blessing of her work. Instead, his assessment of her was meant to belittle her role. He often wrote derisively of "illiterate mechanic preachers...[and] women and boy preachers," all of whom were unsuitable because of their lack of education and training.[12]

As the gathering ended, Mrs. Attaway stood up, offered a prayer of thanksgiving for the occasion, and walked out. Another woman stood and concluded the meeting. In reporting on this meeting, Edwards asserted that Mrs. Attaway left the meeting because she was not fit to argue questions on baptism, but his recording of this lively debate demonstrates her openness to dialogue and diversity of opinion, her embrace of freedom of conscience, her commitment to believer's baptism, and her willingness to walk away from angry retorts.[13]

One hundred years later, "she-preachers" like Mrs. Attaway could be found proclaiming the gospel in colonial America. Early Baptist records indicate that some Separate Baptist women were known for their effectiveness as exhorters and preachers. Originating during the First Great Awakening of the 1730s and 1740s, Separate Baptists were known for their evangelistic preaching, boisterous worship services, and emotional conversion experiences, and some among them also gladly endorsed the service of women as exhorters. Speaking after the "official" sermon, these women testified of their faith and called on "sinners" to repent. Thus, in

---

[11] Freeman, *A Company of Women Preachers*, 7.
[12] Edwards, *Gangraena*, Epistle Dedicatory, B.
[13] Ibid., 1:32.

WHY STUDY BAPTISTS?

some churches, women spoke freely during worship services, addressing the entire congregation, urging the unconverted to come to faith, and pleading with Christians to confess their sins. The most notable of these Separate Baptist women was Martha Stearns Marshall.

Martha Stearns married Daniel Marshall, a deacon in a Congregational church, in 1747. In the early 1750s, the couple spent eighteen months in Onnaquaggy, a village in what is now New York. The Marshalls did mission work with a Native American tribe, hoping to convert them to Christianity. When the French and Indian War of 1754 broke out, the Marshalls left New England and migrated to the South. They first settled in Virginia, where they observed Baptist work being done under the auspices of the Philadelphia Baptist Association. The Marshalls examined Baptist beliefs and concluded that Scripture did indeed teach the practice of believer's baptism. They were soon baptized and attended a Baptist church, which eventually licensed Daniel to preach.[14] Both Marshalls often prayed and preached during worship services, and Martha's zeal apparently equaled that of her husband. Her behavior in worship, however, scandalized Virginia Baptists, who opposed women speaking in public. But among her family and friends, her behavior was a perfectly acceptable way for her to exercise her spiritual gifts.

Martha's brother, Shubal Stearns, also lived in Virginia and was a Separate Baptist pastor. Because Stearns experienced little success in growing a Baptist church in Virginia, he urged his congregation and family to move with him further south to North Carolina. The Marshalls joined with this Separate Baptist experiment and relocated to Sandy Creek,

---

[14] A. H. Newman, *A History of the Baptist Churches in the United States*, rev. ed. (Philadelphia: American Baptist Publication Society, 1898) 293. Other Baptist historians indicated that Daniel Marshall became a Baptist before leaving New England. See Bill J. Leonard, *Baptist Ways: A History* (Valley Forge, PA: Judson Press, 2003) 121, and H. Leon McBeth, *The Baptist Heritage: Four Centuries of Baptist Witness* (Nashville, TN: Broadman Press, 1987) 223. Baptist historians who agree with Newman that Marshall converted to the Baptist faith in 1754 in Virginia include George Washington Paschal, *History of North Carolina Baptists, 1663–1805*, vol. 1 (Raleigh: General Board, North Carolina Baptist State Convention, 1930) 389, and Robert G. Torbet, *A History of the Baptists,* 3rd ed. (Valley Forge, PA: Judson Press, 1963) 25.

"There Is No Area of Religious Privilege Fenced Off for the Exclusive Use of Men"

North Carolina. Stearns founded a church there, and Martha often stood alongside her brother and spoke at worship services. A few years later, she assisted her husband in founding a church about thirty miles away at Abbott's Creek. Martha "was noted for her zeal and eloquence," and her preaching "added greatly to the interest of meetings conducted by her husband." The new church, however, encountered difficulty in that no minister would cooperate in ordaining Daniel because he allowed his wife to preach and pray in public.[15]

Along with pastoring his church, Daniel traveled throughout Virginia, North Carolina, and Georgia, and founded numerous new churches. In 1771, the Marshalls moved to Columbia County, Georgia, to continue their ministry. However, because the Anglican Church was the official state church of Georgia, organizing Baptist work there proved to be a difficult task. At one point, authorities arrested Daniel for violating the law against preaching contrary to Anglican theology. Martha came to his defense, quoting passage after passage of Scripture. Her eloquence and passion deeply impressed the magistrate and the constable, and they both were converted.[16] Eventually, the Marshalls founded the first Baptist church in Georgia at Kiokee. In 1810, Baptist historian Robert Semple wrote of Martha's contributions to Baptist work:

> Mr. Marshall had a rare felicity of finding in this lady, a Priscilla, a helper in the gospel. In fact, it should not be concealed that his extraordinary success in the ministry, is ascribable in no small degree, to Mrs. Marshall's unwearied, and zealous co-operation. Without the shadow of a usurped authority over the other sex, Mrs. Marshall, being a lady of good sense, singular piety, and surprising elocution, has, in countless instances melted a whole concourse into tears by her prayers and exhortations![17]

---

[15] Newman, *A History of the Baptist Churches*, 294.

[16] Tony W. Cartledge, "Woman Preacher's Legacy Spans Generations," Good Faith Media (February 8, 2010) https://goodfaithmedia.org/woman-preachers-legacy-spans-generations-cms-15593/.

[17] Robert Semple, *History of the Rise and Progress of the Baptists in Virginia* (Richmond, VA: John O'Lynch Printer, 1810) 374. Baptist historian George

WHY STUDY BAPTISTS?

Another eighteenth-century Baptist woman preacher was Margaret Meuse Clay of Chesterfield County, Virginia. As a young woman, Margaret was baptized in the James River and soon her gifts became evident. In the 1770s, ministers began calling on her to lead public prayers, and she willingly complied. Apparently, Margaret not only prayed in worship services but preached as well. According to the Clay family tradition, civil authorities summoned Margaret and eleven Baptist men to appear before the Chesterfield court, where they all were charged with preaching without a license. Margaret willingly went before the court alone for her husband was either unwilling or unable to accompany her.[18] The court found all twelve Baptist preachers guilty and sentenced them to be whipped. The eleven men received their punishment, but when it came time for Margaret to be whipped, an unknown man stepped forward and paid her fine, thus sparing her from public humiliation and physical abuse. Following this incident, the civil authorities left Margaret alone, and she most likely continued to pray and to preach.

These British and colonial Baptist women preachers, while apparently quite effective, served only informally. Except for Mary Savage, they were not given official church positions or titles, recognized as ministers, or ordained. Often, their public addresses were not understood to be, or named as, preaching, and their opportunities were extremely limited. Yet preach they did. Most often their preaching tended to be personal and evangelistic, and their voices were heard as they told of their own faith experience and called others to come to faith.

The preaching of these Baptist women was rarely welcomed by male leaders. In England and colonial America, Baptist men seemed to regard public speaking and preaching by women as a threat. Catherine Brekus noted that for colonial men, "female exhorting stood as a vivid symbol of the breakdown of their authority as husbands and fathers...[while]

Paschal, in his *History of North Carolina Baptists*, wrote of Daniel and Martha: "As a result of the labors of this earnest and fervent evangelist, in which he doubtless had the assistance of his saintly and gifted wife, Mrs. Martha Stearns Marshall, great numbers turned to the Lord." See Paschal, *History of North Carolina Baptists*, 1:291.

[18] William L. Lumpkin, "The Role of Women in 18th Century Virginia Baptist Life," *Baptist History and Heritage* 8/3 (July 1973): 165.

154

ministers expressed fears that female exhorting would lead to sexual as well as religious disorder."[19] The response of Baptist men was often to bar women from public praying and preaching, effectively silencing the voices of many gifted Baptist women.

Black Baptist Women Preachers, Colonial and Post-Revolution

From the mid-seventeenth century, black people, especially those enslaved, were drawn to Baptist churches. Historian James M. Washington asserted that black people found the Baptist conviction that salvation was available to all "ethically and spiritually attractive."[20] But such theology did not result in racial equality or inclusion within Baptist churches. During worship services, black members were expected to stand or even move outside if there was not enough space for all the white congregants.

In the South, there were occasional allowances for an enslaved man to preach to white congregants, but black women's voices prior to 1800 were almost completely silent in those churches. No church records yet discovered indicate that black women ever spoke during church meetings, and only a few accounts exist of enslaved women exhorting or testifying on their plantations.[21] Most likely, white ministers, who were reluctant to give white women opportunities to participate or speak, were even more reluctant to offer such liberty to black women. What does exist, however, are oral history accounts of grandmothers and great-grandmothers who exhorted loudly and passionately. Records indicate that black women began exhorting in the nineteenth century, but, according to Catherine Brekus, some "tantalizing clues" point to these women's "refusal to keep silence even before the American Revolution."[22]

---

[19] Catherine A. Brekus, *Strangers and Pilgrims: Female Preaching, 1740–1845* (Chapel Hill: University of North Carolina Press, 1998) 58–59.

[20] James Melvin Washington, *A Frustrated Fellowship: The Black Baptist Quest for Social Power* (Macon, GA: Mercer University Press, 1991) 7.

[21] Brekus, *Strangers and Pilgrims*, 57, 63.

[22] Ibid., 63.

After the Revolution, records suggest that more black Baptist women began preaching, but still the numbers were few.[23] Details about the women and their sermons are scarce, for sermons were rarely preserved in manuscript form, and women's writings were rarely published. White women who dared to write for newspapers or magazines encountered harsh criticism from men, and, as a result, many wrote using pseudonyms. Black women who took up the pen faced even harsher criticism and often were censured by white men and white women.[24]

One black Baptist woman whose voice was preserved was Maria W. Stewart. Born in 1803 in Hartford, Connecticut, Maria was orphaned at age five and was for the next ten years "bound out in a clergyman's family."[25] From age fifteen to twenty-three, she supported herself as a domestic servant. In 1826, Maria married James W. Stewart, an independent shipping agent in Boston. Their wedding was held at Boston's First African Baptist Church, one of the oldest black churches in the nation and the site of the first meeting in January 1831 of the New England Anti-Slavery Society. Maria affiliated with this church prior to and after the wedding, although later in her life she also affiliated with Methodist and Episcopalian congregations.

Following her husband's death in 1830, Maria experienced a spiritual conversion, which she described in "Religion and the Pure Principles of Morality, The Sure Foundation on Which We Must Build," a twelve-page pamphlet written in 1831: "From the moment I experienced the change, I felt a strong desire, with the help and assistance of God, to devote the remainder of my days to piety and virtue, and now possess that spirit of independence that, were I called upon, I would willingly sacrifice my life for the cause of God and my brethren."[26] The pamphlet contains

---

[23] Ibid., 63.

[24] Glenna Matthews, *The Rise of Public Woman: Woman's Power and Woman's Place in the United States, 1630–1970* (Oxford: Oxford University Press, 1992) 83.

[25] *Maria W. Stewart: America's First Black Woman Political Writer*, ed. Marilyn Richardson (Bloomington: University of Indiana Press, 1987) 3.

[26] Maria W. Stewart, "Religion and the Pure Principles of Morality, The Sure Foundation on Which We Must Build," in *Maria W. Stewart: America's First Black Woman Political Writer*, ed. Marilyn Richardson (Bloomington: University of Indiana Press, 1987) 29.

urgent and forceful declarations about the consequences of racial injustice, including segregation, inferior educational opportunities, and poverty, and because of the rhetoric in this pamphlet and other of Maria's writings, some scholars identify her as the first black American woman to write a political manifesto. Other scholars, including Colleen Richmond, believe that Maria was a preacher and that her writings and later public addresses were sermons. This pamphlet certainly had the content and cadence of a sermon.[27] Because her writings are not widely known, "there is considerable ambiguity as to how to classify them."[28]

Collen Richmond argued that Maria's call to preach was foundational, and thus, even though she did not speak from a church pulpit, Maria "may be best understood as a preacher who used the rhetoric of African-American sermons to exhort her people to moral and societal reform, and she created her own pulpit in the press, the public lecture hall, and in her life as a teacher and citizen."[29]

Maria called people to holy living and exhorted black people to work to end prejudice by being moral, working hard, and seeking education. She challenged her readers and listeners, telling them that their goal should be "social reform through religious revival,"[30] and she relied heavily on the writings of the prophets Jeremiah, Isaiah, and Ezekiel but also quoted widely from the Gospels and the Epistles, using familiar biblical phrases and images.

In 1832, Maria published a twenty-eight-page pamphlet titled "Meditations from the Pen of Mrs. Maria W. Stewart, presented to the First African Baptist Church and Society, in the city of Boston." She may have shared the meditations and prayers found in this pamphlet at her church. In 1832 and 1833, Maria made four public addresses. She was one of the first women to speak in public, and like the other women who dared to break gender norms, she caused quite a scandal. In her

---

[27] Collen D. Richmond, "The Preaching of Maria W. Stewart: A Challenge for Harmony and Biblical Justice," *Christian Scholar's Review* 35/3 (Spring 2006): 345–70.

[28] Ibid., 346.

[29] Ibid.

[30] Ibid., 351.

second address, Maria spoke against the "colonization plan," which called for black people to be sent to West Africa. This address began with these words:

> Why sit ye here and die? If we say we will go to a foreign land, the famine and the pestilence are there and there we shall die. If we sit here, we shall die. Come let us plead our case before the whites: if they save us alive, we shall live—and if they kill us, we shall but die.

> Methinks I heard a spiritual interrogation—"Who shall go forward, and take off the reproach that is cast upon the people of color? Shall it be a woman?" And my heart made this reply—"If it is thy will, be it even so, Lord Jesus!"[31]

In her final address, delivered on February 27, 1833, Maria answered criticisms of her public speaking and her willingness to address audiences comprised of both men and women:

> What if I am a woman; is not the God of ancient times the God of these modern days? Did he not raise up Deborah, to be a mother and a judge in Israel? [Judges 4:4] Did not queen Esther save the lives of the Jews? And Mary Magdalene first declare the resurrection of Christ from the dead? Come, said the woman of Samaria, and see a man that hath told me all things that ever I did, is not this the Christ? [John 4] St. Paul declared that it was a shame for a woman to speak in public, yet our great High Priest and Advocate did not condemn the woman for a more notorious offence than this; neither will he condemn this worthless worm.... Again; holy women ministered unto Christ and the apostles; and women of refinement in all ages, more or less, have had a voice in moral, religious and political subjects. Again; why the Almighty hath imparted unto me the power of speaking thus, I cannot tell.... The religious spirit which has animated

---

[31] Maria W. Stewart, "Lecture Delivered at Franklin Hall, Boston, September 21, 1832," in *Maria W. Stewart: America's First Black Woman Political Writer*, 45.

women in all ages, showed itself.... Why cannot a religious spirit animate us now?[32]

Given her sense of calling, her heavy reliance on biblical texts, and her strong defense of her own public speaking, Maria's public addresses may be considered preaching. Had she been born a century later, undoubtedly, she would have been given the title preacher.

Maria used the opportunities she had both in writing and speaking to admonish her readers and listeners toward stronger faith commitments, but her primary concern seemed to be to call them to action, pleading with them to greater activism in working for social, vocational, and economic inequity. Unlike white women preachers of her time, Maria's primary focus was not on religious conversion but on holy living and social reform.

Baptist Preaching Women, 1800–1900

In the nineteenth century, several Baptist bodies began to formally recognize women as ministers, licensing some of them and ordaining others. The number of women recognized was extremely limited, and the practice was not widespread across Baptist denominations. This practice of offering official blessing and provision of titles, however, allows for easier tracking of Baptist preaching women. Every woman who was licensed or ordained had opportunity to preach, and some served as pastors of congregations.

The earliest known inclusion of a woman minister's name in Baptist records actually occurred just prior to the beginning of the nineteenth century. In his 1862 *History of the Freewill Baptists*, I. D. Stewart noted that Mary Savage in 1791 became "the first name on the record as a female laborer in the gospel" among the Freewill Baptists. That year, Mary traveled to New Durham, New Hampshire, and spent nearly twelve months in the town

> doing what she could. The melting power of her exhortations was often irresistible, and so great was the effect with which she

---

[32] Maria W. Stewart, "Mrs. Stewart's Farewell Address to Her Friends in the City of Boston, Delivered September 21, 1833," in *Maria W. Stewart: America's First Black Woman Political Writer*, 68–69.

sometimes spoke at the Quarterly or Yearly Meeting, that a note of the fact was entered upon the book of records. Her knowledge of human nature, and her great spiritual discernment, enabled her to labor with marked success, in reconciling Christians who were at variance.[33]

Stewart concluded,

> There has ever been a difference of opinion, as to the particulate exceptions to the rule that men only are called to preach the gospel. A few women have felt themselves called to this work in different periods of our early history, and while some in the denomination would give them no encouragement, they desired not to stand between them and the full obedience to their honest convictions of duty. Others have thought that women were truly called of God to the work. This number has greatly diminished in later years, so that now it doubtless constitutes a small minority.[34]

In June 1846, Freewill Baptists formally licensed a woman to preach. The Freewill Baptist Home Mission Board commissioned Ruby Bixby and sent her and her husband, Newell Willard Bixby, to minister in Iowa. The couple traveled from their home in Vermont by boat through the canals of New York and made their way into Wisconsin by horse. While in Wisconsin, the Honey Creek Quarterly Meeting of the Freewill Baptists licensed Ruby to preach. The couple then moved on to Iowa, where Ruby's preaching license was renewed each year, and finally she was given a "license without limitation." Although never ordained, "she was not merely an assistant pastor, but was an independent, self-reliant preacher" and was pastor of a congregation.[35]

Ruby and her husband founded a church in Clayton County, Iowa, and the congregation's reports list her as having served as their minister for twenty-eight years, beginning in 1849. She also served as a revival preacher, often as the only minister present. Ruby traveled to the revival

---

[33] Stewart, *History of the Freewill Baptists*, 1:191.

[34] Ibid., 1:192.

[35] "Bixby, Rev. Newell Willard, and his wife Ruby Knapp Bixby," *Free Baptist Cyclopedia*, 56, https://www.nafwb.org/onemag/b.pdf.

160

"There Is No Area of Religious Privilege Fenced Off for the Exclusive Use of Men"

sites, preached, returned home, cared for her family, and then went back out to baptize the converts. The Iowa Yearly Meeting reported in 1853 that there were fourteen churches in the state and that the Bixbys' labors "continued to receive the divine blessing." The report also noted of Ruby: "Sister Bixby was a most consistent and devoted Christian. Love was manifest in her daily example and in her ministry. Her sermons were persuasive; and her ministry, both as pastor and evangelist, was more than ordinarily successful."[36] Indeed, some declared Ruby to be a better preacher than her male counterparts. By the time of her death in 1877, the Freewill Baptists had admitted women as denominational delegates, and, in 1886, the denomination formally initiated a policy of female ordination.

The earliest ordinations of Baptist women began in the 1870s, with the earliest known ordination taking place in 1876. That year, M. A. Brennan was recognized as a minister by the Bellevernon Freewill Baptist Church in Pennsylvania. While specific information about her ordination has not been found, the fact that Brennan was listed on the Quarterly Meeting's annual ministerial list of newly ordained ministers indicates that she indeed had been ordained.

The first ordination of a woman associated with the Northern Baptist Convention, which is now the American Baptist Churches USA, occurred six years later. In 1882, May C. Jones was ordained at a meeting of the Baptist Association of Puget Sound in Washington State. Born in Sutton, New Hampshire, in 1842 to an English physician father and a fearless Scottish mother, May began teaching school at the age of thirteen. At the age of twenty-five, she moved with her husband to the Pacific coast, where they spent more than ten years in California. In 1880, May and her husband settled in Seattle, Washington, and there she preached her first sermon in August of that year. The First Baptist Church of Seattle soon licensed her to preach, and the congregation opened their pulpit to her when their pastor was absent.

On July 9, 1882, an ordination council made up of representatives of churches in the Baptist Association of Puget Sound and British Columbia ordained May, which caused quite a controversy. Opponents charged that First Baptist Church of Seattle had not properly presented a request for

---

[36] Ibid.

161

ordination to the association or scheduled an ordination council. Instead, church delegates, while their pastor was out of the country on a European tour, had proposed to the association that she be ordained that very day after the close of the official meeting.[37] Participants at the meeting who were offended by the proposal walked out, leaving only May's supporters to vote on the recommendation. Not surprisingly, the recommendation was accepted, and following her ordination, she served briefly as the pastor of First Baptist Church, Seattle.

The next year, May began work as a church planter, founding several congregations. She also pastored six Baptist churches, sometimes serving two or three simultaneously.[38] Her last pastorate was First Baptist Church of Spokane, the second largest church in Washington. She served there for four years, preaching, baptizing, and performing weddings. The church grew rapidly under her leadership, but in January 1892, she resigned to care for her invalid husband. Following his death, May engaged in evangelistic work, accompanied by her musically talented daughter, Grace.

Frances Willard and Mary Livermore, in *A Woman of the Century*, described May as having "a flexible voice of marvelous power and sweetness. She speaks rapidly and fluently, with a style peculiar to herself. Added to these gifts is a deep undercurrent of spiritual life."[39]

A second Northern Baptist woman, Frances Townsley, was ordained in 1885. Frances received an excellent public school education, and in 1867, she enrolled at Wheaton College. Her mother's death the next year forced her to seek employment as a teacher, and one day during class, a young Episcopalian woman, Nell Marsh, appeared in Frances's classroom and proclaimed, "Dear, I am convinced that you are to preach the everlasting gospel of our precious Lord!" Frances was shocked, but after much prayer, she began writing sermons and soon was invited to preach in a Congregational church.

---

[37] Frances Elizabeth Willard and Mary Ashton Livermore, *A Woman of the Century, Fourteen Hundred-Seventy Biographical Sketches Accompanied by Portraits of Leading American Women in All Walks of Life* (Buffalo, NY: Charles Wells Moulton, 1893) 426.

[38] James R. Lynch, "Baptist Women in Ministry through 1920," *American Baptist Quarterly* 13/4 (December 1994): 311.

[39] Willard and Livermore, *A Woman of the Century*, 426.

By 1875, Frances had begun preaching in churches throughout New England and holding evangelistic services. A few years later, a church in her hometown of Shelburne Falls, Massachusetts, licensed her to preach. In 1883, she moved to Fairfield, Nebraska, and settled "among a few unchurched Baptists." Together they built a church building, and although she continued to travel and preach, Frances soon was serving as their pastor. In January 1885, Fairfield Baptist Church's deacons, tired of sending for ordained ministers to preside over the Lord's Supper, asked to ordain Frances. After initially protesting, she relented, and on April 2, 1885, following a three-hour examination of her experience, call to ministry, and doctrinal views, the ordination council voted to ordain her.[40] Frances continued to serve in Nebraska until 1898 when she relocated to Vassar, Michigan, to pastor a Baptist church there.

Frances faced opposition throughout her ministry because of her gender, but she responded with scriptural references to Phoebe and Junia, women identified in Paul's Epistles as deacons and apostles. Frances also offered fresh interpretations of restrictive passages, suggesting that Paul's limits on women's speaking were cultural and locational.

While no manuscripts of Frances's sermons survived, her autobiography provides insight into their themes. Of her earlier years in the pulpit as a revivalist, she wrote, "I preached to full houses, to people from the countryside, and the promised city guests [offering] two Sabbath sermons, and leading a twilight service every week, presenting the gospel of love and peace, and forgiving kindness to hearts growing tenderer and minds gradually softening."[41] As a committed temperance leader, she also addressed the evils of alcohol and its impact on family life. But foremost in her preaching was an emphasis on conversion. Frances always extended invitations for response to the gospel message at the conclusion of her sermons and noted that "my gift of song was often used when sermons failed, to lead a soul to Christ or to holier living."[42]

---

[40] Frances E. Townsley, *The Self-Told Story of Frances E. Townsley* (Butler, IN: L. H. Higley Publisher, 1908) 276–81.

[41] Ibid., 180.

[42] Ibid., 192.

The first Seventh Day Baptist woman ordained was Experience Fitz Randolph Burdick, who grew up in West Virginia and had a strong sense of calling as a child. As a young woman, she taught in area schools for several years and then attended Alfred University in Alfred, New York, studying there from 1874 to 1879. At the age of thirty, Experience decided it was time to start preaching, and she knew she needed further education. She returned to Alfred University in 1882 and earned a bachelor of divinity degree in 1885. Church elders in West Virginia apparently affirmed her call. They issued a statement of support in 1883, and in 1885, she was ordained in Hornellsville, New York, becoming the first Seventh Day woman minister.[43]

Experience pastored several Seventh Day churches, the first of which was in DeRuyter, New York. In 1887, she married Leon Burdick, who completed his studies for ministry at Union Theological Seminary in New York City. The couple served in churches in Alfred, New York; Stow Creek, New Jersey; and New Auburn, Wisconsin. Over the course of her ministry, Experience officiated at fifty weddings and ninety funerals, and she preached 890 sermons.[44]

These earliest formally recognized Baptist preaching women share several attributes worth noting. All had some level of education, but only Experience Burdick attended college. None of the women had theological training. All were preaching prior to ordination, and several traveled great distances to preach. While the formal recognition of their ministries may have freed them to preside over communion or baptize converts, none seemed to seek out ordination or view it as necessary to live out their calling.

In addition, none of these Baptist women preachers were members of the wealthy upper class, and all served in less populated towns and regions

---

[43] Minnie Kendall Lowther, *History of Ritchie County: With Biographical Sketches of Its Pioneers and Their Ancestors, and with Interesting Reminiscences of Revolutionary and Indian Times* (Ritchie County, WV: Wheeling News Litho Company, 1911) 630–34.

[44] Patricia A. Bancroft, "Chosen by God: Women Pastors on the Frontiers of the Seventh Day Baptist Denomination," *Baptist History and Heritage* 40/3 (Summer/Fall 2005): 21–22, 24–25.

of the country—and thus were, in some sense, frontier preachers.[45] These women were resilient, overcoming obstacles and objections, and all were exceedingly productive, tirelessly serving multiple churches and causes and preaching hundreds of sermons. While no manuscripts of their sermons have survived, the records available indicate that their sermon content tended to be evangelistic or have a discipleship focus.

Baptist Preaching Women, 1900–2000

The twentieth century proved to be significant for Baptist women called to and gifted for preaching. Women slowly gained entrance into pulpits, and by the end of the century, more and more women were being ordained to the gospel ministry. By the close of the century, several hundred women had been called to pastor Baptist congregations. Following are a few select women who are representative of thousands of twentieth-century Baptist preaching women.

Perhaps the best-known Northern Baptist woman preacher of the early twentieth century was Helen Barrett Montgomery. A graduate of Wellesley College and Brown University, Helen taught school before marrying William A. Montgomery and moving to Rochester, New York. She and her husband generously committed their lives and resources to their church, Lake Avenue Baptist Church of Rochester, where her father, Adoniram Barrett, was pastor. Helen soon organized a women's Bible class that grew to 150 members, which she taught for forty-four years. She often preached in her father's place when he was out of town, and after his death in 1889, she filled the pulpit until the church was able to call a new pastor. In 1892, Helen was licensed to preach by her church.

Both a denominational and ecumenical leader, Helen was elected president of the Northern Baptist Convention in 1921, the first woman to serve as president of any American Protestant denomination. During her

---

[45] In 1880, fewer than four thousand people lived in Seattle, Washington. Clay County, Nebraska, in which Fairfield was located, had a population of fewer than twelve thousand, and Hornellsville, New York, had fewer than ten thousand people living there in 1889.

tenure, the convention found itself embroiled in controversy.[46] Under her wise leadership, the disagreement was settled and division avoided. Helen passionately advocated for world missions and authored eight books on subjects ranging from prayer to missions. Her most notable work is her 1924 translation of the New Testament into "the language of everyday life," making her the first woman to translate the New Testament from Greek to English.

In Rochester, Helen was a pivotal figure for women's rights in educational and civic endeavors. In 1893, she helped organize the Women's Educational and Industrial Union, which served poor women and children. She led, along with Susan B. Anthony, in the women's suffrage movement and campaigned for temperance. She spearheaded the movement to make the University of Rochester coeducational and served as the first woman on the Rochester Board of Education. At the 1923 meeting of the Baptist World Alliance in Stockholm, Helen was one of only two women speakers, addressing the crowd on "New Opportunities for Baptist Women." She proclaimed,

> Jesus Christ is the great Emancipator of women. He alone among the founders of the great religions of the world looked upon men and women with level eyes, seeing not their differences but their oneness, their humanity. He alone put no barriers before women in His religious teaching, but promulgated one law, equally binding upon men and women; opened one gate to which men and women were admitted upon equal terms.... In the mind of the Founder of Christianity there is no area of religious privilege fenced off for the exclusive use of men. In this attitude, Jesus stands absolutely alone among religious teachers.... God has liberated and equipped them [women] in order that they may offer their own mind and soul and body in the service of this Saviour in Whom alone rests the hope of the world.[47]

---

[46] The Northern Baptist Convention was involved in the Fundamentalist Modernist conflict. Montgomery sought unity of diverse factions rather than surrendering to the doctrinal rigidity of the Fundamentalists.

[47] Montgomery, "The New Opportunities for Baptist Women," 99.

"There Is No Area of Religious Privilege Fenced Off for the Exclusive Use of Men"

While Helen embraced the equality promoted by Jesus, she was realistic, recognizing that not every Baptist leader or church agreed. That reality resulted in her concern that Baptists would drive women away by their hesitancy in opening ministry and leadership opportunities to them, a concern that came to be a reality by the end of the century as hundreds of Baptist women left their faith tradition.

In 1929, Helen delivered the initial John M. English lecture in Homiletics at Newton Theological Institute. In her opening address, she offered her thoughts on the centrality of missions in preaching:

> The curse of religion today is churchianity, parochialism, small views of the meaning of the Cross; small enthusiasm for the gospel; the "crumb" Christians who are satisfied with the crumbs that fall from the Master's table when they might sit as guests at the marriage supper of the Lamb; the "mite" Christians who are satisfied with dropping in their "mites," when they might be "hilarious givers" whom God loves. There is no correction for short-sighted views of Christianity like Christian missions.
>
> Scolding accomplishes very little; telling people how worldly and worthless they are pleases a few of those who sit in the seat of the scorner, but leads to few reformations of character. But challenging Christians by the stories of utter nobleness, generosity, goodness, of those who have given their utmost for the love of Christ, stirs heart and conscience.[48]

As a preacher, Helen had extraordinary opportunities for a Baptist woman of the early twentieth century. Her church's frequent welcome of her into the pulpit most likely should be attributed to her father's advocacy of her gifts, her long-term commitment to the congregation, and her faithful leadership. Yet Helen also had a larger stage for her preaching. Her services as president of the Northern Baptist Convention opened doors for her to preach to that convention and at Baptist World Alliance meetings. Helen used those stages to advocate for women in the pulpit and in leadership and to address the issues most critical to her—missions and justice.

---

[48] Helen Barrett Montgomery, *The Preaching Value of Missions* (Philadelphia: Judson Press, 1931) 8–9, 15.

A much-respected twentieth-century Baptist, Ella Pearson Mitchell has been called "a true matriarch of preaching"[49] and "the dean of black women preachers."[50] The daughter of Joseph R. Pearson, pastor of Olivet Presbyterian Church in Charleston, South Carolina, Ella as a young girl rode on the handlebars of his bicycle, accompanying him on pastoral visits to serve communion to those unable to attend worship services.[51] When she was older, she preached for him when he was away. But while Ella's father nurtured and encouraged her calling, her mother did not. In 1941, when Ella enrolled as a religious education major at Union Theological Seminary in New York, her mother "just about flipped."[52]

Ella graduated in 1943 and was one of the seminary's first African American graduates. She then served for two years as minister of education at the Church of the Master (Presbyterian) in New York City, and the church licensed her to preach.[53] But when she requested ordination, the Presbyterian leaders put off granting her request.[54]

In 1944, Ella married Henry Mitchell, whom she had met at Union. Along with her change in marital status came a change in her denominational affiliation. Joining with her new husband, Ella became a Baptist. Together they ministered in churches and in educational institutions for more than sixty years.[55]

After her mother died in the mid-1970s, Ella felt freer to pursue ordination. A Baptist minister agreed to ordain her but later backed out because, he said, the Holy Spirit had told him not to. That same day,

---

[49] Martha Simmons, "An Interview with Ella Pearson Mitchell," *African American Pulpit* 3/4 (Fall 2000): 91.

[50] Samuel K. Roberts, ed., introduction to *Born to Preach: Essays in Honor of the Ministry of Henry & Ella Mitchell* (Valley Forge, PA: Judson Press, 2000) viii.

[51] "A Conversation with Ella Pearson Mitchell," *Union News* (Fall 1993): 2.

[52] Ella P. Mitchell, "In the Same Year That Mama Died, I Also Saw the Lord," in *The Irresistible Urge to Preach: A Collection of African American "Call" Stories*, The McCreary Center Series in Black Church Studies 1, ed. William H. Myers (Atlanta: Aaron Press, 1992) 260.

[53] "A Conversation with Ella Pearson Mitchell," 2.

[54] Mitchell, "In the Same Year That Mama Died," 261–62.

[55] Marvin A. McMickle, "Mitchell, Ella Pearson," in *An Encyclopedia of African American Christian Heritage*, ed. Marvin A. McMickle (Valley Forge, PA: Judson Press, 2002) 74.

however, J. Alfred Smith Sr. told Ella that his church, Allen Temple Baptist Church, a Progressive National Baptist Convention congregation in Oakland, California, would ordain her. In October 1978, after serving thirty-five years in ministry, Ella was ordained.[56]

In the following years, Ella preached all over California. She did not always call it preaching because some of the churches were not open to women in the pulpit, and on one more than one occasion, she was asked to speak from the floor.[57] Yet Ella believed that God called women to be ministers and pointed to Peter's sermon on Pentecost, in which he proclaimed that God promised to pour out the Holy Spirit on "all flesh," which encompassed both men and women (Acts 2:17).[58] Ella asserted that in God's pouring out of the Spirit, God "has dumped the bucket on a whole lot of women a whole lot of times.... It's we faltering humans who have the hangups."[59]

In the final decades of her long ministry career, Ella served on the faculty of Berkeley Divinity School, Compton College, the Claremont School of Theology, and Virginia Union University's Proctor School of Theology. In 1986, she became the first woman appointed dean of Sisters Chapel at Spelman College in Atlanta and soon after, Ella and Henry began team-teaching homiletics as visiting professors at both the Interdenominational Theological Center in Atlanta and United Theological Seminary in Dayton, Ohio. Ella edited four volumes of *Those Preachin' Women*, which features sermons preached by women of color, and edited *Women: To Preach, or Not to Preach*.

Ella's preaching has been described as creative, inclusive, and liberation-oriented. She often pushed back on limits placed on her and other women by society and by the church, and she demanded equal treatment and respect. All these descriptors are evident in her 1999 sermon "All Flesh Is Eligible," in which Ella engaged in a prayerful conversation with

---

[56] Mitchell, "In the Same Year That Mama Died," 262.

[57] Ibid., 261.

[58] Ella Pearson Mitchell, "Introduction: Women in the Ministry," in *Those Preachin' Women: Sermons by Black Women Preachers*, ed. Ella Pearson Mitchell (Valley Forge, PA: Judson Press, 1985) 1:11.

[59] Ibid., 13–14.

WHY STUDY BAPTISTS?

God about "all flesh" and invited her listeners to "turn up" their "spiritual imaginations."[60] Ella began this dialogue with these words: "The Lord made it plain that questions are always welcome and in order. Indeed, we should never be so fearful or presumptuous as to wonder if our questions ever threaten God. Questions are a way of loving our Lord with our minds, as well as our hearts."[61] Later in the dialogue, the Lord says to Ella, "You know very well that I pour out my Spirit, at times, on those whom you call grand rascals. You've seen it countless times, but Ella, you keep forgetting that I said *all* flesh is eligible. If I were to wait to pour out my Spirit on perfect people only, I'd never give a drop away."[62]

Ella's powerful sermons and her personal warmth drew people to her preaching. Her vulnerability in content and her passionate presentation made her one of the best-known and most-loved preachers of the late twentieth century.[63]

Unlike Ella, Addie Davis did not preach on big stages. Instead, most of her preaching took place in small churches located in less populated communities. For forty years, Addie pastored congregations in Vermont, Rhode Island, and Virginia. Yet her name is widely known because she was the first Southern Baptist woman ordained to the gospel ministry.

As a child, Addie felt a sense of calling to preach, but lacking role models, and having a self-acknowledged limited imagination, she remained quiet. At the age of twenty-one, she enrolled as a student at Meredith College in Raleigh, North Carolina, and upon graduation in 1942 served as education director at the five hundred-member First Baptist Church in Elkin, North Carolina.

While this position allowed Addie to minister in a congregational setting, she knew in her heart that she had not been called to be a religious

---

[60] Ella Muriel Pearson Mitchell, "All Flesh Is Eligible," in *Preaching with Sacred Fire: An Anthology of African American Sermons, 1750 to the Present,* eds. Martha Simmons and Frank A. Thomas (New York: W. W. Norton & Co., 2010) 762.

[61] Ibid.

[62] Ibid., 765.

[63] Kirsten Tagami, "Ella Mitchell Obituary," *Atlanta Journal-Constitution* (November 30, 2008).

educator but to be a pastor.[64] She left Elkin in 1946 to take the position of dean of women at Alderson-Broaddus College, a Baptist school in Philippi, West Virginia, and while there, recognized her need for theological education. Addie applied to and was accepted by both Duke Divinity School and Yale Divinity School, but as she prepared to make this transition, a family need took precedence. Addie returned home to Covington to assist her widowed mother in running the family furniture business.

During the next decade she spent at home, Addie served for six months as interim pastor of a rural congregation, Lone Star Baptist Church, which provided her with opportunities to preach and provide pastoral care.[65] In 1960, Addie's mother retired, leaving her forty-three-year-old daughter finally free to pursue theological education. She enrolled at Southeastern Baptist Theological Seminary in Wake Forest, North Carolina, and was among the first women to attend and graduate from the seminary.[66]

During seminary, Addie took a summer-term preaching class and submitted a full-length sermon manuscript to her professor titled "Am I My Brother's Keeper?" Based on Genesis 4:9–16, the sermon addressed the greatest social justice issues of the day: racism, unethical business practices, and poverty. Addie wrote, "Will the color of skin continue to build a wall to divide us? Can we not build bridges of understanding? We do this as individuals occasionally. Most of us know Negros whom we regard highly and who are dear to us; but as a people, we have not bridged the gap of prejudice and misconception. This we need to begin to do, and we must start with ourselves." She also asked, "Should Christianity make any difference in our business practices? Are we ever guilty of false advertising, too much markup, overselling, or unreasonable interest rates?"

In the concluding paragraph of "Am I My Brother's Keeper?," Addie wrote:

---

[64] Addie Davis, interview by Robin McKenzie (Hardison), October 25, 2001.

[65] Addie did not remember the exact dates of her interim pastorate, only that it was sometime during the 1950s.

[66] Addie Davis, Graduation Program, Southeastern Baptist Theological Seminary, Wake Forest, North Carolina, May 1963. Addie Davis Papers, Special Collections, Jack Tarver Library, Mercer University, Macon, Georgia.

WHY STUDY BAPTISTS?

If we permit this transforming power of Christ to work in us we can expect that our attitudes will change and our actions will follow a different pattern. Through him that is at work in us it can be accomplished. When we determine that as far as we are concerned we will follow the leadership of his Spirit and be guided by his truth, then we will begin to live more and more like children of God. God is asking each one of us to be our brother's keeper. This is possible only as we live and act as children of the Most High![67]

As graduation from seminary neared, Addie began an extended search for a pastoral position in Southern Baptist life. When that search proved to be unproductive, she contacted the American Baptist Convention and soon was called by the First Baptist Church of Readsboro, Vermont. On August 9, 1964, before taking on this new position, Addie was ordained at Watts Street Baptist Church in Durham, North Carolina. She was forty-seven years old. For the next eighteen years, Addie pastored American Baptist churches in Vermont and Rhode Island. In 1982, she returned to her hometown of Covington, Virginia, where she co-pastored an ecumenical church until her death in 2005.

In June 1985, Addie preached at Baptist Women in Ministry's annual gathering, held in Dallas. She preached a sermon titled "A Dream to Cherish," which concluded with these words:

May God richly bless each of you as you follow your dream; and hopefully as God opens doors so long shut by prejudice and lack of understanding, He will continue to unfold His will for modern day women. The frontier is limitless in the realm of God's spirit. We humans become the stumbling blocks, often holding back the free flow of God's spirit. Women have always been pioneers, so keep on dreaming and cherish the dream God has given you![68]

---

[67] Ibid.

[68] Addie Davis, "A Dream to Cherish," *Folio* (Autumn 1985): 1, in *The World Is Waiting for You: Celebrating the 50th Ordination Anniversary of Addie Davis*, eds. Pamela R. Durso and LeAnn Gunter Johns (Macon, GA: Smyth & Helwys, 2014) 21.

"There Is No Area of Religious Privilege Fenced Off for the Exclusive Use of Men"

Many of Addie's sermons were similar to this one in that she offered words of encouragement to her listeners, acknowledging the challenges of the day and assuring them of God's continuing presence. On occasion, she addressed social issues, but the majority of her sermons, written for and preached to her congregations, were filled with comfort and hope, and she delivered them in a quiet, calming manner.

The first black woman ordained by the Progressive National Baptist Convention was Prathia Hall, a civil rights activist, pastor, and seminary professor who was the daughter of Baptist pastor Berkeley Hall. Prathia earned a degree in political science at Temple University in 1962 and joined the Student Non-Violent Coordinating Committee (SNCC). Following college graduation, she was one of the first women organizers for SNCC, serving in southwest Georgia as a field leader, canvassing door-to-door to register voters, and teaching classes designed to help potential voters pass registration tests. In mass meetings in Georgia, Prathia was moved by the "power with which...songs and prayers were infused and transcended the objective reality of our situation, fashioned fear into faith, cringing into courage, suffering into survival, despair into defiance, and pain into protest."[69]

On September 9, 1962, two Georgia churches were burned down by the Ku Klux Klan. The next day, a prayer vigil took place where one of those churches, Mount Olive Baptist Church, had stood. Prathia and Martin Luther King Jr. attended the service, and she led the group in prayer, repeating the phrase "I have a dream." Inspired, King sought and received permission to use the phrase in his own sermons, where he immortalized it, less than a year later, as the foundation of his famous "I Have a Dream" speech during the March on Washington in August 1963.[70]

In 1977, Prathia was ordained, and the following year she began serving as pastor at Mt. Sharon Baptist Church in Philadelphia, the

---

[69] Prathia Hall, "Bloody Selma," in *Hands on the Freedom Plow: Personal Accounts by Women in SNCC*, eds. Faith Holsaert et al. (Urbana: University of Illinois Press, 2010) 174.

[70] Courtney Pace, *Freedom Faith: The Womanist Vision of Prathia Hall* (Athens: University of Georgia, 2019) 59–60.

church her father founded forty years earlier. A few years later, she enrolled at Princeton Theological Seminary, where she earned a master of divinity degree in 1982, a master of theology degree in 1984, and a doctor of philosophy degree in 1997, specializing in womanist theology, ethics, and African American church history. The same year she completed her doctoral degree, *Ebony* magazine named her first in their list of the fifteen greatest black women preachers in America. [71] She was "among the first group of women preachers in the twentieth century, of any race, who achieved national notoriety."[72] Prior to her early death, Prathia taught at United Theological Seminary in Dayton, Ohio, and Boston University School of Theology, where she held the Martin Luther King Jr. chair in Social Ethics.

As a preacher, Prathia confronted all forms of oppression, including racism, sexism, and classism. She boldly called out injustice "with a womanist vision of liberation for all people."[73] Her preaching was prophetic, poetic, pastoral, and powerful.

In 1992, during a Hampton University Ministers' Conference, Prathia shared about her journey toward embracing her ministry gifts and God's calling. She had ministered for years but had never been given the title of preacher, and she herself was reluctant to take on that title: "I never wanted to admit I was preaching, but time after time, when I spoke, miracles would take place—God did bless."[74] In a conversation with homiletician Donna Allen, Prathia admitted: "This is a vocation by which I was not even pursued but I was possessed. What I finally realized about my own call was that, all that time I thought I was running from God, God was holding me while I ran. I was running nowhere but into the hands of God. God was using my experiences to prepare me for ministry."[75]

---

[71] "Prathia L. Hall," in *Preaching with Sacred Fire: An Anthology of African American Sermons, 1750 to the Present*, 687.

[72] Ibid.

[73] Pace, *Freedom Faith*, 4.

[74] Ibid., 112.

[75] Ibid., 112–13.

"There Is No Area of Religious Privilege Fenced Off for the Exclusive Use of Men"

One of Prathia's best-known sermons, "Between the Wilderness and the Cliff," was preached at the same conference. In her introduction, she proclaimed Jesus' sermon in Luke 4 to be the greatest sermon ever preached, and then asked, "if what we do in the pulpit is not good news to the poor, deliverance to the captives, sight to the blind, healing for the broken, and freedom for the oppressed, it may be sweet, it may be eloquent, it may even be deep, but it ain't preaching."[76] Prathia addressed the context for the sermon—Jesus went alone into the wilderness, where he was tempted by Satan to surrender his identity. She then told her listeners: "We are not strangers to the wilderness, and the wilderness is no stranger to us. Our sainted fathers and mothers called the wilderness a low ground of sorrow. We know about the wilderness. We know we've been wandering through the wilderness.... My friends, there are no shortcuts through the wilderness. The only way out of the wilderness is through the wilderness." When Jesus came out of the wilderness, he preached his first sermon, after which the crowd drove him out to the edge of a cliff, hoping to hurl him over, but Jesus escaped. Prathia concluded her sermon with a challenge:

> So preachers, teachers, servants of God, don't you get tangled up between the wilderness and the cliff. Don't surrender your identity. Sister preacher, whether they believe you or not, you better know who you are. The God who has called us is the God who has consecrated us, is the God who is right now, right now anointing us. And that God is with us, with us, with us. So go, preach, pray, heal, bless, hold, help, and in this desert, in this wilderness, prepare ye the way of the Lord, for every valley shall be exalted, every mountain and hill shall be brought low, every rough place is being made smooth.[77]

Many of Prathia's sermons focused on the biblical narratives featuring women, and her most prominent theme was liberation. Historian Courtney Pace noted,

---

[76] Prathia L. Hall, "Between the Wilderness and the Cliff," in *Preaching with Sacred Fire: An Anthology of African American Sermons, 1750 to the Present*, 689.

[77] Ibid., 694.

She used the Biblical text to demonstrate equality, justice, and the necessity of Christian commitment to liberation. Her preaching demonstrated that salvation is not merely the deliverance from personal sin but necessitates dismantling systemic oppression, bridging personal faith and social justice, and calling Black churches to remember their heritage as mediators of the people's struggles for liberation and justice and to honor that heritage in their ministries.[78]

Charles Adams, former president of the Progressive National Baptist Convention, believed Prathia to be "the best preacher in the United States, possessing proven ability to exegete, illustrate, celebrate, and apply the scriptures healingly to the problems, pains, and perplexities of the people who sit ready to hear a word from Yahweh." He also noted, "She strikes a beautiful balance between addressing individual problems as well as the social-political-structural condition that helps to determine the equality of individual being and behaving."[79]

Like many Baptist preaching women, Nancy Hastings Sehested was the daughter of a preacher. As a young Southern Baptist woman, she sensed a call to pastor and enrolled at Union Theological Seminary in New York. Graduating in 1978, she began the search for a church to pastor, but few Baptist churches had women serving on their pastoral staffs, and only a handful had women pastors. Nancy eventually received a call as associate pastor from Oakhurst Baptist Church in Decatur, Georgia, where she preached regularly. The church ordained her in 1981.

In 1983, Nancy was a driving force in the founding of Baptist Women in Ministry, a nonprofit organization that connects, networks, and advocates for Baptist women called by God. At the first annual gathering of this new organization, Nancy preached a sermon based on 2 Corinthians 4:7–12 titled "We Have This Treasure."

---

[78] Courtney Pace, "She Had a Dream: The Freedom Faith of Prathia Hall," BJC-Baptist Joint Committee Blog (March 15, 2021) https://bjconthehill.medium.com/she-had-the-dream-the-freedom-faith-of-prathia-hall-a629d0394830.

[79] Charles Adams to Maxine Beach, April 11, 1997, PHP 4:097, in *Freedom Faith: The Womanist Vision of Prathia Hall*, 216.

"There Is No Area of Religious Privilege Fenced Off for the Exclusive Use of Men"

We live in the great in-between time. We are ready, but still waiting. We are called, but not confirmed. We are trained, but not employed. We are willing, but not able. Pastors tell us their congregations are not yet ready and able to accept us. Congregations tell us their pastors are not yet ready and able to accept us. We are to our convention like Paul's early Gentile converts.

We live in the great in-between time. Our calling is clear, and our gifts are manifest. But the desert is a severe, unforgiving place. Many have already parted company, taking on other careers in other denominations. Are there many among us who have not entertained such options? For those who have moved on, we bid God-speed. Some of us feel that if we had any sense, we would do the same. But we remain. It is no special virtue, no special righteousness. Stiff upper lips will not do.

We cannot fully understand why we stay, although all of us would have some partial reasons. The deepest reason is not fully fathomable. The best we can say is that this is where we are called to be. And that is enough.

We live in the great in-between time. We hope for brighter futures, assured of nothing but God's continued fidelity to undergird our spirits and nurture our souls. We see glimmers of light here and there, shining in the darkness, and we celebrate and cultivate it. But we know that light shines from a great distance. It will be a while yet before the whole room is lit up.[80]

In 1987, Nancy was one of thirty-three founders (only three of whom were women) of the Alliance of Baptists. That same year, she was called to pastor Prescott Memorial Baptist Church in Memphis, Tennessee, where she found and honed her preaching voice. As she learned, her congregation also learned. From her interview with Nancy, Leah Grundset Davis wrote, "If [Nancy] preached a particularly tough passage—such as from the prophet Jeremiah, she would receive chicken casseroles the next week because people thought she needed to be cheered up. They were not

---

[80] Nancy Hasting Sehested, "We Have this Treasure," in *This Is What a Preacher Looks Like: Sermons by Baptist Women in Ministry*, ed. Pamela R. Durso (Macon, GA: Smyth & Helwys, 2010) 6.

accustomed to hearing a woman offer the challenging words of a biblical prophet. Soothing words were more the social norm for the public words from women."[81]

As a result of Nancy's call as pastor, Shelby County Baptist Association voted to withdraw fellowship from Prescott Memorial. The public attention that resulted was exhausting. She remembered, "I put extra pressure on myself as a pioneer to prove that I could do it...[but] it was clear I couldn't keep up the pace I was going."[82] Nancy left Prescott Memorial after eight years, which led to a "profound sense of having failed at being a pastor" and "in being able to balance attention to family and husband and children and my own soul."[83]

With her family, Nancy relocated to North Carolina, served as interim pastor of a small church, and then embraced a new ministry role as state prison chaplain. She worked for thirteen years in two high-security prisons for men, ministering as "a priest in the village of the damned."[84] During her early years as a chaplain, Nancy, her husband, Ken, and Joyce Hollyday founded a church, Circle of Mercy, in 2001 in Asheville, North Carolina, and together the three served as co-pastors. Nancy retired from her chaplaincy work in June 2013 and retired from Circle of Mercy in August 2021.

Nancy was a pioneer as a Baptist woman pastor in the South. Her preaching was prophetic and most often justice oriented. While she excelled as a preacher, Nancy encountered the hard realities that many other Baptist women experience. Securing a ministerial position was extremely difficult because few churches were open to woman pastors, and for those women who did receive a call from a church, living up to their own expectations and those of their congregations was often overwhelming.

Like so many other Baptist preaching women in the twentieth century, Isabel Docampo had few female minister role models, but she, too,

---

[81] Leah Grundset Davis, *Believe the Women: A Journey of Liberation with Alliance of Baptists' Women* (Macon, GA: Nurturing Faith, 2019) 29.

[82] Norman Jameson, "Women in ministry pioneer seeks glimpses of holy as prison chaplain," *Baptist News Global* (July 27, 2011) https://baptistnews.com/article/women-in-ministry-pioneer-seeks-glimpses-of-holy-as-prison-chaplain/.

[83] Ibid.

[84] Ibid.

"There Is No Area of Religious Privilege Fenced Off for the Exclusive Use of Men"

found her way to seminary and to ministry. Isabel grew up in New Orleans, the child of parents who had emigrated from Cuba. She experienced a diverse Central American and Caribbean church subculture that was part of a white Southern Baptist church. She learned early in life "to move in and out of different groups and languages very easily and to embrace the diversity as gift, even when perplexing and jarring."[85]

Sensing a call to ministry, Isabel enrolled at the Southern Baptist Theological Seminary in 1979. She was the only Latina enrolled in the master of divinity program and the only woman in her preaching classes. During her years in Louisville, Kentucky, Isabel helped found a church among Puerto Rican military personnel and their families. Following her graduation from seminary, she was appointed as a home missionary by the Southern Baptist Home Mission Board, serving as a co-chaplain to seafarers and as a Christian social minister for the Judson Baptist Association in Baton Rouge, Louisiana, where she worked with refugees and immigrants. In 1985, Broadmoor Baptist Church in Baton Rouge ordained her to the gospel ministry.[86]

A few years later, as a result of controversy within the Southern Baptist Convention about the acceptable roles of women, the Home Mission Board defunded Isabel's position. Forced to piece together ministry work, she served in local retirement homes. In 1987, she found a new Baptist home with the Alliance of Baptists.

In 1996, along with other Alliance leaders, Isabel made a trip to Cuba, and in 1999, she was invited to preach at First Baptist Church of Matanzas, Cuba. She had not preached in Spanish in a long time and had never preached from her chosen text, Mary's Magnificat. She struggled in writing the sermon, aware that she was preaching in a Communist state and knowing that in Cuba "people cannot be motivated to rise up and protest government! I was worried that I might jeopardize the ministry.

---

[85] Isabel Docampo, "This is what a minister looks like," Baptist Women in Ministry Blog (July 3, 2015) https://bwim.info/this-is-what-a-minister-looks-like-isabel-n-docampo/.

[86] Ibid.

So, I asked [the pastor] what I should do. He said, 'You preach what God has put on your heart, don't worry about us.'"[87]

In light of her preaching context, Isabel saw the Magnificat to be "about remembering people who are isolated and caught up in occupation. She saw that in "this Magnificat, you have liberation personally and communally. In this Magnificat, you have the intersection of oppression and liberation—it speaks of both."[88]

A manuscript of Isabel's 1999 sermon is not available, but in November 2016, she preached from this text again at Grace United Methodist Church in Dallas, and in her sermon, she asked the question, "Can Mary's song be our song?" Her answer: "I think so." She then proclaimed:

> Mary's Magnificat reveals how our world today is also distorted far from what our Creator intended. It makes us stop and assess if we have accepted the limitations of identity forced upon us and that separate us from one another, if we have accepted a fatalistic view of our current situation as unchangeable. *It is what it is.* The Magnificat makes us think about power—the power that we have as individuals to do extraordinary things for love and justice's sake. It makes us think about our power as a group. Do we pretend to be powerless and unconsciously allow our power to be used to oppress others, or do we stay awake to understand how our group's power is channeled for ill or for God? Mary's song is a call to stand up so that the world might be a place where all creation can flourish—as God had intended from the very beginning.[89]

In her preaching as well as her ministry, Isabel has been a bridge builder, drawing people together across difference, including cultural, geographical, and theological differences. Her preaching has demonstrated both awareness of context and prophetic courage. Pastor Leah Grundset Davis interviewed Isabel and wrote, "To stand in a pulpit as an ordained Baptist woman, [Isabel] Docampo believes she is a witness to freedom and

---

[87] Davis, *Believe the Women*, 38.

[88] Ibid.

[89] Ibid., 42.

"There Is No Area of Religious Privilege Fenced Off for the Exclusive Use of Men"

liberation. As she stands there, God is breaking down barriers and weaving freedom with grace."[90]

These six Baptist women represent the hundreds, if not thousands, of other women who preached during the twentieth century. By century's end, Baptist preaching women became increasingly common, at least within congregations affiliated with the Alliance of Baptists, the American Baptist Churches USA, the Cooperative Baptist Fellowship, and the Progressive National Baptist Convention. The great majority of congregations affiliated with the National Baptist Convention of America and the Southern Baptist Convention, however, did not encourage women to preach and did not welcome women into their pulpits, and those denominational bodies stood firmly against women preachers.

Throughout most of the twentieth century, many of the Baptist women who were preaching and those who found their way into the pulpit were not automatically identified as preachers. They answered to other titles such as "speaker" or "teacher," and their sermons were labeled as "talks," "messages," or "speeches."

Interestingly, numerous twentieth-century Baptist preaching women were the daughters of preachers, and for many of them, their fathers both encouraged their preaching and opened doors of opportunity for them. This trend seems to be true for both white women and women of color.

Twentieth-century Baptist preaching women gave attention to justice issues of their time, such as racism and sexism, tended to preach more from the New Testament than from the Old, generally favored preaching from Gospel texts, and most often were narrative preachers, weaving together biblical, cultural, and personal stories into their sermons. These Baptist preaching women also tended to preach in first-person plural rather than second-person singular. They included themselves when offering instruction or challenges, preaching from a place of "we should, we must" rather than "you should, you must." These Baptist preaching women also were often vulnerable in their preaching, spotlighting their own struggles and sharing openly about their personal heartbreak or pain. While most twentieth-century Baptist women had limited access to pulpits and few opportunities to preach, they found places in which they could use their voices,

---

[90] Ibid., 39.

often advocating for themselves or relying on affirming Baptist male pastors to make space for their callings and gifts.

Conclusion

Many Baptist preaching women have told a similar story: they had encountered someone opposed to women in the pulpit. Some of these encounters took place in churches, before or after the woman's sermon. Some of these encounters occurred at community events, when the woman was introduced as a minister, or her preaching was referenced. The shared story goes like this:

> Opponent of women preaching: "I don't believe in women preachers."
>
> Woman preacher: "I am standing right here in front of you. I am a woman preacher, and I am real. Women preachers do exist. You may not believe that women should preach. You may be opposed to women in the pulpit. But you cannot deny that women do preach. I am standing right in front of you. I preach."

For more than four hundred years now, skeptics have questioned whether Baptist women could or should preach. They have kept women out of pulpits and have withheld ministry titles from women. And yet...called and gifted Baptist women have been preaching and using their gifts since the earliest days of Baptist existence. As far back as the 1630s, Baptist women have been faithfully using their voices and finding places to preach, sometimes creating those opportunities by preaching in the streets or in their homes, and Baptist women continue to use their voices to preach the gospel. Baptist preaching women are part of our past, our present, and our future. They are standing right in front of us. They are real.

"Do You See Her?" A Sermon on Luke 7:36–50

Meredith Stone

In the mid-nineteenth century, a French journalist and author, Alphonse Karr, published a work which included an anonymous verse that some have attributed to Abraham Lincoln. It translates to something like "you may complain that rose bushes have thorns; But as for me, I rejoice and give thanks to the gods, that thorn bushes have roses."[1]

It's a quote about perspective. One can look at a rose bush and protest that the presence of prickly thorns diminishes the beauty of the roses. But, on the other hand, one could look at the very same plant and see a thorn bush that miraculously produces splendid flowers. It all depends on our perspective.

One of my former professors at Texas Christian University, David Gunn, often used the image of a painting to talk about the importance of perspective in how we view the world and read the Bible. In the introduction to his book *Gender, Power, and Promise*, he writes,

> Imagine a large blue painting on a wall at the far end of the room. Yes, just blue, nothing but blue. [As] you try to suppress speculations about how much the gallery paid for it...you walk toward it to examine it more closely. [When you realize,] actually, the blue is not just blue. It is textured and variously hued. But more than that. There are red dots on/in the painting. Mostly around the margins, but a few scattered through the center, randomly, it would appear. Your interest is suddenly piqued. You even begin to ponder this painting. How do you feel about it? What does it mean? Is it a picture about blue or red? Is it, perhaps, about the importance of blue? Or, there again, the subversion of the dominant blue by the apparently subordinate red? (So does that make the red more important—after all, isn't it the red that is lending the blue its meaning?) And who knows? Scrape the blue, and perhaps there are rivers of red beneath....

---

[1] https://quoteinvestigator.com/2013/11/16/rose-thorn/.

The question of meaning is becoming more complex than you thought.[2]

When we read the Bible, we find a painting which from far away, and from particular perspectives, looks blue. But when we start to examine it closely, we find the blue intermingled with red. The blue exists simultaneously with the red. Dominant stories, themes, and interpretations coexist with auxiliary ones.

With this in mind, we come to the story found in Luke 7:36–50.[3] A similar episode in which a woman pours extravagant oil onto Jesus' feet and wipes them with her hair appears in each of the Gospels (Matt. 26:6–13; Mark 14:3–9; John 12:1–8). But Luke's version has several differences and unique elements.

First, when Luke tells the story, he begins by introducing this woman and calling her "a woman in the city who was a sinner" (Luke 7:37, NRSV). Most interpreters have thus assumed that the woman was a prostitute. Supporting their assumption is the fact that the woman has an expensive perfume, which must have been bought with the earnings of her ignoble profession. As further evidence, the interpreters point out her engagement with Jesus in a physical manner—weeping at Jesus' feet and kissing them while touching them with her unbound hair—with the claim that physicality and a sexual profession must go hand in hand.

Still another difference we find in Luke's account, relative to other Gospel writers' narratives, is that Jesus doesn't describe the woman's act as a burial anointing (Matt. 26:12; Mark 14:8; John 12:7). Instead, in Luke's account, the event takes place in the home of a Pharisee named Simon, whom Jesus speaks to about what the woman has done. Jesus tells Simon a parable about the forgiveness of a great debt and then speaks of the

---

[2] Dana Nolan Fewell and David Gunn, *Gender, Power and Promise: The Subject of the Bible's First Story* (Nashville, TN: Abingdon Press, 1993) 9.

[3] This sermon's exegetical interpretation of Luke 7:36–50 is largely based on the excellent scholarship found in Barbara Reid, "'Do You See This Woman?' A Liberative Look at Luke 7:36–50 and Strategies for Reading Other Lukan Stories Against the Grain," in *A Feminist Companion to Luke*, ed. Amy-Jill Levine (New York: Sheffield Academic Press, 2002) 106–20.

woman's actions toward him as great love shown in response to forgiveness (Luke 7:40–50).

Focusing on the large debt, again most interpreters have emphasized this woman's, this prostitute's, great sins. They assume the story is about some harlot who intrudes on a private dinner at a respectable Pharisee's home and performs an inappropriate act in touching and kissing Jesus' feet, but whose great sins Jesus forgives anyway. He even speaks about how such a wretch can demonstrate great love toward him.

Certainly, the gist of that message is true. Jesus is the great source of forgiveness, and all people, sinners and righteous alike, can pour out their lives in a demonstration of love toward Jesus who saves us.

But when I look for the red dots in this story, the roses among the thorn bushes, there are a few things that I wonder about.

I wonder why most interpreters have decided that the woman in the city, who was a sinner, was necessarily a prostitute, a harlot. All the passage says is that she was, past tense, a sinner. It says nothing about the nature of her sins. Yet because she was a woman who was also a sinner, people have assumed her sin must have to do with her gender and be sexual in nature.

In the very same Gospel, in Luke 5:8, when Peter is being called by Jesus to become a disciple, he himself says, "I am a sinful man." But we never seem to speculate about the nature of Peter's sins. Even while Peter declares his state in the present tense, I am a sinner, he is commonly characterized as a disciple. But this woman, who, the text says, was, past tense, a sinner, gets fully and completely characterized by a very particular kind of sin.

This woman was sinner, and so was Peter, and so am I. And her sin may have been sexual promiscuity, but it also could have been pride or greed or just about anything else. If anything, greed might actually be a better guess since the fact that she has an expensive jar of perfume might mean she was a wealthy woman of some means.

So, a woman who formerly had committed some sins of an undisclosed nature goes to the Pharisee's house where Jesus is eating. She pours a jar of expensive perfume on Jesus' feet, weeps so intensely that her tears cover his feet, and then wipes them with her hair and kisses them (Luke 7:38).

WHY STUDY BAPTISTS?

At this point, the second red dot I have considered is why this woman's act has been interpreted as inappropriate, the kind of thing only a harlot would do. Because if it was an inappropriate thing to do, why did it not elicit a response from her host or anyone around her? Her actions are not the concern of Simon the Pharisee, the host of this gathering. Simon does not kick her out or question her right to be there. She might have even been an invited guest; we do not know. Simon also doesn't stop her from touching Jesus' feet; instead, he questions Jesus and wonders whether Jesus is a prophet (Luke 7:39).

This woman did not touch Jesus inappropriately. She was performing a pious act of worship, and the Pharisee didn't question it. Instead, the Pharisee's questions were about who Jesus really was, and that's something the woman already knew.

At this point, Jesus, perhaps sensing the Pharisee's suspicion about him, tells him a story about a person who forgave two people debts of 500 and 50 denarii. As is the case with most good parables, Jesus ends the story with a question: "Now which of these will love him more?" The Pharisee answers as we suspect, "The one who had the bigger debt," which Jesus deems to be the right answer (Luke 7:40–43).

Jesus then asks another question, a question which some who see the red dots in this story would say is the focus of the entire episode. Jesus says, "Do you see this woman?" (Luke 7:44) Do you see her?

Before the Pharisee can answer the question, Jesus apparently assumes his answer would be no, so Jesus tells him what he should see. He should see a woman who devoted herself to serving and honoring Jesus when the Pharisee did not even offer him water for his feet, did not greet him with a kiss, and did not pour oil on his head. All these acts, Jesus says, were performed as a response of great love to the fact that her sins had been forgiven (Luke 7:44–48). That's why she *was* a sinner, past tense. And thus, we must assume that this Pharisee, who had shown little love to Jesus, was the one who still had many sins which had not been forgiven.

While the woman who was a sinner has been branded a harlot by interpretation, Jesus says the bigger sinner in the story, the one who has been forgiven little and thus has not responded to Jesus in great love, is actually the Pharisee. This woman *was* a sinner, but Simon the Pharisee *is* a sinner. While the editors of the NIV translation (2011) labeled this story

"Do You See Her?" A Sermon on Luke 7:36–50

"Jesus Anointed by a Sinful Woman," maybe it would be better named "A Sinful Pharisee Watches as Jesus Is Anointed by a Forgiven, Loving Woman."

The woman in this story is the example to follow: she shows how to respond to Jesus' forgiveness. Jesus asks the sinner, the Pharisee, do you see her? Do you see her great love? Do you see this disciple?

In continuing with the Gospel of Luke, I have to wonder if we should see her in other places, too. When Luke mentions women disciples in various places, I wonder if this woman—this forgiven woman who shows great love, this disciple—I wonder if she's there.

Because right after her story, the next verse in Luke 8 reads,

After this, Jesus traveled about from one town and village to another, proclaiming the good news of the kingdom of God. The Twelve were with him, and also some women who had been cured of evil spirits and diseases: Mary (called Magdalene) from whom seven demons had come out; Joanna the wife of Chuza, the manager of Herod's household; Susanna; and many others. These women were helping to support them out of their own means. (Luke 8:1–3, NIV)

I wonder if this woman, this woman who had means, whom Jesus has held up as a model of discipleship, I wonder if she became a disciple and followed Jesus with the twelve and these other women.

When you look into the crowd of disciples following Jesus and supporting his ministry, do you see her? Do you see the anointing woman there, traveling from town to town serving with the other disciples and sharing the good news of forgiveness?

These women disciples traveled with Jesus throughout Galilee until eventually Jesus' ministry took him to Jerusalem, where his arrival was heralded by some, but where he was also betrayed, arrested, and sentenced to death by crucifixion.

When Luke describes the scene at the crucifixion, he mentions that many were watching when Jesus breathed his last from the cross, "all those who knew him, including the women who had followed him from Galilee, stood at a distance, watching these things" (Luke 23:49, NIV).

When you look into that scene of Jesus' followers mourning, do you see her? Do you see her again weeping, this time over his cruel death?

Later when it was time for Jesus to be buried, Luke tells us, "The women who had come with Jesus from Galilee followed Joseph and saw the tomb and how his body was laid in it. Then they went home and prepared spices and perfumes" (Luke 23:55–56, NIV).

Do you see her? Do you see her witnessing Jesus' burial and once again tapping her wealth for another jar of perfume for the one who had forgiven her?

Then, on the first day of the week, Luke says these same women disciples went to the tomb with the spices and perfumes but found that the stone had been rolled away. Jesus' body was not there. And two men in gleaming white clothes asked them, "Why do you look for the living among the dead?" And the women remembered his words, that he would die and be raised on the third day, and they went back to tell these things, it says, to the eleven and to all the others (Luke 24:1–10).

Notice it doesn't say to tell the disciples, but rather to tell the eleven and the others, because they were disciples just like the eleven! And even though the eleven did not believe them (Luke 24:11), they were faithful to proclaim the resurrection of the savior—these women disciples.

Do you see her? Do you see this woman who used to be a sinner? Do you see her there, the one who poured out great love for Jesus because he forgave her of her sins? Do you see her there proclaiming that Jesus is alive? Do you see her?

She is a red dot, a rose among the thorn bushes. She is not the main character in the story, the Gospel doesn't even give her a name. But she's there, being faithful and serving as an example to others, even though later interpreters have failed to do justice to her story.

I really think if we look closely, we not only see her in that dinner party in the home of the Pharisee. We can also find her, the faithful forgiven disciple, following and serving Christ, weeping for him, spending all she had for him, and even proclaiming him in the face of adversity.

Today, in this generation's attempt to see and understand Jesus, who are the people that we do not see? Who are the unnamed people in our story of trying to be the church today? Who are the people giving all they have to demonstrate their love of Christ? Who are the people who you could never even imagine might be held up as an example of discipleship?

At Baptist Women in Ministry, we are working to make sure that all the women disciples of today are seen and honored for their acts of discipleship because sometimes, when we view the landscape for Baptist women serving in ministry and leadership, all we see is a painting of blue. And when we try to live out our callings, we sometimes feel misunderstood, branded a sinner, and even invisible.[4]

But step a little closer to that blue painting, squint your eyes, and tilt your head a little to the left. Do you see the red dots? Do you see the rivers of red about to emerge from the blue? Do you see her?

Because that faithful, forgiven woman who poured out great love for Jesus, she's everywhere, even among Baptists! She's following, serving, ministering, leading, pastoring, preaching, and proclaiming the resurrection even in the face of adversity.

But she's not the only disciple whose example is often not seen by the church.

The story of the woman in Luke 7 compels us to more closely examine how our notions of discipleship have been formed to exclude instead of include. We cannot let our biases blind our ability to see what serving Christ really means. There truly are roses among the thorn bushes. We just have to learn how to see them.

---

[4] For a more complete picture of the current realities of being a woman in ministry among Baptists, see the *State of Women in Baptist Life Report 2021* from Baptist Women in Ministry. https://bwim.info/state-of-women-in-baptist-life-2/.

The Mountain behind the Mountain: The Spirituality of Appalachian Mountain Religion Seen from the Life of an Appalachian Mountain Preacher

In memory of Bro Harold McKinnish and in honor of Bro Bill Leonard

Linda McKinnish Bridges

This work places the study of Appalachian Mountain religion, an early research focus of Bill Leonard's, in the context of a distinctive spirituality of mountain faith expressed in the first-person account of a Southern Appalachian Mountain preacher, Brother Harold Lloyd McKinnish (1933–2013). This spirituality—"the mountain behind the mountain," akin to the ancient Celtic tradition of the region's ancestors—anchors multiple iterations of religion in the Appalachian Mountains and may serve all of us as we search for a faith place to call home in the tumultuous religious environment of this historical moment.

It was the winter of 2008—a very cold mountain winter in western North Carolina. Snow and ice had blanketed even the lowest peaks of the Blue Ridge Mountains. Daylight hours were short; night came quickly. The winter solstice sun started sliding down the ridge about 3:30 P.M. The back roads were closed because of ice. The others remained open, covered with snow, but were so dangerous, with hairpin curves and missing guardrails, that a slight nudge of the wheel in the wrong direction could result in a lethal slide down the mountain. With no experience driving these roads, a weary traveler faced a fairground's white-knuckle thrill.

Seminarians, young and old, were driving in from the south and north, east and west—from Mercer University in Atlanta; Lancaster Theological Seminary in Pennsylvania; Yale Divinity School in Connecticut; Wesley Theological Seminary in Washington, DC; Baptist Theological Seminary in Richmond, Virginia; and Wake Forest School of Divinity in Winston-Salem, North Carolina—into Yancey County, North Carolina, for the very first time. Yancey County—elevation three thousand feet,

The Mountain behind the Mountain

nestled between Madison and Buncombe Counties, beside Mount Mitchell rising six thousand feet in the air as the highest peak east of the Mississippi River—must have seemed like a faraway place. The ultimate destination of these uncommonly brave pilgrims was a lesser-known retreat center called High Pastures, situated off the main road, down a remote back road, then a smaller gravel road, located in a remote area outside of Burnsville, the county seat. There in these backwoods twenty people, of all ages and places, committed ten days of their lives to living, studying, eating, praying, listening, talking, and learning about these mountains, from sunrise to sunset and beyond. And it was cold—mountain cold.

For those students who drove in from large urban areas, the darkness of the night on an unfamiliar back road deep in the woods without any lights was eerie scary. They were committed. This course, aptly named "Fierce Landscapes: Listening to the People of Appalachia," required by some of their institutions in order to fulfill a cross-cultural credit, became more like a danger-charged religious pilgrimage. Contemplative travel demanded cutting a path through obstacles, challenges, and fears (both literally and figuratively). A simple decision to stop to pump gas at a dimly lit, one-pump family gas station, standing alone on the side of the mountain road, would have appeared as a big obstacle, an existential threat, with even the possibility of physical danger for some of the travelers.

One of the students, an African American man from a large urban area in the North, was fearful not only of the travel conditions in the dark and snowy night, but also for his own personal safety from the perceived harsh prejudices of the mountain people. He had carefully reviewed the route before starting the journey, much like brothers and sisters had done to check the safety of the roads as they traveled through the deeply prejudiced South of the 1960s. It was only after arriving safely, unpacking his suitcase, and settling into a comfortable chair in front of the roaring fire in the warm house that this weary traveler could finally relax. After a long breath of release and a cry of relief, the pilgrim declared: "Why, these roads are so far back in these hollers they are not even listed in the Green Book!"[1]

---

[1] Harlem postman Victor Hugo Green (1892–1960) published a guide for African Americans traveling in the Jim Crow era. Known as *The Negro Motorist*

Bill Leonard and "Fierce Landscapes"

This was Bill Leonard's course, "Fierce Landscapes: Listening to the People of Appalachia," guided by his own personal and professional research interest in this subject area of American church history and over four decades of scholarly research and writing.[2] Working with the Appalachian Ministries Educational Resource Center in Berea, Kentucky, founder Mary Lee Daugherty had the courage to create a graduate center devoted to contextual education in her own heritage of Appalachia, and raised an endowment to cover the expenses of courses throughout the thirty-

---

Green Book or *The Travelers' Green Book*, this work helped the traveler identify the roads, inns, hotels, and restaurants that were safe and hospitable to black travelers. Green wrote: "There will be a day sometime in the near future when this guide will not have to be published. That is when we as a race will have equal opportunities and privileges in the United States. It will be a great day for us to suspend this publication for then we can go wherever we please, and without embarrassment." I hope we are closer to a time of full racial equality, but on that day, deep in the mountains of western North Carolina, the student was following the Green Book as he traveled to Leonard's "Fierce Landscape" course. See Jeff Wallenfeldt, "The Green Book," *Encyclopedia Britannica*, August 31, 2020, https://www.britannica.com/topic/The-Green-Book-travel-guide. Accessed September 5, 2022.

[2] Some of Bill Leonard's writings on Appalachian religion include: Bill J. Leonard, "Historical Overview," in *Foxfire 7*, eds. Paul F. Gillespie and his students (New York: Anchor Books, 1980), 13–27; *Christianity in Appalachia: Profiles in Religious Pluralism*, ed. Bill J. Leonard (Knoxville, University of Tennessee Press, 1999); Gary Farley and Bill J. Leonard, "Mountain Preachers, Mountain Ministers," in *Christianity in Appalachia: Profiles in Religious Pluralism*, 153–63; Bill J. Leonard, "Ministering in Appalachia," *Then and Now* 13/3 (1996); Bill J. Leonard, "The Bible and Serpent Handling," in *Perspectives on American Religion and Culture*, ed. Peter W. Williams (London: Blackwell Press, 1999); Bill J. Leonard, "Goodbye to Old-Time Mountain Faith," in Terry Mattingly's *On Religion*, September 29, 2011: https://www.tmatt.net/columns/2011/09/goodbye-to-old-time-mountain-faith; Bill J. Leonard, "Leave Your Medicine Outside: Bioethics, Spirituality, and the Rhetoric of Appalachian Serpent Handlers," in *After the Genome: A Language for Our Biotechnical Future*, eds. Michael Hyde and James A. Herrick (Waco, Texas: Baylor University Press, 2012).

member seminaries.[3] Leonard brought the course to Wake Forest as founding dean of the divinity school when he arrived in 1999, and in 2008 he invited me to help lead the travel portion of the course. For several years I shepherded the group through the North Carolina mountains with a most formidable team of experienced educators and preachers from Madison and Buncombe Counties, the Reverends Tommy Justus of Mars Hill Baptist Church and Polly Binkley Cheek, now deceased.

I had known of Leonard's interest in Southern Appalachia since the 1970s, our shared Southern Seminary years, and I watched him work with a "there but by the grace of God go I" sense of relief. I had come "out" of those hills via Raleigh, Taipei, Louisville, Richmond, and Beijing. I had worked hard to understand another way of living out my faith without all the hollering and loud singing. I had spent time learning the stately hymns from the hardback, green 1956 Baptist hymnal and had stored my soft-cover, brown, shaped-note Stamps-Baxter *Songs of Praise* in the back closet. I learned to write out manuscripts of sermons and, yes, even wrote offertory prayers from time to time. I slowly realized that not everyone needed to pray out loud at the same time during the service to be heard by God, and that silence in worship did not mean that the Holy Spirit was absent. And although the lessons were hard, I learned in seminary to adapt to a service where both the choir and the preacher wore long black gowns and carried their sermons and songs in a written manuscript and fancy songbook, not just deep in their heart. I was happy that Leonard was working in this area of mountain religion, but it was not for me. I had worked hard to leave those mountains, and I was not about to look back. "I was outta there." Or so I thought—until Leonard called.

For four consecutive winters, I led these students back to my mountains—my ancestral lands. We visited the churches of my youth—the "whoop-and-holler" ones that I had left when I finally discovered the interstate out of the mountains on I-40 East and went away to college. I helped the seminarians learn to sing "shaped-note" music—the kind of

---

[3] https://www.amerc.org/; Mary Lee Daugherty introduced Bill Leonard to the world of serpent handling as sacrament in "Serpent Handlers: When the Sacrament Comes Alive," in *Christianity in Appalachia*, ed. Bill Leonard (Knoxville: University of Tennessee Press) 138–52.

WHY STUDY BAPTISTS?

singing that I had rejected when I went to college and studied "real" music. We visited with people in cabins beside the "crik" where they grew and raised their own food—the kind of cabin with an outhouse by the barn on a small tract of land just like my mountain grandma knew.

We talked to church people who lived their lives by the King James Bible and the *Farmers' Almanac*—"by the signs," as my nanny would say. The power of *Jesus* and the power of the *moon* are not in contradiction in this ancient mountain way of thinking. We danced Irish jigs with a bluegrass band and professional cloggers from Mars Hill University, thanks to my childhood friend and pastor of Mars Hill Baptist, Tommy Justus. Yes, these were my people. I had left those hills to see the big world beyond the mountains, and now I returned to the mountains with a host of theological students to help them see what I had left behind. I was ready—finally. And it was like I was seeing it all again "for the first time." T. S. Eliot wrote these words in 1943 about his own return to the little Anglican community in Huntingdonshire, England, formed some 300 years before:

> We shall not cease from exploration
> And the end of all our exploring
> Will be to arrive where we started
> And know the place for the first time.
> Through the unknown, unremembered gate
> When the last of earth left to discover
> Is that which was the beginning;
> At the source of the longest river
> The voice of the hidden waterfall
> And the children in the apple-tree
> Not known, because not looked for
> But heard, half-heard, in the stillness.[4]

---

[4] T. S. Eliot, "The Little Gidding," in *Four Quartets* (Boston: Houghton Mifflin Harcourt, 1943) 59.

The Mountain behind the Mountain

Bro Harold McKinnish and
"Fierce Landscapes"

The greatest gift of all was that Bill invited my dad, the Reverend Harold Lloyd McKinnish, a southern Appalachian Mountain pastor for almost seven decades, to be a primary witness of this mountain religion to eager seminary students.[5] Dad's teaching and first-hand accounts brought this course to life. He personally recommended the places for our church visits and carefully chose the pastors who could both comfortably guide and confidently challenge these seminarians. On several occasions, Dad (Bro Harold) spent a full day with us on the mountain, meeting the students, talking to us in front of the roaring fire, playing gospel bluegrass on his old guitar, and telling stories of mountain faith that brought tears to all our eyes. Leonard wrote these kind words shortly after Bro Harold's passing in August 2013: "Harold McKinnish was one of the great mountain preachers of his generation, a legacy stretching back to the Separate Baptist preacher Shubal Stearns, who came to North Carolina in 1755."[6]

I was always proud of both Mom and Dad and their lives so sacrificially lived for others, but I have never been so moved by their presence as I was those days on the mountain. All those sermons that I had to endure as a child growing up in the Baptist parsonage began to make more sense than ever before. And to think that our simple life—a busy yet modest one, lived in and between the life cracks of travel to countless summer-camp meetings and fall revivals; Tuesday night "cottage prayer meetings"; Wednesday night prayer meetings with long altar calls in tiny churches scattered on small, mountain dirt roads; dinner interruptions with telephone calls from hospitals with a sick church member; funeral homes that knew our phone number by heart with information about grieving folks who wanted Bro Harold; and unexpected front-door visits from anxious mothers searching for lost, addicted sons—was something others wanted

---

[5] See the video produced the week of his passing in Henderson County, North Carolina (August 21, 2013) by Eddie Swan of the Regal Media Group in Mills River, NC, and Kyle and Linda McKinnish Bridges: https://www.youtube.com/watch?v=Gpn_dt_Ps_o

[6] Bill J. Leonard, "Memories of a Mountain Preacher," September 12, 2013: https://baptistnews.com/article/memories-of-a-mountain-preacher-2/

to study and ponder was beyond my imagination. All I seemed to know then was that everybody in our little mountain village was always looking for the "preacher." We had to sneak in summer family vacations between the annual Southern Baptist Convention and Vacation Bible School and try to live happily beside the church in someone's else house that everybody else seemed to own except us. It was the world we knew, not anything special. But Bill Leonard thought differently. This was his way of doing research in the study of Appalachian Mountain religion, and both his personal humility and his scholarly maturity were clearly revealed when he wrote, "As we look to the future, we need to listen to the mountain preachers who have devoted their lives to calling people to a Christian world view.... Many have tended to look down upon the mountain preachers and have scorned their premodern, 'traditional' views as out of date or inadequate—as seriously in need of rejection or at least significant change. But now it seems that we were wrong."[7]

Leonard, in the late 1990s, challenged the perceived scholarly and religious critique of mountain religion as "backward" by calling out the elitist attitudes of those folk who were more "missionaries of modernity than missionaries of the gospel."[8] He urged the confession of these paternalistic notions by religious scholars and ministry leaders and wrote these powerful, even proleptic words: "If rapprochement can occur among the various ministry types, then the next decades will be exciting times for ministry in Appalachia. These years might involve several important projects."

The first of those projects listed by Bill Leonard and Gary Farley, now the basis for this chapter, is simply stated: "First, mountain ministers might inform our understanding of Christian spirituality...the life of prayer, study of the Scriptures, religious experience, and the 'practice of the presence of God.'"[9] And to Leonard's goal, we open a window into the

---

[7] Farley and Leonard, "Mountain Preachers, Mountain Ministers," 162.

[8] Ibid.

[9] Ibid. Leonard suggests other potential areas of research and reflection including spirituality, cross-cultural communication studies, and issues of mountain injustice along with the traditional themes of sin and redemption, the individual callings of the mountain preachers, and their willingness to serve and do the work regardless of salary, formal education, and convenience.

spirituality of Appalachian Mountain religion through the life of Bro Harold McKinnish.

This heritage, as crazy and strange as it is, is mine. It is rough, raw, loud, and gentle, lyrical, and soft, all at the same time. It is what you see, and yet there is much more there than what can be seen. Kathleen Raine, a poet in the Celtic tradition, describes that understanding, which is deeper than what can be fully expressed but is still there waiting to be explored:

> I came too late to the hills: they were swept bare
> Winters before I was born of song and story,
> Of spell or speech with power of oracle or invocation,....
>
> Yet I have glimpsed the bright mountain behind the mountain,
> Knowledge under the leaves, tasted the bitter berries red,
> Drunk water cold and clear from an inexhaustible hidden fountain.[10]

And southern Appalachian religion, as taught by Bro Bill and lived by Bro Harold, became my path to "know the place for the first time" and to understand that there was more here than what I had understood as a child, *that the mountains hold an ancient spirituality that can guide all pilgrims, no matter the generation or historical context.*

"Listen Well to the Mountain Preacher"

To a serious researcher, primary sources are always the best. To understand your subject, depend on someone's evaluation of another (secondary)— only if you must. With only a secondhand knowledge, many scholars have attempted to define Appalachian Mountain religion. The information has not only been scanty but also presumptuous, patronizing, arrogant, and faulty. Deborah McCauley, seasoned scholar of Appalachian Mountain religion, states:

---

[10] Kathleen Raine, "The Mountain Behind the Mountain," in *The Collected Poems of Kathleen Raine* (Washington, DC: Counterpoint, 2001) 132.

The starting point, then, for too many scholars' "firsthand" information about religious life and traditions distinctive to Appalachia's mountains regions has been the observation and interpretations of home missionaries and social uplift workers, past and present.... Primary sources from within the mountain religion have yet to be identified and collected in any systematic manner for one basic reason: mountain religion is principally an oral tradition.[11]

How does a scholar, however, work with primary oral sources if those oral voices have been silenced by time and death? How does that work if the *primary holders of the tradition, the ones who really know the story—the mountain preachers*, pass on into eternity without any written traces of their thoughts, ideas, dreams, or aspirations? To be certain, the diaries, memoirs, journals, written manuscripts of any kind of the mountain preachers are almost nonexistent.

This absence of written materials is not the product of an unlearned clergy who cannot read or write, as some patronizing secondary sources have concluded. Quite the contrary. This dearth of primary source materials is central to the theological tenet of mountain spirituality, which clearly acknowledges that words are holy—so holy that they are to be *spoken* aloud, not written. If you write them down, you enslave those words to the limits of either medieval parchment or even digital algorithms. In that confined place, the Spirit of God cannot be present.

The sacred oral mountain tradition has ancient antecedents. The Hebraic and Celtic notion of speaking and listening, of both raging prophets and druidic bards, finds a home in the Appalachian Mountain tradition, where God is present in words, in spontaneous, spoken ones—not written ones. God's spirit moves in the flowing sounds of the wind that beat deeply in the heart, not in static parchment, print, or paper.

This cultural reality presents a huge problem for Appalachian religion scholars. McCauley, Leonard, and others point to the lopsided and incorrect assumptions of mountain religion *without* primary sources. McCauley gives some of those accounts. The home missionary of the mid-nineteenth

---

[11] Deborah Vansau McCauley, *Appalachian Mountain Religion: A History* (Chicago: University of Chicago Press, 1995) 20.

century writes an account of the preacher and the mountain people: "They go to hear the 'larned' preacher, and to see the new-fashioned plow,...and then they return home...and cling tighter to the old rickety plow, and to the see-saw, hum and spit preacher, feeling that improvements are for others."[12] Like Leonard, McCauley minces no words about these nineteenth- and twentieth-century missionaries who were trying to "save" the people they demeaned when they wrote about mountain religion as "systematic degeneration, regression, and stagnation infesting mountain culture."[13]

The mountain preacher, according to McCauley, "deserves much, much better than most of what has been published so far." The need now, she writes, is "to begin to identify this oral religious culture—the preaching, singing, praying; the visions, dreams, and trances; the conversion narratives and testimonies; the material culture of church houses and religious art; the private letters, dairies, and memoirs."[14] McCauley urges scholarship with primary sources, not secondary, to understand the heart of Appalachian Mountain religion. Both Leonard and McCauley know this fact:

> Only through the resources of this oral religious culture—resources that are primarily flesh and blood, people who graciously allow us to enter the intimate realm of their religious lives that they so carefully nurture and fiercely guard as perhaps the clearest and most cherished expression of who they are—will we begin to hear and understand mountain religion in a way that will allow a more authentic portrait to emerge in secondary literature.[15]

Bro Harold—A Primary Source, Both Oral and Written

One of the distinctives of the life of Bro Harold, the southern Appalachian Mountain preacher, is that not only did he speak like a wild mountain

---

[12] Ibid., 27–28.
[13] Ibid., 28.
[14] Ibid., 34.
[15] Ibid., 35.

preacher man, but he also wrote like a mild-mannered accountant.[16] Bro Harold kept meticulous written records of the more than 17,000 sermons he preached during his lifetime. Many of those sermons, mostly written in outline form, were handwritten with a fountain pen on onionskin paper, 4 by 6 inches in size, and carefully inserted with needle and thread into the pages of his very worn King James, big, black-leather Bible, a tradition he began at fifteen years of age when he prepared to go on his first missionary journey throughout the counties of the Southern Highlands. He continued this tradition of hand sewing written sermon outlines into the spine of his Bible when he became a full-time pastor of Liberty Baptist Church near Bat Cave, North Carolina, at the age of sixteen. Entering the pulpit with his Bible held high in his right hand, he would place his right foot out in a deep lunge (with the preaching posture of a Billy Sunday) and preach the Word, free of manuscript, but not without notes!

Bro Harold was different from his mountain preacher colleagues because he believed that words, both spoken and written, were holy artifacts. He left preaching dairies, dozens of black books, some small, some large—more than thirty bankers' boxes full. Bro Harold even recorded each sermon title, numbering each one and dating each service—sometimes two or three services daily. These entries spanned over six decades of mountain preaching. With each entry, he carefully documented the following information: the title of the sermon, the name of the church, the names of the people saved, who sang the special music, the amount of the free-will offering, and then, at the end, he recorded the "spiritual barometer of the service." In relation to each sermon he preached, he noted the response of the listeners with this following metric: "cold," "lukewarm," or "on fire." This treasure trove is enough to keep the researcher focused for more than a few months. But there is more. Bro Harold wrote more than thirty poems and songs, some written on backs of envelopes, some hand printed with pen or pencil on notebook paper, and some typed out on a typewriter

---

[16] With access to sermons, diaries, poems, songs, cassettes, videos, and Bibles belonging to Bro Harold and tons of personal memories, the work of preparing his memoir continues in the soon-to-be-published book *PASS IT ON: The Story of Harold L. McKinnish, An Appalachian Mountain Preacher*, with special thanks to the staff of Library Partners Press at Wake Forest University.

The Mountain behind the Mountain

and bound in binders. Bro Harold also kept cassettes, CDs, and reel-to-reel tapes of the services, including his 1949 ordination sermon, that he had preached all over the mountains. Revival brochures, personal correspondence, pictures of creek baptisms, dinners on the ground, and congregational photos of mountain churches are all part of the collection now being curated by the Z. Smith Reynolds Library, Wake Forest University, in the Baptist archives.[17]

Bill Leonard cautions that "the religion which developed in Appalachia is in transition. As a more mobile, secular generation moves in and out of the mountains, the changes created affect all facts of life, including religion."[18] To document the preaching and life of mountain preacher Bro Harold is to provide a window in time before the dramatic changes of the late twentieth century. Bro Harold not only has provided a written account of the oral world of mountain religion, but his life also serves as a historical bridge to a time almost lost to historians.[19] Born in 1933, Bro Harold's cultural and religious influences came from the late nineteenth century and perhaps even earlier, due to the cultural isolation of the mountain region

---

[17] See the Reverend Harold L. McKinnish, Special Collection and Archives, the Z. Smith Reynolds Library, Wake Forest University: https://wakespace.lib.wfu.edu/handle/10339/98696. Special thanks to Tanya Zanish-Belcher, associate professor and director of special collections and university archivist at Wake Forest University, and her staff, who have been a tremendous help in digitizing this collection.

[18] Leonard, "Historical Overview," 26.

[19] Ronald D. Eller makes this convincing argument in *Miners, Millhands, and Mountaineers: Industrialization of the Appalachian South, 1880–1930* (Knoxville: University of Tennessee Press, 1982), when he quotes a personal letter written by William and Wilma Wirt, Tennessee mountain farmer, to Peggy Westerfield in 1938 after the logging boom and the construction of the Fontana Dam by the Tennessee Valley Authority: "One day we were the happiest people on earth. But like the Indian we are slowly but surely being driven from the homes that we have learned to love.... Now what are we going to do, move on and try to fit in where we do not belong or undertake to face the situation and gradually starve to death? In the little mountain churches where we once sat and listened to the preaching of the gospel with nothing to disturb us, we now hear the roar of machinery on the Sabbath day. After all I have come to believe that the real old mountaineer is a thing of the past and what will finally take our place, God only knows" (242).

in the early 1800s. With confidence, the researcher can know this mountain preacher gave witness to the religious and cultural phenomenon in the mainly isolated region of western North Carolina in the late years of the nineteenth and the early years of the twentieth centuries.

Bro Harold is a valuable first-person (primary) witness because he wrote what he felt in a culture that did not favor written religious speech. In addition, he is a valuable witness because his life and the influences on this life (1933 to 2013) represent a defined cultural and historical moment in the southern Appalachian Mountains that is now almost lost to modernity and global commerce. Leonard and Farley remind us, "Those who remember need to tell their story while they are able. The children of the new era may well have forgotten, repudiated, or reinterpreted the practices and traditions of the past. They need to be reminded of those events which shaped the faith of the forebearers."[20] Leonard describes it this way: "Thus, the stark 'Sacred Harp' hymns of the shape-note era gradually gave way to the cheery gospel quartets of the radio era, which were then blitzed by the pop-rock 'praise bands' of the Contemporary Christian Music era. What happens when the mountain churches and their traditions are gone?"[21]

Listening to Bro Harold

Amid a changing religious world that for too long has focused on the structures of the tradition, such as ecclesiastical architecture and doctrinal rightness, perhaps it is time to listen to the mountains to understand a spirituality that works in small brush arbors and intimate communities, one that employs more heart than reason and which extols humility and grace above catechetical rightness. D. McCauley describes the impediment to this kind of listening when she relates that

> the dominant religious culture has always been deeply frightened of mountain people's distinctive religious culture: in part because American Protestantism could not control it; in part because it

---

[20] Farley and Leonard, "Mountain Preachers, Mountain Ministers," 27.

[21] Leonard, "Goodbye to Old-Time Mountain Faith," *Terry Mattingly's On Religion* (blog), September 29, 2011: https://www.tmatt.net/columns/2011/09/goodbye-to-old-time-mountain-faith

The Mountain behind the Mountain

was so "other," even though mountain people shared the same racial, ethnic, and national origins, as well as the same religious heritages, as their counterparts in mainstream Protestantism; in part because mountain religion's communal worship traditions—centered on the emotional, nonrational experiences of the individual—made American Protestants feel too vulnerable, too exposed, and too threatened; in part because mountain religion's primary theological values of grace and humility "convicted" American Protestantism's overweening pride expressed through its values promoting individual and institutional merit and achievement; in part because mountain religion challenged American Protestantism's will to power pursued through its colonial-type dominance of the less powerful...; in part because mountain religion's own institutional structures were very small, very local, and very autonomous, in complete opposition to the national hierarchical institutionalism of denominationalism.... Fear translated into loathing, and even into outright hatred.[22]

But not on that mountain on a cold, winter, January day. No fear, no loathing, no outright hatred, just an honest desire to listen and learn. Bro Bill was more than willing to listen to Bro Harold—his personal humility and his professional curiosity as a church historian demanded it. Bro Harold was more than willing to talk. And those listening learned not only of the historical features of mountain religion, they were introduced to a different kind of spirituality that seemed both ancient and current, all at the same time.

Bro Harold was a different kind of mountain preacher. He could "whoop and holler" like the rest of them. He could jump the pulpit and the mourner's bench rail when the Spirit moved him. He could take off his suit jacket and loosen his tie as he entered the preaching pulpit to do the "Lord's work." He knew the cadence and the rhythm of the mountain preacher, almost singing the alliterative points of his Sunday sermon.[23]

---

[22] McCauley, *Appalachian Mountain Religion*, 12–13.

[23] Howard Dorgan, who studied mountain preaching as a university professor of communication arts, writes, in *Giving Glory to God in Appalachia: Worship Practices of Six Baptist Subdenominations* (Knoxville: University of Tennessee Press,

The conversion stories that he told of the mountain people that he knew and loved brought lots of tears and people to the altar at the sermon's end. Bro Harold recalled the words of preaching advice he received from a trusted mountain elder: "Get all the schooling you can. Read the sermons by great preachers. Polish yourself like newly polished shoes, then *preach like a wild man*."[24]

Bill Leonard writes that the most effective type of mountain preacher is "distinguished by a certain charisma—gifts of spiritual insight, homiletical flourish, and pastoral concern.... Added to this is an ability to perform in worship to the standard expectations regarding good gospel preaching: colorful sermon content, the ability to touch the deepest emotions, and the recognition that he is merely an instrument of the Holy Spirit."[25]

The connection that Bro Harold had with those seminary students and with others throughout his life was born of the Spirit—that intangible space of holy where God is present, almost undefinably so. The warmth of his personality drew the students to him, and, as his dear friend and mountain relative Sissy Corn Thompson said about him at his death, "people were drawn to him like moths are driven to the light." Bro Harold spoke of the love for the land, his special places of holy on the land, his love for people, his love for God. He also made it clear to Bro Bill and the group that he was *not* a snake-handling preacher. We all laughed. Bro Harold confessed that he had handled lots of snakes in the church through his years of ministry, but they were walking on two legs, not slithering on

---

1987), what I knew to be true about Bro Harold's preaching: "Intensely emotional, extremely rhythmical, and highly physical, the typical Southern Appalachian Baptist sermon pours out in furious volleys of rhetoric that build, hold for ten or twelve minutes on high plateaus of exuberance, subside, and then build again, over and over. Extending from forty-five minutes to two hours in length, this prototypical sermon is delivered with a passion that demands all the energy a preacher can muster. This fervor engenders the mountain congregations a type of responsive behavior seldom seen outside of rural black churches" (56). See also Dorgan's research on mountain preachers and preaching in *In the Hands of a Happy God: The "No-Hellers" of Central Appalachia* (Knoxville: University of Tennessee Press, 1997).

[24] Words from preacher, friend, and mountain evangelist P. E. Kuykendall to young preacher Harold in 1950.

[25] Farley and Leonard, "Mountain Preacher, Mountain Ministers," 154–55.

The Mountain behind the Mountain

the floor, and were sometimes called Baptist deacons.[26] And we laughed some more.

Mountain Spirituality:
The Land Is Holy

Bro Harold loved the mountains. He could identify every mountain that surrounded his twenty-acre family farm off the Howard Gap Road and the names of every tree, bush, and wildflower that grew therein. Bro Harold hunted rabbits, squirrels, and mountain bears. He collected hunting dogs and constructed dog runs for his precious hunting companions in every parsonage backyard; he even wrote sermons about them. Bro Harold laid brick, built a log cabin, and loved working with stone. He was the type of mountain preacher described by Leonard and Farley: "The more effective, or 'successful' of this type of preacher usually is distinguished by a certain charisma—gifts of spiritual insight, homiletical flourish, and pastoral concern. His skills may include the 'manly' tasks of the mountain culture, such as hunting, fishing, various sports...strenuous manual labor. Abilities in music and storytelling are also prized."[27]

---

[26] Some of the excitement in the course "Fierce Landscapes: Listening to the People of Appalachia" was directly related to Bill Leonard's early research and field work of snake-handling churches in Kentucky while a young seminary professor at Southern Baptist Theological Seminary. He describes meeting his first snake handlers while teaching in the Appalachian Ministries Education Research Center (AMERC) with Mary Lee Daugherty, a well-known authority on the tradition, at Berea College in 1990. See Leonard, "The Bible and Serpent Handling," 228–40. Students in the "Fierce Landscape" course visited snake-handling churches deep in Madison County. The church and the snake boxes, however, were closed. The early January mountain weather was too cold, even for snakes and perhaps the Spirit to be awake. Read Leonard on this "undomesticated spirituality" of snake handling in "Spirituality in America: Signs of the Times," *Religion and American Culture: A Journal of Interpretation* 9/2 (Summer 1999), reprinted in the course pack of readings for "Fierce Landscapes: Listening to the People of Appalachia," Wake Forest University School of Divinity, December 2005, for the Appalachian Travel Seminar, December 30, 2005 to January 8, 2006, at Valle Crucis Episcopal Retreat Center, Valley Crucis, North Carolina.

[27] Farley and Leonard, "Mountain Preacher, Mountain Ministers," 154.

It is no surprise that the shape and texture of the land seeped into Bro Harold's soul. We become what we see—if we are around it long enough. His paternal ancestors (McKinnish) had claimed the land around Dryman Mountain in Leicester, close to Asheville, and named it McKinnish Cove when they emigrated from Scotland in the early 1800s. His maternal ancestors (Pace) came through Jamestown, Virginia, then to Saluda, North Carolina, then to the Howard Gap Road. For almost three centuries the mountains had both nourished and sheltered, liberated and insulated the threads of Bro Harold's family—the clans of Smiths, Collinses, Paces, Wagners, and Wolfs—in the hollers of what is now known as Buncombe and Henderson Counties, deep in the Blue Ridge.[28]

While the culture of the Blue Ridge Mountains may have changed through time, with fancy interstate roads and busy Walmart parking lots, this range of mountains has stayed the same—for *millions of years*. The Blue Ridge belongs to a portion of the huge Appalachian mountain chain that spreads over 550 miles from southern Pennsylvania through Maryland, West Virginia, Virginia, and both North and South Carolina, all the way down to northern Georgia. This land mass of strength and wonder began forming more than four hundred million years ago. Bro Harold lived in the middle of these amazing towers of blue strength, called the Blue Ridge because that stretch of mountains, filled with wooden statues of oak and hickory trees, gives off various shades of blue reflected from the sky. These hills influenced everything about him—his speech patterns, the music that he played, the food that he ate, the shape of his house, his life calling, his family.

Catherine L. Albanese writes about the power of the physical landscape to shape the "mountain character": "Marked by traditional habits of mind, mountain character formed the basis for ordinary religion in the hills. Like many other Americans, mountain people were sometimes mystics and dreamers. Unlike many others, the quality of the landscape led them to foster these traits. Thus, ordinary religion among these

---

[28] John M. Coggeshall, *Something in These Hills: The Culture of Family Land in Southern Appalachia* (Chapel Hill: University of North Carolina Press, 2022).

The Mountain behind the Mountain

Appalachians grew out of their temperament and landscape, the one supporting the other."[29]

These mountains, or holy hills, create holy spaces that traditional denominationalism historically scorned, but now, with the tottering of ecclesiastical steeples, church leaders look at them with great interest. Brandon Wrencher and Venneikia Samantha Williams, in the newly published work *Liberating Church: A 21st Century Hush Harbor Manifesto*, represent a portion of this movement beginning to grow among black churches as they write that "churches exist only to serve people and planet. The church is not an empire....The church is not a building.... The church is not 'professional holy people' that keep things running, or personalities that fill up mega-stadiums.... We are honestly called to abandon, disengage from, to desert the American systems of death into which we have been inculcated...to walk away from the death march."[30] These black scholars and religious leaders issue a powerful call to return to the "hush harbors" as alternatives to the church-industrial complex.

The words of bell hooks must be invoked as one who certainly understood the "solace of wild things," and she writes from her experience as a black mountain woman from Kentucky: "Reclaiming the inspiration and intention of our ancestors who acknowledged the sacredness of the earth, its power to stand as witness is vital to our contemporary survival."[31] This gifted scholar knew that those Kentucky hills were "a constant reminder of human limitations and human possibilities. Much hurt has been done

---

[29] Catherine L. Albanese, *America: Religions and Religion* (Belmont, CA: Wadsworth Publishing Company, 1999) 330.

[30] Eds. Brandon Wrencher and Venneikia Samantha Williams, *Liberating Church: A 21st Century Hush Harbor Manifesto* (Eugene, OR: Cascade Books, 2022). This idea of returning to the hush harbors of the years of enslaved peoples was birthed during a 2016 retreat at the Highlander Research and Education Center in Tennessee as black clergy activists struggled with deep questions of belonging and becoming—in church. The wisdom of the hush harbor became clear as the group engaged in ethnographic research with ministries in black communities in the South (Dallas, in Texas, plus the North Carolina cities of Greensboro, Winston-Salem, Salisbury, and Charlotte). This research was funded by a pastoral study research grant from the Louisville Institute.

[31] bell hooks, *Belonging: A Culture of Place* (New York: Routledge, 2009) 48.

WHY STUDY BAPTISTS?

to those Kentucky hills and yet they survive. Despite devastation and the attempts by erring humans to destroy these hills, this earth, they will remain. They will witness our demise. There is divinity here, a holy spirit that promises reconciliation."[32]

Bro Harold knew that a mountain existed behind the mountain, and so did his ancestors. Brush harbor meetings—a mountain expression for hush harbor meetings—were common about August camp meeting time in Baptist and Methodist meetings in the early 1960s. The site of the camp meeting was a large tent with a sawdust floor pitched on a large patch of land outside town. Nearby, the men would also clear a thicket in the forest in order to pray before the nightly camp meeting services. And one by one, they would enter the thicket and pray until their shirts were soaking wet with a combination of sweat and tears. While my mother was driving the car down the dirt road to meet Dad for the night revival service under the tabernacle, my little brother and I, who sat in the backseat, could hear the men weeping and praying in the brush harbor. They then walked out of the woods, with their hands in the air with shouts of holy praise, one by one. Dad led the men from the brush harbor to the tabernacle. And the service began—again. Leonard Visage tells of his memory of the brush harbor in the early 1900s in *Foxfire 7*: "They'd make little benches to sit on. They'd put that brush up there to knock the sun off you and it'd turn a light shower if it would rain, but if it rained pretty hard, you'd get wet!"[33] Without a beautiful sanctuary with padded pews and stained glass, the presence of God was felt by the faithful, who were able to find places of holy even in a deep thicket of woods.

Mountain spirituality sees the land as holy. Like the ancestral Irish who knew that hill mounds and wells were special places for the unseen and holy to dwell, the mountain settlers in the Blue Ridge claimed special places on the land as holy with brush harbors, hush harbors, and family praying grounds.[34] Bro Harold knew it to be so, both at the camp meeting

---

[32] Ibid., 52.

[33] Gillespie, *Foxfire*, 190.

[34] John O'Donohue understands that civilization has tamed place: "Below the asphalt roads, the leveled floors, the worked ground to produce homes and

The Mountain behind the Mountain

sites and on his own home place. In 1986, he built a small log cabin on the family farm off the Howard Gap Road. This was his own hermitage for prayer and meditation, a stone's throw from his grandmother's praying ground. John O'Donohue suggests that the "shape of a landscape is an ancient and silent form of consciousness. Mountains are huge contemplatives. Rivers and streams offer voice; they are the tears of the earth's joy and despair. The earth is full of soul."[35]

And Bro Harold tapped into that soul-filled consciousness of prayer and place, of presences and presence, when he wrote this poem in 2011,

"Our Grandmother's Praying Ground."
There is a cabin in the woods where I relax and meditate,
Built with trees from the seedlings completed in nineteen and
ninety-eight.
These woods have been my friends with a thousand memories.
Not just the old house but the beauty of the flowers and trees.

A lad of five, helping Grandmother gather firewood, wanting to
play,
The cabin now stands among the laurels where she knelt to pray.
Grandmother now is in heaven probably singing beneath a tree,
Rejoicing with her sister, the writer of the song, "How Beautiful
Heaven Must Be."

Thanks to Lois, Linda, and Jim for room to spend many hours on
this ground,
My prayer is you will retain thoughts of pleasure and not gloom.
For me the memories are blessed and here in the cabin, all around.
You who follow, may your thoughts be precious, bring a smile and
not a frown.

---

cities lies a landscape that invites us to the loyalty of stillness and great presence" (*Anam Cara: Spiritual Wisdom from the Celtic World* [London: Bantam Press, 1997] 116).

[35] Ibid., 115.

Remember where the cabin now stands was once our Grandmother's Praying Ground.

Mountain Spirituality:
The People Are Holy

Bro Harold spoke these words to his son, Jim, who asked, "Dad, how do you want to be remembered?" Bro Harold responded, "I want to be remembered as someone who cut a trail through the jungle of this life so that those who follow might find their way a little easier in their journey." And what a mountain trail he left us—with more than thirty bankers' boxes full of his own recordings, pictures, sermon notes and sermons, revival posters, preaching diaries. In these boxes, his life appears as a kind of misty pattern. Misty because of the tears in my eyes, but a clear pattern of life emerges in this retrospective "rearview mirror" of his life. We all thought it was that way in the living of his days, but we did not stop to think about it. People seemed to matter a great deal to him—all kinds of people. He never met a stranger and was utterly convinced in that mountain way of being, that all people put their "britches on the same way" and that there were "no big 'I's and no little 'u's," as he was prone to say almost every Sunday morning from the pulpit. And that everyone, everyone, was redeemable through God's grace.

But one day I asked him why. We talked this way in the last year of his life, not realizing that these were his final months before his death in 2013. I asked, "Why have you stayed in these mountains and cared for the needs of these people all of these years? What compelled you to give your life in this manner?" I knew that he had forgone his salary on several occasions when the mountain mill was shut down and the workers' pay was slim and sometimes even nonexistent. I knew that he spent hours traveling those mountain roads to care for sick and aging parishioners who needed not only spiritual care, but also a stockpile of wood and food. I knew that the funeral home called him every week, sometimes two or three times, to care for a grieving family and to provide the eulogy over their loved one. I knew that he had given much of his energy to carrying the heavy load of a bi-vocational mountain pastor, teaching vocational education in the local high school and doing "brick jobs" for people in the community to

The Mountain behind the Mountain

compensate for his low salary in the small mountain churches. And I wanted to hear his "why." And he knew what I was asking.

Bro Harold paused, cleared his throat, and slowly began to explain this way: "Linda, I didn't aim for position. I didn't aim for prestige or salary. I really did this life work as a minister of the gospel because I really do love people. I have always been interested in people—to be a part of their lives and to be an encouragement to them along life's journey." And I listened to the words and to the heart of Bro Harold, who was often called the "Baptist Bishop of Henderson County," and we both cried a little.

And then he preached his final sermon, perhaps number 17,001, on July 7, 2013, in Hickory Grove Baptist Church, at the foot of the mountain in Rutherfordton. He knew that this was his last one. We didn't. We had followed him so many times, with one of us always carrying his big black Bible, stuffed with preaching notes and clippings, so he could shake hands with the people before the service. At the end of those long revival services, I would fetch his heavy wool winter overcoat from the church coatrack where he had hung it when he came in the front door. Mother was afraid that he would catch cold because his shirt was dripping wet when he left the pulpit after another rip-roaring, hellfire sermon, loving and admonishing the lost with every ounce of his energy.

We knew he was not well that summer. He continued to push on like he always had. In late spring of 2013, he managed to direct the clearing of the land at the homeplace. He drove his old Datsun truck daily to the store for a gallon of milk or to the post office to mail a letter. But his health was declining faster than we anticipated. He knew, however. He often quoted John 21:18 at the breakfast table: "Verily, verily, I say unto thee, When thou wast young, thou girdedst thyself, and walkedst whither thou wouldest: but when thou shalt be old, thou shalt stretch forth thy hands, and another shall gird thee, and carry *thee* whither thou wouldest not." He wanted to preach his final sermon on his own. He called on an old friend from the mountains, a preacher boy from Middle Fork in Bat Cave, the Reverend Wade Huntley, whom he had known in high school at Edneyville, at Fruitland Baptist Bible College, and at many revivals in shared churches through the years.

Bro Harold called me on the phone and asked, "Linda, do you think that I should call Brother Wade and tell him that I want to come now. He

211

WHY STUDY BAPTISTS?

asked me several months ago to come and preach for him anytime. But I had not felt the time was right—until now. And I want to preach but I don't want to seem bold or self-serving." (This is also a mountain way of being in the world—humility).

"Call in the standing invitation," I advised, not thinking this might be his final sermon but rather another opportunity to do what I knew that he loved to do—almost above anything else (other than hunting in the woods)—and that was preach. He called and the invitation came. Bro Harold wanted to make sure that both my brother and I were free to join him that Sunday. He knew that his wife, Lois, would be there with him, as she had always been. Bro Harold planned this final sermon with the same precision and intentionality as if he were planning his own funeral service. He wrote the sermon notes out in long hand, with his distinctive printing, not cursive, style on a piece of paper torn from a composition book. At the top of the paper are these words "Pass It On" II Tim. 1:1–7. No one else would have to "gird" this mountain preacher man. He was on his way home.

The preaching notes told the story. The points missing from this outline revealed his life work. This was his "last will and testament"; therefore, one would expect a sharp outline of beliefs, of doctrinal stands, of church expectations and protocol, of denominational faithfulness. Yet this outline, and later this preached sermon, would have none of that.[36]

With a walking cane, he walked up the five steps to enter the pulpit. I moved to help him; he pushed my help aside and instructed me to return to my seat. He did not want to be "girded" for he had a mission to accomplish. He stood with great confidence, looked at the eager listeners waiting for the "word from the Lord," and then told a joke. The congregation laughed; they were with him now.

When the laughter subsided, with a strong, polished, oratorical voice belonging to the fine training in elocution at the mountain high school and years of practice in front of the barnyard chickens and lots of sleepy parishioners through the years, his voice seems to boom as he raised his hand to the heavens and introduced his sermon with this question: "Who

---

[36] Listen and see the service here: https://wakespace.lib.wfu.edu/handle/10339/98865

The Mountain behind the Mountain

touched your life? Who introduced you to the Christian faith?" And he then said, "If this sermon had a theme, which I hope it does, it is 'Pass It On.'" Of course, the sermon had a theme; his entire life had a theme. And it was people and faith, and faith and people, that was it. Nothing more, nothing less.

The sermon began with a timeline of people, beginning in 1901. The pastor of Middle Fork Baptist Church near Bat Cave, the Reverend Billie Huntley, had booked a revival with the Reverend Hiram Rich of First Baptist Asheville, who was known for his spiritual depth and great preaching ability; he had performed the wedding of Bro Harold's grandparents, Alice Whiteside and James Harold McKinnish, in 1870. Bro Rich became ill and could not lead the revival. In his stead, Reverend Huntley asked Wade Sinclair, the son of Mrs. M. K. Huntley Sinclair, to do the preaching for the revival.

"Where is this sermon going," I remember thinking during the service. Bro Harold continued to follow the chronological timeline by remembering that several people were saved in that meeting, including a thirty-seven-year-old man, a local mountain moonshiner who shut his operation down to come to the revival and was "gloriously saved." That man was Samuel Huntley, who became a minister and eventually Bro Harold's pastor at Ebenezer Baptist Church on the Howard Gap Road. Huntley served this church, the oldest congregation in the county, founded in 1816, for twenty-seven years. Sam Huntley was then asked to preach a revival at Middle Fork the night that W. C. (Buck) Huntley was saved. Buck Huntley then became a preacher and was asked to lead the revival at Middle Fork at which S. D. Rhodes and J. G. Allred were saved and "surrendered" to the ministry. Then, in 1944, Allred was the pastor of Moore's Grove Methodist Church when Bro Harold was saved at the age of eleven years old. In 1945, Allred and Huntley were preaching at the local tent revival meeting in Fruitland when a little twelve-year-old girl named Lois Griffin was saved. That little girl, some six years later, married Bro Harold at Ebenezer Baptist Church on October 7, 1951.

At this point in the sermon, I think I realized that this was probably the last sermon that I would hear from Bro Harold. Through the tears, I knew what I was not hearing. I was not hearing a harsh admonishment from the religious establishment to follow the rules of the righteous legalism. I was not hearing for a renewal of the "six-point record system" which had kept Baptists in line for many years, literally checking a box if you stayed for Sunday School, read your Bible, paid your tithes, and planned to stay for preaching. This was not your typical mountain preaching of the late twentieth century, where denominationalism had ruled the day with its own brand of religious protocols.[37]

This was mountain preaching at its best. With heart, with emotion, with focus on the Spirit as the life guide and goal, and with an emphasis on the love of people and how people are the clear channel to what is good and right in the world. An "unfeigned faith" was the subtext of this sermon from II Timothy 1:5 (KJV, of course). An "unfeigned faith" was not learned in six-point record systems, or four spiritual laws, or catechetical classes for confirmation, or clever Sunday school brochures. This "unfeigned faith" was a matter of the heart, grown in humility, strengthened by solitude, prayer, and study, and revealed in a deep willingness to love all people, even the lowest of sinners.

This was Bro Harold's *Summa Theologica*, preached six weeks before he would leave this earth. He answered the question "What is the greatest of these?" with these final words from a lifetime of thinking, praying, living, and loving as a southern Appalachian Mountain preacher. His understanding of God's revelation, a key point in any robust theological discussion, was not going to be left to chance or speculation as Bro Harold prepared to leave this world. He acknowledged the traditional paths of Bible, the created order, and Jesus Christ. Bro Harold's life had been shaped by the Bible, shown by the hours of sermon preparation, the underlined books, and the file folders and boxes stuffed with sermon notes. But Bro Harold did not stop there.

---

[37] Read McCauley's treatment of denominational influence as she quotes Loyal Jones's words: "No group in the country, in my estimation, has aroused more suspicion and alarm among mainstream Christians than have Appalachian Christians, and never have so many Christian missionaries been sent to save so many Christians than is the case in this region." Loyal Jones, "Old-Time Baptists and Mainline Christianity," in *An Appalachian Symposium: Essays in Honor of Cratis D. Williams*, ed. Barry Buxton (Boone, NC: Appalachian Consortium Press, 1977), 120–30, quoted by McCauley, *Appalachian Religion*, Part 4, "The Home Mission to "Mountain Whites" (341–464).

The Mountain behind the Mountain

Yes, Bro Harold firmly believed that God is revealed through nature. He dearly loved these mountains. He found so many sermons in the created order—the discarded dogwood thrown out on the mountain road became an entire sermon on being lost and being found; the variety of coon dogs represented the varieties of church personalities; and the sunrise was present every morning to reveal the glory of God on the mountain ridge. But Bro Harold did not stop there.

Yes, Bro Harold believed that God had revealed God's self in Jesus Christ. He had spent his entire life telling this "Old, Old Story" of a first-century carpenter from Nazareth and his death for all on the mountain of Golgotha and his powerful resurrection, conquering death and sin for all of us. He had a deep personal relationship with Jesus as friend, with whom he spoke regularly in the solitude of his home study, in the woods hunting for rabbits, or in the mountain cabin. But Bro Harold did not stop there.

The final sermon, which, like a deathbed memorial, stands as a true testimony to his deepest understanding of faith. When all is said and done, it's the people. We know God through God's creation—God's people.

Mountain Spirituality:
All of Life Is Holy

Robert Morgan, the poet, novelist, and retired English professor from Cornell University, knew Bro Harold well. He had grown up listening to him preach revivals in churches around Green River, near Tuxedo, North Carolina—Mt. Olivet, Green River Baptist, Cedar Springs, and Mountain View Baptist. It is not a surprise that Bro Harold was the inspiration for the character Preacher McKinney in his 2001 novel, *This Rock*.[38]

In Morgan's novel, young Muir, age sixteen, wants to be a preacher. His mom, Ginny, is busting proud of her son but struggles to understand what preachers really do. She knows one man down the holler who can bring down fire when he stands behind God's holy desk. She knows another mountain preacher named Brother McKinney, who is a little different from the rest and "can change the air in the church and in a congregation, and in a whole community." She describes him as a preacher "who

---

[38] Robert Morgan, *This Rock* (New York: Simon and Schuster, 2001).

can make the trees and rocks seem witnesses to the power of the Bible." She says that this preacher can "make time itself seem like a testimony of grace meant for us."[39]

Ginny studies preachers. She wants to guide her young son. She recalls that the best sermon she ever heard was at a funeral where Preacher McKinney was leading the service: "It was preached in the afternoon in the little church up on Mount Olivet. It was the funeral service for one of the Tankersleys who had gone to Preacher McKinney's revival." She describes the funeral and the preacher: "It was the brightest day you ever saw. The trees were green and the mountainsides were green, and the weeds along the road were green.... Preacher McKinney stood calm and cool in the pulpit.... There was great peacefulness and poise in him.... And he said, 'Our lives might be hard, but they was not too hard as long as they had meaning, as long as we could see far enough ahead, to the plan of salvation.' He said that 'our labor was our wisdom.'"

Ginny, author Morgan's literary character, described Preacher McKinney: "Can you feel the hand of Sister Tankersley leading us into the sunlight and into the day and across the threshold to the rest of your life?" Preacher McKinney finished his funeral service saying, "In the heart of a Christian, it is always eternal morning. I am not here to mourn, and I am not here to accuse and threaten. You are all children of the Savior, and you are all my brothers and sisters."[40]

To note again, Preacher McKinney was based on the life and preaching of Bro Harold. Yes, he was a mountain preacher, but he was different. He was able to tap into the ancient tradition of the mountains—the mountain behind the mountain. That ancient spirituality shaped by the land, the people, and the harsh living of life was filled with wisdom. Divine Wisdom came from the soil, the air, and the trees. A fine sanctuary with stained-glass windows and comfortable pews was not always necessary. God can be found anywhere.

Bro Harold wrote these words on one of those early mountain mornings when he would rise before the others in the house to commune with

---

[39] Ibid., 22.
[40] Ibid., 24.

The Mountain behind the Mountain

the Spirit of God. The original trappings of religious talk are missing: the setting is the kitchen counter, the words are close and real, the day is holy:

Hello, World
Hello world how are you doing?
It's good to see you, to hear you, to be a part of you—however small.
It seems I've known you for a long, long time, and yet I know so little about you.
The Sun still gets up in the Morning and the Light drives away the Darkness of the Night.
Then in evening the Sun goes elsewhere and my part of you is Dark again.
They tell me that you've been around a long time and many others knew you before I was introduced.
I don't really know how they felt about you, but I just want you to know that I think it really Blessed that we got acquainted.
Harold McKinnish (2011)

The ancient Celts understood that life was teeming with the holy. The Appalachian Mountain religion probably left behind the fairy mounds and the leprechauns in the Great Migration, but the center remained.[41] All of life is holy. Elizabeth Barrett Browning, not a Celt or an Appalachian native, expressed this mountain spirituality with these words: "Earth's

---

[41] For a strong introduction to Celtic Christianity, see Ian Bradley, *Celtic Christianity: Making Myths and Chasing Dreams* (Great Britain: Edinburgh University Press, 1999). For a sample of ancient Celtic prayers and hymns, see Alexander Carmichael, *Carmina Gadelica: Hymns and Incantations* (Hudson, NY: Lindisfarne Press, 1992). To hear the voice of modern Celtic poets, see the works of John O'Donohue's *Anam Cara* and *Beauty: The Invisible Embrace: Rediscovering the True Sources of Compassion, Serenity, and Hope* (New York: Harper Collins, 2004). For a quick review of the feminine presence in the tradition, read Linda McKinnish Bridges, "Brigid, Mary, and Lottie: An Irish American Baptist Woman of the South Looks at the Blessed Virgin Mary," *Review and Expositor* 96 (1999).

crammed with heaven, And every common bush afire with God, But only he who sees, takes off his shoes."[42]

Bro Harold was constantly "taking off his shoes," claiming that the land, people, and all of life was holy, even the rough places. His awareness of holy was not confined to the ecclesiastical structures or denominational programming. He walked through life with the sense that in all places, in all people, in all ways, God was present. I remember we sometimes had family prayer meetings by the living room stereo console. A special song would be playing, the Spirit would be present, and Dad would begin to pray. He would have us all stop and just listen to the words and the sounds for he was finding a place for the Divine, even from the 1960s stereo cabinet.

Barbara Brown Taylor calls preachers "detectives of divinity." The mountain preacher Bro Harold McKinnish was always on the lookout in both common and uncommon places where God is present.[43] A walk through the woods became the background for a spiritual truth for tending to the path of faith. Caring for a pack of hunting dogs became a revelation of God's variations of care. For Bro Harold, the earth was "crammed with heaven" and his life's work was to identify it, take off his shoes, and tell somebody about it.

Conclusion

I don't claim to know the future of Christianity. I am not even sure about the church at the corner next week. But this I do know. We are searching for something more. The traditional models, however strong and mighty in the past, are not working right now. We need a fresh breath of air. Might we be able to "lift up [our] eyes unto the hills, from whence cometh my help"?[44] Might the life of Bro Harold and his ability to see God everywhere, much akin to his Celtic ancestors, lead us to a new universal sacrament where all the world is sacred? Would a study of Appalachian

---

[42] Elizabeth Barrett Browning, "Earth's Crammed with Heaven," from the epic poem *Aurora Leigh*, Book 7.

[43] Barbara Brown Taylor, *The Preaching Life* (Boston: Cowley, 1993) 49.

[44] Psalm 121:1 (KJV).

The Mountain behind the Mountain

Mountain religion enable us to have a better understanding of faith in this moment?

We not only need to study and learn of this religious tradition from the Appalachian Mountains as cultural and historical artifacts expressed by the life of Bro Harold. There is more. We also need to see the mountain way of understanding God—the spirituality of the mountains ("the mountain behind the mountain")—for our own current predicament and human condition.

This distinctive Appalachian Mountain spirituality does not rest in tall steeples nor finely-turned theological paragraphs, which are already gradually receding in the religious landscape, but rather in the everyday world of smooring fires, growing corn, building cabins, making poetry and music, honoring your neighbor and the land, and loving this world for the sake of this world and the world to come.

This moment, as the church becomes "decentered" in our world,[45] challenges us to see beyond what we can see, to look for "the mountain behind the mountain." Perhaps the study of Appalachian Mountain religion, as Leonard and Farley suggested, and as expressed in the spirituality of the Appalachian Mountain preacher Bro Harold, just might give us some new direction. And if so, Bro Harold is still preaching. And we are listening. Pass it on!

---

[45] The concept of the "decentered church" was first introduced to me by my colleague and friend Dan Aleshire, executive director emeritus of the Association of Theological Schools, when we talked about the challenges of theological education, specifically the closing of Baptist Theological Seminary at Richmond in 2019, when I was the school's final president. One of the challenges to a changing culture that no longer features the steeple as the center of the town is not only the reformation of theological education, but changes to our individual spiritual focus as well. As theological education, as we have known it, and church, as we have known it, become less influential in our culture, what remains? In other words, where do we go from here? Aleshire concludes that spiritual formation will become the center of theological education in his published work *Beyond the Profession: The Next Future of Theological Education* (Grand Rapids, MI: Eerdmans, 2021): "We need practices that cultivate moral maturity, relational integrity, and spiritual maturity. Authority will accrue to leaders who have deep identity as Christian human beings." https://faithandleadership.com/the-task-new-day

Studying with *Doktor Bruder*:
On Being Bill Leonard's First Graduate Student
and Living to Tell about It

Andrew Manis

The first time I ever saw Bill Leonard was in a picture in a catalog of the Southern Baptist Theological Seminary (SBTS) in Louisville, Kentucky. Since he was in his first year of teaching at the seminary I was considering as the next stop in my educational journey, and never having heard of him up to that point, I found both the picture and the professor intriguing.

Studying the authoritative finger gesticulating to explain the word "*Didache*" scrawled behind him on the quaint pedagogical tool then known as a chalkboard, some impressions of him began to form. The picture showed what appeared to be an intense teacher. If memory serves, a shaggy-haired, young professor was wearing a pair of thick-rimmed— plastic not wire—aviator-shaped glasses and a mustache curling slightly around the corners of his mouth. "Why, this guy is young enough to be my brother," I thought to myself, adding that he must be okay since he wore his dark, curly hair, his glasses, and his mustache very much like my own. Even though I resent that his hair is still thicker and darker than mine, I am nonetheless honored to have been asked to write this tribute to him.

In the mid-1970s, the Southern Baptist Theological Seminary was by reputation the most intellectual, and probably the most liberal, of the Southern Baptist seminaries. It was in first place as my eventual theological destination. The pastor of my home church, however, was a New Orleans Seminary man. Like Leonard, he was from Texas and in his first post-seminary pastorate, and he took me under his wing, baptized me, and rescued me from possibly a lifetime of mean-spirited Fundamentalism. When the Reverend Daniel Stammann saw a catalog from Bob Jones University in the backseat of my car, he reflexively snatched it up, shook it almost in my face, and said, "You are *not* going to this place." He confiscated it, and as God does with our sins, he tossed it "as far as the east is

Studying with Doktor Bruder

from the west." I never saw it again. I wish I could say the same thing for my sins and the Bob Joneses all over the Southern Baptist Convention (SBC).

"Brother Dan," as we called him, knew I was a preacher boy from the time we were first introduced. Even before he baptized me at the Seventh Street Baptist Church in Bessemer, Alabama, I had already preached a few times, my initial time being at the Morgan Methodist Church, which I attended with a friend of mine. The minister at Morgan was a very loving yet quite conservative graduate of Asbury Theological Seminary in Wilmore, Kentucky, named Clark Pope. An intense stickler for Wesleyan doctrine, he preached against Baptist views of "once saved, always saved" about once a month.

Then my sister and brother-in-law, who was serving the First Baptist Church of Arab, Alabama, took their youth choir on a mission tour to the Midwest one summer. There they encountered a very Calvinist pastor-evangelist from St. Louis, Missouri, named the Reverend Bob Whitehead. A powerful preacher with a deep bass voice, Whitehead's doctrine was impossible to ignore. Never willing to concede a theological point and never willing to take a gentle approach, even with a young convert, Whitehead shook my confidence in Clark Pope's Arminianism. After a weekend revival under Whitehead's preaching, I returned home convinced I had to make up my mind for myself. The extreme views of both Pope and Whitehead caused me to believe this doctrine was nonnegotiable. Whichever arguments prevailed would determine my denominational home. Several weeks of reading every book I could find on the subject of "eternal security" led me to conclude that the Baptist view was correct—not realizing until much later that many Methodists believed in "once saved, always saved" and many Baptists did not. In my incomplete and youthful theological education—*and* with the active encouragement of my sister and brother-in-law—I followed my sister out of the Greek Orthodox Church into which we had been born and opted for the Baptists. A high school friend who attended Seventh Street Baptist Church introduced me to Brother Dan Stammann, who treated me like a younger brother and whose pastoral care won me into his flock. In September 1971, I officially was immersed into Baptistdom. Not long after, Stammann confiscated my Bob Jones catalog and, without me realizing it, my pilgrimage out of Fundamentalism had

221

begun. Samford University and, later, the Southern Baptist Seminary, and still later, the takeover of the SBC, would move me farther and farther from Fundamentalism.

Stammann insisted I apply to Samford University, the Southern Baptist school in my hometown of Birmingham, Alabama. He taught me theology in late-night bull sessions at his home, coached me on how to craft a sermon for the two or three times he invited me to preach from his pulpit on Youth Sunday, and took the time to critique the sermons as if he were my homiletics professor. Dan really wanted me to go to his alma mater. He nurtured me so well, so tenderly, that I felt I owed it to him at least consider New Orleans Baptist Theological Seminary (NOBTS).

Then one day I learned the new president of New Orleans Seminary was coming to Samford to preach in chapel. That morning, I hustled over to Reid Chapel to hear him. He seemed nice enough, but waxing eloquent, he made the pronouncement that "if everybody in the world had Jesus in their hearts, there would be no more long lines at the welfare office or soup kitchens, and every social problem in society would disappear."

I will refrain from naming names, but the historians who read these lines can ferret out his identity for themselves if they are so inclined. I wondered, "Has this guy ever been a member of a Baptist church?," an institution with Jesus in lots of hearts but hardly the utopia this Big Preacher had described. I left that experience knowing three things: First, I was a sophomore, and he was a seminary president. Second, that was the stupidest thing I had ever heard a supposedly educated minister say from a pulpit. Three, if that was the best he could do, I wasn't going to *his* seminary. That was the day Southern Seminary won the contest for my matriculation.

By the time I graduated from Samford, I knew I would go for the PhD, and since I had majored in both religion and history, I was torn between majoring in New Testament (being of Greek descent, I was pretty good in Greek language) and church history. I wish I had been wise or informed enough to say I was torn between going to an SBC seminary, which I knew would accept me, and a university-related divinity school, where acceptance would be more competitive and whose cost would be prohibitive. All my Samford profs were products of SBC schools, more than half from SBTS and a couple of others from NOBTS. They were all

Studying with Doktor Bruder

wonderful persons who nurtured us "preacher boys" and shaped us into better human beings. But their universes were small, and they couldn't predict what was soon to happen to the SBC.

Nobody else could either. Not even Bill Leonard, nor the other professors at Southern Seminary. If I had known Southern Baptists were beginning to be transformed into a full-fledged Fundamentalist denomination, with serious ramifications for students who hoped to find teaching positions in the future, I probably would not have stayed at SBTS for my PhD or even remained a Baptist.

By the time my generation of grad students finished our doctorates, SBTS graduates were trapped on a theological—and please pardon the male-dominant phraseology here—"no-man's-land." University divinity schools and state university departments of history or religious studies would not hire us because they thought our educations had been provincial and determined by the church rather than by the academy.

Apart from Baylor University, the upper-echelon Baptist schools (University of Richmond, Furman, and, increasingly, Mercer) wouldn't hire us because they could hire candidates from the Ivy League or the Southern Ivy League (Emory, Vanderbilt, Duke). Lower-echelon Baptist schools (in which I would include the six seminaries of the new SBC and other Baptist colleges) wouldn't hire us because we had attended SBTS and were deemed too liberal. Though some of us managed to get jobs despite a horrendous job market, we sought teaching jobs in an atmosphere where "Southern" (the region) was strike one, "Baptist" was strike two, and "seminary" was strike three. With few exceptions, we were out.

Our professors at Southern Seminary cannot be blamed for the advice they gave to rising graduate students asking, "What should I do?" As the Fundamentalist Takeover advanced, their own jobs were increasingly in grave jeopardy, and no professor will devalue the work of the place where they teach by recommending that their potential students seek their PhDs elsewhere. Still, I wish someone had said to me what I later came to say to my own students who were interested in theological education: With the exception of Union Theological Seminary in New York City, do not seek a PhD from a seminary—any seminary, free-standing or denominationally connected. If you want to maximize your chances of getting a teaching job, apply to as many university-related schools of theology, divinity schools,

WHY STUDY BAPTISTS?

or history departments as you can. If you are accepted at more than one, choose the one with the best academic reputation.

After a year pastoring a small rural church near Monroeville, Alabama, I was completely unaware of the dark clouds forming over the SBC and its "liberal" seminary. So off to Louisville my wife of five months and I went, unpacking a small U-Haul truck on August 16, 1977—the day Elvis and at least part of the music died. My vocational calling still uncertain, I was not only wavering between studying New Testament and church history, but I was also torn between pastoral ministry and a career in the professoriate. Bill J. Leonard clarified both of my dilemmas almost immediately.

Somehow (or providentially), in my first semester I was assigned to take church history with Bill Leonard. By then, having heard of his reputation as a classroom teacher, I was eager to get started. Leonard's classroom has converted innumerable students to at least an appreciation for the history of Christianity. He effortlessly and regularly surprised "history buffs" that the history of the Christian church could not only be interesting and relevant to contemporary church life, but also extremely amusing. Bill Leonard is possessed of the most natural sense of humor I have ever encountered. Along with his deft use of humor, he eloquently preached the history of Christianity to young preachers, and like a *good* Baptist preacher, he always went for the heart. Like the last seasons of the television series *M*A*S*H*, he could bring an audience, either from a lectern or a pulpit, to belly laughs in one moment and to tears in the next. Once I had spent one semester with him in Church History Survey, I knew immediately that I wanted to spend my years of active ministry trying to do in my own class what Leonard did in his.

Having decided that I would apply to PhD programs in church history or the history of Christianity, I had to decide what area of that history in which to major. This was a difficult choice because every era of the history of Christianity fascinated me, and if I ultimately remained at SBTS for the PhD, all the professors in the Church History Department were among the more respected superstars on the faculty.

E. Glenn Hinson, with a doctor of theology in New Testament from SBTS and a DPhil in patristics from Oxford University, had already established a strong reputation among scholars outside the Baptist orbit.

224

Studying with Doktor Bruder

Walter B. Shurden, then in charge of the area of Baptist studies, was perhaps more limited in his field of influence but was an underrated scholar and excellent classroom teacher. Bill Leonard (PhD, Boston University) and Timothy George (PhD, Harvard) were budding superstars in their respective fields of American religious history and Reformation history, but they were still young enough that their now-universally respected reputations were still in the future.

In addition, these church history professors were also clearly the best preachers on the faculty, which, to potential graduate students who would not have careers in academia, was another selling point for Southern's Church History Department. It certainly would not have hurt me to emulate Bill Leonard the preacher. If I had just half of his sense of humor or talent as a wordsmith, I might have tried. From the pulpit, Leonard can deliver that humor with kindness, not denigrating theological or ecclesiastical evildoers, but showing, instead, that even the "villains" from the church's past have something important to teach us, even in the twenty-first century.

Besides the entertainment value of getting to spend a lot of time with Bill Leonard—I'll mention the educational value as we go along—a lesson from my undergraduate days played a major role in my decision to ask him to be my graduate advisor and/or major professor. I had majored in American history at Samford University, where one of the greatest historians of the South, J. Wayne Flynt, had been my advisor. Since I was still trying to decide which subject to study in my future graduate work—New Testament or church history—I took courses in ancient Greece and the Roman Empire that were useful but not taught by Flynt. I have long regretted that I had had the chance to take two additional upper-level courses with Flynt and didn't do it. I did take three courses with him, however, including American Social and Intellectual History, which featured Sydney Ahlstrom's classic *A Religious History of the American People* as the main text. As a Southernist, Professor Flynt put his own spin on the course, introducing me to at least part of the history of the American South beyond what I had learned in my American history survey classes. Ahlstrom's text blew me away. What college sophomore knew, at that stage of development, that a PhD could be earned in the history of *American* religion? Since I had enjoyed Flynt's courses so much, and since Bill Leonard,

225

WHY STUDY BAPTISTS?

though younger than Flynt, had equal brainpower and a greater sense of humor, I knew studying with him would be an enjoyable as well as educational experience. Finally, the thought of being his *first* graduate student held an additional attraction for me.

At some point in college I also became acquainted with the early writings of Martin E. Marty of the University of Chicago Divinity School. Chicago's reputation—plus Marty's regular appearances in print and on television as an expert on religion—put the dream of a Chicago PhD in my head. If my grades at the MDiv level were good enough, maybe I would be accepted there.

I applied for my doctorate at two schools, Emory and the Southern Baptist Theological Seminary. I am uncertain why I failed to apply at the University of Chicago, but after Emory turned me down, I must have thought, "If I couldn't get into Emory, why bother with Chicago." I was accepted at SBTS, but soon a "cloud of unknowing" formed regarding my being allowed to start my PhD studies in the fall of 1980.

Routine graduate-degree paperwork became a minor crisis when I wrote in Bill Leonard's name as my preferred doctoral supervisor. The then director of graduate studies, Joseph Callaway (or "Joltin' Joe," as I began calling him), informed me that I could not list Leonard as my supervisor because (1) he was scheduled to be at Yale on sabbatical during the 1980–81 academic year, (2) he was not yet tenured and thus not certified to take on graduate students, and (3) he would not be certified until he returned from sabbatical and went through the tenure process. "Is there really any doubt that Dr. Leonard will be tenured as soon as he returns from sabbatical?," I asked Dr. Callaway. His answer was no, but there were proper procedures that must be followed. When I asked if the extenuating circumstances of Dr. Leonard's sabbatical might allow for an exception in this case, Callaway asserted, "No exceptions." He then shook his finger in my face and said, "Young man, you are trying to do things no other graduate student is trying to do!" "Dr. Callaway, all I'm trying to do is start my doctoral studies on schedule," I replied, trying to control my anger, "and I'm going to find a way to do it. What about my university work? Do you have any objections to me doing my university work during my first semester and then finding a temporary adviser for my second semester?" He was getting tired of me, saying with a sigh, "I suppose not." I then got up

226

Studying with Doktor Bruder

and exited his office as quickly as I could before he changed his mind or before I spoke out loud the choice words that were bouncing around in my head.

I went straight back to my Fuller Hall apartment, looked up the phone number of the University of Chicago Divinity School, and within a few moments I was talking to Martin Marty. I told him I understood that it was too late for me to apply to enter their PhD program for that fall, but that Southern's program had a component that required doctoral students to take six hours of work at a PhD-granting university. Could I come study at the Div School in the fall as a "special student"? "Of course," was Marty's answer. Once I realized that the recently probated will of my late mother had yielded a small inheritance just large enough to cover the semester's tuition at the University of Chicago, and once my wife agreed to let me go off to school six hours away while she stayed in Louisville supporting us both with her teaching job, the plans were set.

So while Leonard went off to New Haven, I spent the fall of 1980 in Chicago taking a course with Marty called Religion in Turn-of-the-19th-Century America and a course with Jerald Brauer called Regionalism in Colonial American Religion. In doing so, I was both fulfilling my university work requirement at SBTS while at the same time trying to elbow my way into the PhD program at Chicago by impressing Professors Marty and Brauer with the quality of my work.

Early on in my masters of divinity work, I had told Leonard of my interest in possibly doing a PhD with Marty. With no self-consciousness whatsoever, he was pulling for me to make the cut there. When Chicago didn't work out, Leonard wrote me a kind note from Yale, sensitive to my disappointment but promising to make my SBTS PhD as challenging as what I would have had at the University of Chicago. I worried that I might have implicitly demeaned Dr. Leonard by letting him know I would have headed for Chicago had I been accepted. By extension, I feared I was sending the message that, having been blocked from developing a professor-student relationship with Martin Marty, I was "settling" for Bill Leonard.

Sometime during one of my MDiv courses with Leonard, I discovered a book entitled *Living in the Shadow of the Second Coming: American Premillennialism, 1875–1982*, which had originally been author Timothy Weber's Chicago dissertation, supervised by Marty. In his preface, Weber

WHY STUDY BAPTISTS?

thanked Marty for being enthusiastic about his work and then called him his *Doktor Vater*—his teacher-father. Because of Leonard's age difference from me, because he allowed all of us grad students to address him by his first name (unthinkable with Marty), and because I was his *first* graduate student, I felt that his relationship to me was more that of an older brother showing me the ropes of being a professional historian of the church. To me, and I am sure to others in the department, Leonard became our *Doktor Bruder*. In fact, neither I nor any of my fellow graduate students *ever* felt we were *settling for* Bill Leonard, either as a major professor or as a member of our graduate committees. In reality, it was much more like we were all *settling in with* him—us settling into the role of historians of Christianity, and he settling into a new role as trainer and model of how to become a historian. And, I might add, it didn't take him nearly as long as it took us.

As a side note, because of Marty's academic fatherliness, I *was* still able to retain a relationship with Mr. Marty, as he was called at the Divinity School. He unexpectedly came to my first presentation at a meeting of the American Academy of Religion, scaring the hell out of me when he left early. Happily, I learned that people always came in and out at such sessions and no one but rookies took it personally. More happily, in 1992, an address on Christian Reconstructionism that I presented at a Baptist Center for Ethics conference led Marty to reach out to me. Having read my piece in *Report from the Capital*, Marty wrote me a warm letter, complimenting the article. He also praised my dissertation/first book, *Southern Civil Religions in Conflict: Black and White Baptists and Civil Rights, 1947–1957*. He added: "I use the book in class, and every time I do, I think how proud I would have been to have supervised it as a dissertation. I think that, in your case, Chicago made a mistake and let a good graduate student slide by." If I could find where I filed that letter, it would be framed and hanging on my wall somewhere. But such is the gracious nature of Mr. Marty, and the letter says more about him than it does me.

I came back to Louisville with three emphases. The first was a commitment to a Chicago-style of analysis, combining traditional historiographical methods supplemented by insights from the sociology of religion. This meant including the areas of American religion with my eventual supervisor, Bill Leonard, patristics (the early church) with E. Glenn Hinson, and sociology of religion with Larry L. McSwain. These

228

Studying with Doktor Bruder

were choices I believed would emulate the methodology most prevalent at the University of Chicago. This, in turn, convinced me that this arrangement of subject matter would give me some additional skills and increase the likelihood of my landing a teaching position in the future. At the time, however, I worried that my decision to focus on sociology of religion meant I couldn't study Baptist history with Walter B. Shurden. I feared he might take my decision as a slight of both him and his area of expertise. This might also have presented a problem because Shurden was set to be my temporary adviser while Leonard was finishing up his sabbatical at Yale. This was a salient example of an overly cautious graduate student worrying himself over a matter no busy seminary professor, not to mention one whose primary job was that of dean of the School of Theology, had time even to notice.

A second emphasis came from Jerald Brauer's Regionalism in Colonial American Religion course in Chicago. Having written a paper that took a regional look at Baptist John Leland's arguments for church-state separation and having been fascinated by the concept of "civil religion" after taking Wayne Flynt's American Social and Intellectual History in college, I returned intending to do a dissertation on civil religion in the American South. A few weeks after coming to this decision, however, while book hunting at Hawley-Cooke bookstore in Louisville, my heart sank when I found a brand-new book that had scooped my dissertation idea. What is now a classic study in Southern religious history, Charles Reagan Wilson's *Baptized in Blood: The Religion of the Lost Cause, 1865– 1920*, was personally devastating insofar as he was the first scholar to apply the civil religion concept to religion in the South, forcing me to find another way to analyze the subject. I did have the opportunity to review the book in the fall 1981 semester, Leonard's first semester after returning from Yale. That fall, I attended the 1981 Southern Historical Association meeting at Louisville's Galt House Hotel, where my former college mentor, Wayne Flynt, introduced me to Wilson, who was eager to see my review of his book. That began a long friendship with Charles, and after an exchange of a couple of letters, he suggested that I look at how civil religion(s) in the South looked during the civil rights movement.

The third emphasis I brought back from Chicago was a departure from the traditional ways Baptist history had been done not only at

WHY STUDY BAPTISTS?

Southern Seminary but at virtually all the SBC schools. My sojourn in Chicago convinced me that writing the history of the Baptists could no longer depend *solely on* sources created by Southern Baptists, but rather needed to be written in dialogue with both secular and religious historians of the American South, analyzing historical materials as cultural rather than filiopietistic denominational history. When Leonard assumed his doctoral supervisory responsibilities in the fall of 1982, he was not known as an expert in the history of the South, and especially not the Deep South. His training was with both Southwestern Baptist Theological Seminary's Robert A. Baker and with William R. Estep, two excellent scholars trained as traditional church historians. The same was true of his mentors at Boston University, Earl Kent Brown and C. Allyn Russell. Baker had done the most work dealing with the South, seen primarily in his classic text *The Southern Baptist Convention and Its People* and *Relations Between Northern and Southern Baptists*. But Leonard believed strongly that his and our scholarship must reflect interaction not only with scholars who studied religion in the South using traditional assumptions from the American Academy of Religion and the American Society of Church History, but also with those who leaned toward a more secularist approach at the Southern Historical Association, the American Historical Association, or the Organization of American Historians. The lines between these historians' guilds were often blurred. What mattered to Leonard was that the budding historians who left his tutelage went out into the academic jungle, did not hide in denominationally oriented Baptist history, and took their scholarship into a mixture of these non-Baptist, mainstream organizations. We had to defend our work against all comers, against those sensitive to religious faith and those who were not.

In any case, Leonard was a quick study and picked up the literature of historians of the South in record time. I think my presence, and that of several others who included the work of sociologists of religion and that of secular Southern historians, in his first crop of grad students pushed him in that direction. But the major force moving him into the ranks of the historians of Baptists was the titanic struggle that became known as the Fundamentalist Takeover of the SBC. Thus, by the time he published *God's Last and Only Hope: The Fragmentation of the Southern Baptist Convention*, in 1990, he had become a master of both sociological and

Studying with Doktor Bruder

Southern sources. Oddly, this Fundamentalist-Moderate Controversy, which eventually ran most Liberal-minded professors and churches out of the SBC and spawned several new organizations, including, most importantly for Leonard, the Wake Forest School of Divinity, turned Leonard into the historian of Baptists with the loudest megaphone in America.

A Leonard graduate seminar was just as entertaining as his undergraduate courses. He was almost always light-hearted and jovial as he commanded the rapt attention of his student-fans. I would be hard put to name a professor under whom I have studied or even known from afar with as much natural charisma as Bill Leonard. His sharp mind was always attentive to the ironic or the absurd in any discussion of a historical topic. He treated us like colleagues and consistently gave the impression that he was learning almost as much from us as we were from him. His questions about our book reviews and research papers always pushed us to look deeper and read and analyze more perceptively. He was usually generous and very encouraging in his evaluations of our research papers. In two seminars and two or three colloquia, I can recall only two occasions when he took a hard line in his criticisms. I will only describe one of those occasions, in my unwillingness to embarrass any of my former classmates, which would happen even if I didn't attach a name. I feel perfectly free to name names on the other occasion because the name to be dropped in this case is my own.

Leonard's first official graduate seminar in the fall 1981 semester reflected both his research at Yale and the subject of his forthcoming faculty address. A ritual tradition for faculty at SBTS was to sign the school's Abstract of Principles, the seminary's own confession of faith. Before a professor earned tenure at the seminary, he or she was required to sign the document, always done publicly in Alumni Chapel, after delivering her or his faculty address. Serving as the public conclusion of the tenure process, the ritual of signing a confession of faith always seemed to contradict the Baptist tradition of non-creedalism. The seminary tried to soften that contradiction by pointing out that the Abstract of Principles was self-imposed and had been written by the seminary's founders. The statement combines both the non-creedalism of the Separate Baptists and the Calvinism of the Regular Baptists, the two strands that merged to create an originally inclusive Southern Baptist Convention in 1845.

The topic of our seminar was "Religious Experience in America." For my book review, I chose the classic text by philosopher William James, *Varieties of Religious Experience.* I found the book dense and at times tedious, but typically, the more difficult a book, the more detailed my review. Professor Leonard was kind and helpful in his response. For the moment, there were no fireworks.

When the day came to present my research paper, however, the pyrotechnics were hot enough to singe my shorts. "Varieties of Revivalism in the New South" was my topic, which compared and analyzed the revivalistic preaching and techniques of the famous Methodist evangelist Sam Jones with a much lesser-known Presbyterian evangelist named Edward Guerrant. I had great difficulty framing a thesis for this paper. One reason was a dearth of primary materials focusing on Guerrant. What differences I detected between him and Jones seemed attributable to their denominational differences. The ultimate result was a hodgepodge of biographical vignettes of both preachers and quotes from each of them. My descriptions of them told a great deal about each evangelist but offered a very weak argument that their messages were designed to speak to the conditions of the New South. Leonard was not gentle in his criticisms; he was not wrong for leveling those criticisms. All of these were scrawled in larger letters than his usual handwriting, and he concluded with, "This is the worst paper you've ever written for me."

Only one other professor in my entire education had ever been that tough on me: Walter B. Shurden. In my second semester in seminary, I had written a paper on "Southern Baptists' Responses to the Assassination of Martin Luther King Jr." I worked on it diligently and tried to write it as best I could. When I got it back, I had never seen so much red ink on a paper. With detail, Professor Shurden showed me how to write more clearly and with an economy of words. Like most young students who thought they were good writers, I tended toward long, complex sentences that showed off my vocabulary of polysyllabic words. All the red ink shocked me into understanding that less is more and that short sentences are usually clearer sentences.

Likewise, Leonard's tough critique taught me that thesis sentences had to be specific and supported by strong evidence, preferably from primary sources. After class, a couple of classmates tried to console me, some

Studying with Doktor Bruder

of them thought Leonard had been unusually and unnecessarily harsh in his evaluation of my paper and his treatment of me. A couple of days later, I knocked on his office door to ask for clarification of his critique and offered a couple of pitiful excuses for the uncharacteristically poor quality of the paper. The professor stuck to his guns regarding the weakness of the work, but his pastoral nature kicked in when he offered a small dose of consolation. "Damn, Andy," he confided, "I just expect so much more from you." I took that as a compliment, and despite my bruised ego, I left feeling better. Looking back on that paper years later, in preparing this short memoir and after thirty-eight years teaching students and grading papers, I don't think that paper was as bad as Leonard insisted. It did have a weak and weakly argued thesis, but the research was thorough and, except in two or three spots, the writing was clear. I am convinced Professor Leonard just wanted to take a hard coaching line and toughen me up a bit as a scholar. He was teaching me to defend my positions more confidently. He was teaching me not to settle for half-baked, half-convincing arguments. Between Shurden's response to my writing and Leonard's demand for stronger arguments for stronger theses, I was gradually becoming a historian.

I passed my preliminary examinations, a story I will mercifully abbreviate, although preparing for Leonard's exam was a monumental challenge. I recall studying for those exams twelve hours a day, seven days a week, for three months. After celebrating the passing of my prelims, I began preparing a prospectus for a dissertation comparing civil religious expressions among white Baptists and Methodists in the South in the 1950s. Leonard seemed excited about this plan, but he became even more enthusiastic about my proposal thanks to an unexpected development.

By 1983, my graduate committee was in a state of flux. Professor E. Glenn Hinson, my professor in patristics, left SBTS to teach in the religion department at Wake Forest University. Stepping into this new vacancy on my committee was professor of Christian ethics Glenn E. Stassen. Professor Stassen remained on my committee for a relatively short time, but he did serve during the crucial point when my dissertation prospectus was up for approval by the graduate faculty. Stassen supported my basic topic of civil religion as an important field of research, but he thought my comparison between white Baptists and Methodists was likely to

233

produce similar kinds of evidence. He candidly said, "I would be much more excited about this dissertation and support it more fully if you would consider switching from the Methodists to comparing images of America in the civil religions of white Southern Baptists with black National Baptists." He recommended I write to a friend of his at Union Theological Seminary, in New York City, Dr. James Melvin Washington. A few weeks later, I received a very gracious letter from Washington complimenting the basic thrust of the dissertation proposal and providing me with several ideas for finding civil religion among black Baptists. Washington was later offered a position at SBTS replacing Walter Shurden as the go-to professor in the history of Baptists. Unfortunately for SBTS and my dissertation, Washington opted to remain at Union.

Taking the suggestions of Stassen and Washington to Leonard, we both agreed that Stassen's suggestion made the dissertation proposal much stronger and Washington's suggested research strategy would make the research more interesting. We both found ourselves much more enthusiastic about the dissertation. This, once again, underscored how fortunate I was to have a dissertation advisor with as open a mind and as generous a spirit as Bill Leonard. It is not hard to imagine an advisor—particularly one dealing with his first set of graduate students—having professional jealousies about other professors offering too much input to his graduate students. Fortunately, he did not feel threatened by those contributions that did not come from him. For Leonard, what mattered was the quality of the work, and he was wise enough to realize he was not the sole fount of knowledge of American religious history.

As he guided the writing of my dissertation, which was entitled "Civil Religions in the South: Desegregation and Southern Images of America, 1947–1957," Bill Leonard was unfailingly supportive, offering encouragement when I was depressed about the quality of my work. As I was writing the dissertation, I typically joked with classmates that whenever I put the final period on a chapter, I would lean back and say to myself, "Well, there's the biggest pile of crap I've ever seen!" To my happy surprise, each time the adviser and the advisee met to discuss the latest chapter, Dr. Leonard's consistent comments were excited and complimentary of the work, pushing me forward to finish what he thought was going to be a publishable dissertation.

Studying with Doktor Bruder

Finally came the endgame of the process. I completed the epilogue and turned it in to *Doktor Bruder*. He celebrated with me as we waited for the day of the oral defense. I gathered with my committee of Bill Leonard, Larry McSwain, and Timothy George. None of their questions sought to catch me in any errors. We spent two hours in lively discussion of the concept of civil religion with my work critiquing both the Liberal pro-civil rights, antiracist version and the more exclusionist version often detected in Southern Baptist Convention policy and preaching. Leonard related to me as a proud older brother who had taught and demonstrated how to be a professional historian. All three committee members assured me that my work had met their standards and had passed with flying colors. They became the first persons ever to call me "Dr. Manis." Even Timothy George congratulated me for producing "a good piece of theology," although he and I both knew I was more attuned to the sociological aspect of the subject. As is the case with everyone who completes a PhD, it was a wonderful day.

Perhaps a week or so later, my quarterly copy of *Church History*, the journal of record in the discipline of the history of Christianity, arrived in the mail. I casually browsed the table of contents, looking for articles or book reviews that particularly interested me. As I scanned the titles, I spotted in the book review section the listing of Dr. Leonard's first book, *Early American Christianity*. It was an introduction to several major classic primary source writings dividing early Christian beginnings in America, divided into five major categories: colonial beginnings, denominational development, revivalism, missions, and major religious controversies. Leonard included introductions to and excerpts from colonial, early national, and antebellum authors such as William Bradford, Roger Williams, John Woolman, Jonathan Edwards, Francis Asbury, John Carroll, Alexander Campbell, Peter Cartwright, Charles G. Finney, David Brainerd, and Timothy Dwight. He also included writings produced by various religious schisms in America: Ralph Waldo Emerson on transcendentalism and Mother Ann Lee on the Shakers. He concluded with opposing views of the slavery controversy with Richard Furman's "Slavery, an Exposition" and Theodore D. Weld's *American Slavery As It Is*. Originally published by Broadman Press, Leonard hoped to show the diversity and depth of early versions of Christianity transplanted to American soil to Southern

235

Baptists, especially those who had a triumphalism about their Baptist identity. I was crestfallen to discover that the reviewer, a well-respected member of the guild, offered a less-than-stellar appraisal of the book.

Sometime later, I wandered into the graduate student lounge in the seminary library, a sacred sanctum where most PhD students of any discipline went to relax with their friends. Occasionally, we celebrated our victories, but mostly we complained about some injustice done to us. One might say that each afternoon enough steam was blown off in that room to power the paddleboat the Belle of Louisville for several miles down the Ohio River. That day, having recently finished my dissertation and having read the very negative review of *my supervisor's book*, my contribution to the Belle's power source had grave repercussions.

To the "congregation" gathered there, and thinking only of myself and my future marketability for teaching positions, I groused out loud about how my work, supervised by a mentor so rudely introduced to the readers of *Church History*, would be poorly evaluated on the job market. A day or so later, as I worked my shift at the seminary bookstore, one of my colleagues on the staff answered the phone and announced, "Andy, Dr. Leonard wants to talk to you." Always happy to speak to *Doktor Bruder*, I greeted him cheerfully. "Could you come up to my office?" I asked, "Now?" "Yes," was his terse reply.

I headed quickly up the stairs and knocked on the door. "Come," he called out. He immediately got to the point: "I understand you had some choice words about the review of my book in *Church History*," he said before I barely settled into my chair in front of his desk.

Cold chills in my arms and legs immediately ensued. I knew he could hear my heart thumping as he sat across his desk from me. In formal writing such as this, I don't use the contemporary colloquial expression that Americans now almost-universally use, but there was enough anger etched on his face to fill all of Norton Hall. My academic life, I just knew, was about to end. It seemed that a younger graduate student in church history who heard my graduate lounge comments had almost immediately reported my insensitive words to Professor Leonard. I was surprised that Leonard named the name of his informant, and I made a mental note to visit the student's carrel in the library as soon as I got out of that office. I spent the next ten minutes "walking back" my comments, as the

236

newscasters now express it. "Aw, Bill, I am so sorry. You know I didn't mean that. I was just blowing off steam in a place I thought was a safe space to utter outrageous complaints and other inanities about people, even people we love. I can't believe that so-and-so turned right around and told you what I said. As far as I am concerned, he violated the sacredness of the confessional, and you can bet your life [I didn't use the word "life"] that I am going to speak to him about it."

After we exchanged a few more comments—with me apologizing my head off and him gradually calming his justifiable anger—he finally dismissed me, saying something like, "I'm sure every graduate student ever, including me, has said such stupid things not intended for their supervisors' ears. I forgive you. Now go on and get out of here."

I left feeling sad, relieved, and wondering if I had just ruined my relationship with the best teacher I had ever had. I also left very angry. Without going back to work, I almost sprinted to the second floor of Boyce Library to the grad student carrels. When I turned the corner, there sat the budding historian who had ratted me out.

"Why the hell did you tell Leonard what I said about the review of his book?," I demanded.

"Uh...well, Andy, I don't think you realize how intimidating you are in seminars. I thought your comments were very cold," he mumbled.

"So naturally you felt the need to hustle up to his office and tattle on me?"

After thrashing the conversation out for another five or ten minutes, he apologized; my anger subsided, and we are still friends. In that category, I count both my fellow grad student and especially Dr. Leonard. Until now, I don't think I've ever talked to either of them about the incident. I trust we'll still be friends after they each read about it in these pages.

In the years since he hugged and congratulated me on that graduation day in December 1984, Bill Leonard has continued to teach me by word and example, to congratulate me on my successes, to write letters of recommendation for me for countless job applications without ever expressing a hint of exasperation or impatience, to make a special effort to see me at professional conferences or when he came to preach or lecture in some church or college nearby. He has loved me as his student and as a brother. He also prayed for me and checked on me almost every day via Facebook during my almost fatal two-month hospitalization for COVID-19 in 2021. Words cannot express how much I respect, honor, and love him.

Bill Leonard has been my greatest teacher (*Doktor*) and loving brother (*Bruder*) for forty-five years. One or two of my classmates finished their dissertations under Dr. Leonard's supervision before I finished mine because their original supervisors (Shurden and Hinson) left SBTS earlier than expected. Nevertheless, I still claim to be Leonard's first graduate student. If I were to put that fact on my curriculum vitae, it would be without question my proudest accomplishment of all. I will always be grateful that I was *Doktor Bruder*'s first graduate student.

Wrapping the Gospel in Humor and Fidelity:
A Tribute to Bill J. Leonard

Molly T. Marshall

It is a privilege to offer some reflections on the unparalleled ministry of Bill Leonard, a long-admired fellow worker in the vineyard of theological education. He was just beginning his storied career at Southern Baptist Theological Seminary when I entered the PhD program in 1979. His classes were packed, and when he preached in chapel, those who often used that time for a coffee break showed up. (I always wanted to preach like Bill, and I have consciously emulated him, especially in the use of humor). His was a fresh voice, having traveled from the plains of Texas to the lofty climes of Boston to study American Christianity, his chosen discipline. His presence brought vitality and thoughtful perspective to the Church History Department, as well as the whole School of Theology at the seminary, which I joined in 1984.

Vivid images come to mind as I look back over the shared years at Southern. I remember Bill walking attentively with toddler Stephanie across the expansive lawns; I remember his loving presence at Maundy Thursday foot-washings on campus; I remember his perceptive questions at faculty meetings as the Fundamentalist SBC battles heated up in the early 1980s. Wrapped in humor, his prescience about the gathering storm warned his colleagues. He was prophetic in that he knew well some of the earlier schisms in our vexed Baptist tradition and recognized the threat in the machinations of adverse Fundamentalist opponents. In each of these settings (family, students, and faculty colleagues), I recall how fully present Bill was, bringing his array of gifts to whatever the moment required. He was beloved by both students and colleagues there. He left a graceful imprint as he shared in the thick relationships of that community, even as it was fracturing.

My reflections from our shared time at Southern are dated, to be sure, hopefully more than anecdotage (a term I learned from Duke McCall). Over the years, however, as Bill served at Wake Forest University School of Divinity as dean and I served as president of Central Baptist Theological Seminary, we were often in the same room, primarily at events convened by the Cooperative Baptist Fellowship. I was able to witness his dream for a more expansive Baptist identity on the other side of the SBC rupture, forged out of conflict and renewed conviction about freedom and conscience. Often at break time in these meetings, Bill, David Garland, Alan Culpepper, and I would gravitate toward a corner to talk. In Bill's words, "you tend to stick with those with whom you shot the rapids." Indeed, we had done so. And morning and evening we continued to "sow the seed," as Basil Manly's seminary hymn instructed. Bill has a great capacity for friendship, and he has been invariably generous over the years with the many students, colleagues, and congregations who call him friend. That is the hermeneutic that guides this recollection of his areas of contribution.

Advocate for Scholarly Freedom and Dissent

Bill J. Leonard saw more clearly than most what was at stake in the ever-narrower demagogic rhetoric of Southern Baptist Fundamentalists. He had been drawn to Southern after his doctoral work at Boston University because it promised a horizon of freedom for his scholarly pursuits. Southern was then known as a pioneering seminary in many areas, and he joined that trajectory of free inquiry. Yet the freedom of the classroom was soon to be threatened and ultimately eclipsed as definitions of Baptist identity were being dictated by those engineering the hostile takeover of the convention. (In the ensuing years, we have learned how deeply malevolent some of the principal characters were and that their motivation was hardly purely theological in nature. Power and profit were key factors, to be sure).

Professor Leonard practiced and welcomed scholarly freedom. It was a charism to be offered in service to the church. In his classes, students explored new terrains as his wide-ranging scholarship ignited their curiosity of the varied ecclesial traditions. His own ecumenicity kindled curiosity about other ecclesial traditions, even those such as snake handling and foot-washing sects scorned by the presumably cultured learning at Southern. He practiced respect for the lived religion of others.

From Bill I learned about a spirituality of dissent. His careful reading of Baptist sources elevated how dissent has shaped authentic Baptist identity. Whether in matters of religious freedom, liberty of conscience, church polity, or biblical interpretation, Baptists have shaped their gathered communities to welcome dissenting voices. The truncation of dissent in the resurgence of Fundamentalist forces was telling.

One of his treasured PhD students, Andy Pratt, says this about Bill's privileging of dissent:

> It is my sense that the dissenting seed was always present in Bill. The decisions he made in light of the changes at Southern and in the Southern Baptist Convention were informed by the dissenting tradition in Baptist thought. The theme of dissent became more robust as Baptists in the US became more political, more right-wing, more discriminatory toward women, and more expressive of white supremacy. All of this called forth dissenting speech, writing, and actions. Also, Bill's growing awareness of and sensitivity to disability, gender, and race realities called forth dissenting speech.[1]

Advocate for Racial Justice

Professor Leonard probed the structural racism in Baptist life and beyond. He intentionally pursued learning from black students for he knew his own narrative was a product of the Jim Crow South. Fascinated by the writings of Will Campbell, he drew his students into deeper conversation about the role race has played in the formation of Christian identity. Before the surfeit of writings in the last two decades on white supremacy and the Christian origins of racism, Bill began to interrogate his own place of privilege. While teaching at Samford University in Birmingham and then while serving at Wake Forest University School of Divinity in Winston-Salem, Bill and his family joined historic black churches. It was more than a gesture; it was transformative.

To hear him speak of his pastors was luminous, and he adopted that lovely "greet one another with a holy kiss" practice of which I was the

---

[1] Email from Andrew Pratt received August 16, 2022.

beneficiary on many occasions. His concern for racial justice grew as he was steeped in a venerable tradition of preaching that elevated social justice as the necessary exemplar of gospel faith. While I have never heard him break forth in song while preaching, he echoed some of the best of black preaching in verve and emphasis.

Bill's growing appreciation for the black Baptist traditions was palpable. He realized that white and black Baptists had too long existed in a parallel universe, and he sought to learn from the narrative of black Baptists as they reframed an oppressive history into a story of liberation and justice. His concern to add persons of color to the faculty while he served as dean at Wake Forest University School of Divinity was clear, and his persistent attention to cultivating a more robust presence of BIPOC students was admirable. That the deans who followed him were first a woman and then a black man speaks to the preparatory work he accomplished.

Advocate for Women in Ministry

Bill was regularly invited to preach at the ordination of women students. Not only did he relish the occasions, but Professor Leonard also wrote about them. After Cindy Harp Johnson's ordination, Bill wrote "Good News at Wolf Creek,"[2] celebrating the freedom this small Baptist church had exhibited in ordaining this fine minister. Even though this affirmation of women in pastoral leadership went against the new symbol system reinforcing the patriarchy that was incrementally being erected at Southern—the retrenchment of male authority, complementarity in marriage, and the pernicious notion that for a woman to claim her rightful place as a pastoral leader meant that she did not "believe the Bible"—Bill, in the ensuing years, nevertheless encouraged women to pursue their vocations in an unhindered way.

Frankly, he grew in this advocacy. When Daniel Vestal began thinking about how to wrest leadership away from the Patterson-Pressler cabal, he visited Southern and requested time to meet with several faculty members. When I learned of the proposed meeting, I remarked to Bill that no

---

[2] Bill J. Leonard, "Good News at Wolf Creek," *Christian Century* (May 2, 1984): 455.

242

Wrapping the Gospel in Humor and Fidelity

women had been included. He responded by observing that Daniel was perhaps more conservative than some of us, with the implication that if I were included, it might have negative consequences. Providentially, during the same week that Vestal was to visit, homiletician Fred Craddock was offering lectures in the seminary chapel. A day before the proposed meeting, Craddock preached on the Ethiopian eunuch, an outsider who was included, who did find posterity among the people of God. It was deeply moving to me—and to Bill—and as we greeted one another after the lecture, it "seemed good to the Holy Spirit and to us" that I should attend the meeting with Vestal. I tempered any raging feminism and was on my best behavior! We both grew in this epoch as we shared the task of dismantling patriarchy at Southern, which sadly has experienced virulent expansion during the presidency of Al Mohler.

A significant aspect of Bill's legacy is his support of women in ministry; there are many women who call him a mentor, advocate, and friend. Many of the graduates of Wake Forest's divinity school are leading pastors among progressive Baptists, women and men who are reshaping the church toward gender equity. Just as Bill saw the racial injustice that was pervasive in Baptist life, he saw the untoward behavior women faced as they made their way toward their God-beckoned places of service. It is not surprising that many women who graduated from WFU School of Divinity are flourishing in ministry, and their male colleagues have been formed to consider them "partners in Christ's service," to use Jane Parker Huber's winsome wording.

Advocate for Renewed Focus on Jesus

At some Baptist gathering, Bill and I engaged in a good-natured theological debate (with a circle gathered around us) about what the most pressing doctrinal issue is for our time. I said it was to find a way to make trinitarian confession constructive for congregational life. He said it was how to think about Jesus. We are both right, of course, yet his concern may have precedence, as one cannot think about trinitarian thought without the ontological movement of God as the Incarnate One.

Over the past decade or so, Bill has consistently written essays on what following Jesus means in our day. More recently, his series in *Baptist*

243

News Global on the "meaning of Jesus in these odd times," written in the spring of 2022, offers a deep sounding into the various ways Jesus has been conscripted for political purposes and yet how Jesus cannot be contained by those who want to domesticate his identity. That Jesus' identity is contested is a thread throughout these four essays, and Professor Leonard seeks to disentangle the contemporary cultural Jesus from the biblical Son of God.

Jesus, as rendered by Professor Leonard, is hardly the warrior of the right or the heroic figure of American mythos; he is, rather, the vulnerable one, condemned as a criminal whose own experience of Gethsemane and Golgotha accompanies our human suffering with intimate knowledge and fidelity. The suffering of Jesus did not come to an end in the first century but is present with those lynched, those bombarded in Ukraine, and those who suffer oppression throughout this groaning world of injustice.

Drawing from the works of Thomas Merton, Marcus Borg, N. T. Wright, Frederick Buechner, Howard Thurman, and his good friend Frank Tupper, Professor Leonard sketches a vision of Jesus who continues to accompany those who suffer. That he has gone before us grants us confidence, and that he makes the slow way with us ensures companionship and hope.

This brief tribute seeks to articulate Bill Leonard's great contribution to generations of scholars and students. It has been a privilege to learn from him and be his junior colleague over the years. His kind of Baptist identity and Christian wisdom are sources of inspiration and renewal for which I join many others in giving thanks.